COVERED WATERS

Also by Joseph Heywood

FICTION:

Taxi Dancer

The Berkut

The Domino Conspiracy

The Snowfly

Ice Hunter

Blue Wolf in Green Fire

"On Becoming an Aspirinaut" was previously published in *RIVERWATCH*.

Versions of "The Little Munoscong Academy" and "Mister Tom's Cabin" appeared in Flyanglersonline.com.

JOSEPH HEYWOOD

COVERED WATERS

TEMPESTS OF A
NOMADIC TROUTER

THE LYONS PRESS

GUILFORD, CONNECTICUT

AN IMPRINT OF THE GLOBE PEQUOT PRESS

The Lyons Press is an imprint of The Globe Pequot Press.

Printed in the United States of America

10 9 8 7 6 5 4 3 2 1

The Library of Congress Cataloging-in-Publication Data is available on file.
Library of Congress Cataloging-in-Publication Data

Heywood, Joseph.
Covered waters : tempests of a nomadic trouter / Joseph Heywood..
p. cm.
ISBN 1-58574-766-1 (hc : alk. paper)
1. Trout fishing—Anecdotes. 2. Heywood, Joseph—Journeys. I.
Title.
SH687.H44 2003
799.1'757—dc21
2002156058

To my mother and father, Wilma and Ed, my grandfathers Harry and Atley, my grandmothers Mary and Catherine, and to all the Heywoods and Hegwoods for the DNA that has somehow propelled me from then to now.

· CONTENTS ·

· PROLOGUE ·

ON BECOMING AN ASPIRINAUT

Most trouters endeavor to learn to expect the unexpected and somehow to embrace it. Gazing in the rearview mirror is fine, but when you are immersed in the deep fecundity of now, the past is often pretty worthless. The old vets in my USAF squadron always insisted that life's most useless commodities were the runway behind and the altitude above. I have always focused less on what was than on what is and can be.

When I was a USAF student navigator in the sixties, we were all required to ride the "puke chair," a sort of barber-dentist seat in which we were spun and expected to perform certain simple maneuvers, such as resting an ear on a lap pad between our knees and lifting our heads from there to a headrest, the idea being to stimulate fluid movement in our inner ears, the insidious plan being to get the fluids in our semicircular canals sloshing about on multiple axes, the normal result being cold sweats, nausea, and the Holy Grail of the undertaking: projectile vomit. Most mortals stumbled directly and shakily from the chair to a nearby door that led to a small lawn outside, there to collapse and puke under the northern California sun.

This exercise was contrived to teach us about the real world of vertigo and it was far more memorable than similar demonstrations in altitude chambers which familiarized us with explosive decompressions and our personal symptoms of hypoxia. I would add that I did not succumb to the puke chair's sirens. However, I subsequently lost my cookies at least once in virtually every model of military aircraft I flew in.

A month or so before the millennial rollover and some thirty-four years after riding the spinning chair in California, my friend Bob Lemieux and I were in his Suburban, driving north from the village of Schoolcraft where we had breakfasted. Suddenly I felt cold sweats and major vertigo. My head was still, the road smooth, and my ear canals had no good reason for acting erratically; I knew these were inauspicious signs, especially when my left arm and left leg declared themselves inoperative and refused to obey commands from the cockpit of my brain. After Bob pulled up in front of my office, I swung my feet down from the passenger's seat, but my legs wouldn't bear weight, so off we motored to Immediate Care, which led to a siren-less meat wagon ride to the emergency room at a local hospital.

I asked one of the EMTs why no siren, and he said, "Because you're stable." I thought this a pitiful snap judgment.

An admitting nurse asked me if I felt threatened.

"You mean right now?"

"Anytime during your life," she said by way of clarification.

"I was in a war. Does that count?"

She wrote down a yes.

"Who wants to know?"

The nurse shrugged. "The state, I think."

So began my journey, not wading in a river but *as* a river.

Over the next three days in the hospital I began to imagine strange parallels to fishing. The scrubbies (doctors, nurses, techies, aides, etc.) were like anglers exploring new water: the River Me. I underwent CAT-scans, X rays, echocardiograms (outside in and inside out), and MRIs—all taken to read the water, to search for structure, to see if clots were waiting like ripening nymphs to wend their way to the surface.

Like serious fly fishers, the scrubbies were conversational minimalists while pursuing their quarry. They willingly revealed little, cottoned no small talk, and invited few questions. After all, they were fishing and I was merely the riparian ecosystem, the host, if you will; the true quarry dwelt somewhere inside me. The somethings that had hatched inside me were eventually classified as a "series of strokes," scrubby prospecting having revealed (from several half-moon-shaped black holes in my brain) that I had had three or four over a couple of weeks, one of which I recognized, one of which I didn't, another which was diagnosed by doctors as low blood sugar, and the ball-breaker that put me into the hospital.

The neurologist called me on the phone in my room and said, "We want to do another echocardiogram, and by the way, you have diabetes, but you'll have to talk to your own doctor about that." A friend of mine, a former colleague, nurse, and writer, assures me that doctors find diabetes "boring." Especially specialists. How I went from having passed out from supposed low blood sugar to being diagnosed with diabetes, which is a condition of elevated blood sugar, was never addressed, much less explained.

The stay in the hospital was filled with weird moments. There being no MRI equipment in the main building, I was stuffed in a wheelchair and taken by ambulance to the building where it was housed. The ambulance attendant got my foot caught in the handicap lift of the ambula-van. My second morning I was examined by Occupational Therapy and informed I did not need inpatient therapy. The next day people from the same organization came to move me to another floor for inpatient therapy. I told them their own people had declared the day before that this wasn't needed. They did? That would be a roger, folks. I was bed-bound and not bathed for three days.

In the middle of the night during a blood draw my vampire had problems, and I bled all over myself. I also watched him, with bare hands and no rubber gloves, dip a sample of my urine out of a container. I felt like Alice down the rabbit hole. On the day of my release my doctor did not show until nearly 5 P.M., and then spoke with one foot pointed at the door. I told him I had left word early that morning that I wanted to talk to him (about special care at home, etc.). I added that I had heard his voice several times in the corridor and that it was my impression he was avoiding me. He hauled a list out of his pocket and said with a whine, "I had seven patients to see." Maybe he ought to drop his number, I thought. Or find a new profession. A B-52 pilot that can't manage eight engines ought not to be flying B-52s.

I did not go back to see him. Instead, I got the name of a neurologist fifty miles north in Grand Rapids, and my wife, Sandy, and I went to see Dr. Herman Sullivan. He took a lot of time and answered all the questions the first neurologist had not. He said the location of the stroke was such that it had nearly been catastrophic and he concluded, "Enjoy your new life." I worry some about ending up back in the local hospital, but I also figured I frequently fish up north and most stroke-folk from up there get medevaced by helicopter down to Grand Rapids, so I hoped I was covered.

Having been a river, I suddenly became an aspirinaut, one of that proliferating legion of people my age now taking plain old aspirin every day to prevent platelets from clumping like gawkers at a traffic accident. This practice is intended (hoped?) to stop or reduce the severity of another stroke or some other form of cardiovascular crapout. Herman Sullivan explained that there is a small percentage of the population that spontaneously "throws clots." He doubted I was in this number, but a battery of blood tests subsequently revealed that because I was close enough on some statistical parameters, I should act as if I had passed (failed?) the test. Thus, I became a daily aspirin consumer.

My hospital roommate during my three-day Joe-as-a-river phase was Waldo, a snow-haired German-born man in his eighties. His stroke had taken two languages from him. I tried to comfort him in the middle of the night when it was just the two of us against our demons and the hospitrouters were busy plumbing other rivers. I learned later that Waldo had designed the legs of the lunar lander and that he had been through this before, which only added to his frustration. I didn't like contemplating return engagements.

During my three-day hospital stay, my friends came to visit; I knew Robochef Bob Peterson was wondering if the stroke would erode my poker-playing acumen, so I preemptively announced (like any in-role poker player on the bluff) that the doctor had said I should be even more adept at the game.

After the hospital sojourn, I was freed to be an angler again, navigating with less than my customary coordination. I suddenly had trouble with sleeves and socks, coordinating knives and forks, turning pages, picking things up, opening envelopes, two-handed typing, riding in vehicles, remembering events of a minute before, standing up in a shower, acting normal, feeling normal. After a stroke, there is a tendency to feel like you are walking around with your own dedicated stalker-sniper inside you. The heat of showers made me dizzy and left my head reeling. Sitting on a dining-room chair and riding in a car had the same effect.

All through this I was filled with bizarre thoughts, buoyed by remnants of USAF Survival Training: stay with the bird, make a signal, stay calm. I wondered whether I would be able to wade again, tie one of my inept fishing knots, do any of my flawed trouting again. The idea of picking up a Size 22 fly, much less affixing it to a 7X tippet, seemed daunting. Was I done wallowing solo in Michigan's rivers and streams? Done writing, living the way I had for so long?

All my life I had thought of myself as a nomad. Over my fifty-six years, most of the houses I'd lived in had been torn down. Even the corporation that employed me for nearly three decades had been largely and unceremoniously subsumed in various mergers. Normally people die and don't suffer the inevitable changes and erasures behind them, but I have lived to see a lot of my own tracks obliterated, smoothed over, rendered nothings.

During those days in the hospital bed I had felt overwhelmed by the need to be alone outdoors, neither lost nor specifically located; rather, I wanted to be on a journey with no timetable, no specific route, ETD or ETA, winder-wandering to avoid the snicker-snack of the Big Bye-Bye.

I began to summon memories rarely thought of.

As I took refuge in memories, I was reminded of Michigan poet Bob Hicok's line, "Tests show within seconds, recall's fiction that we create more than remember." We tend to remember the past the way we want to—not as it actually was.

I decided that it might be time to write down what I could remember, acknowledging that those facts and events as I could or chose to remember them, may not necessarily be as they were or are. I also knew that having considered embarking on such a task, I first had to confer with God.

Lest you panic, this God is not the exalted deity of monotheistic religions; he's my trouting partner. For real. This, let me assure you, has absolutely nothing to do with religion (not counting the unabashed adoration of trout).

Godfrey Grant (aka God) was born and raised in Baton Rouge in the 1930s. He keeps his waders up with straps jury-rigged with baling wire, the same gauge most people use to hang their favorite Elvis-on-velvet next to a small, faded Rebel flag and the ratty head of a mosshead buck gotten in the way-back of a favorite bayou. As eloquent as he is frugal, God in one of his former lives was a professor of English, and in those days pay for untenured academics was just slightly better than for indentured servants; baling wire was the all-around fix-it-up material that Super Glue and duct tape later became. Habits learned early tend to persist, even for God.

Our shared southern roots (his in Louisiana and mine in Mississippi), and the fact that both of us had once lived in Texas and had ended up in Michigan chasing trout, helped seal our friendship.

God is now retired from full-time corporate servitude, still teaches non-trout season literature classes at Western Michigan University, and operates as a freelance technomedical writing consultant under the rubric of "The Word of God."

It was months after the strokes, during our first trouting venture, when I told him about what I had in mind.

"You want to write a book about *not* catching trout?" God asked.

"I figure I should write about what I know best."

God is the sort of trouter who likes to cover a lot of fast water quickly. I'm more an adherant of the Lugubrious School of the Interminable Gawk and Slow Mosey. He fishes so hard and with such singular focus that by dark he's often lost; I get temporarily disoriented once in a while, but rarely lost. I can walk back to a spot where I dropped a dime five hundred miles from here in 1961; he has difficulty finding his car in an empty parking lot. Away from the river God cooks brilliantly, eats slowly, keeps two cats and Tipper the Dog, is married to the Lovely Laurie (I was God's best man), lives well and likes to mull things over.

"Who you think's gonna wanna read this book?" he asked.

"Most trouters. If it's true that five percent of the fishermen catch ninety percent of the fish, then I have something to say to the ninety-five percent of us who subsist on the ten percent. Near as I can tell, nobody ever writes about or to this group. We're the forgotten trouters."

God briefly mulled this over. "Doesn't sound like a bestseller."

"Art's not about money."

"Art?"

"Defined as making something out of nothing."

Which coincidentally described the quality of fishing I knew best. "I suppose you'd rather read about some jamoke with a creel filled with twenty-five-inch browns?" Extended mull mode was followed by a slow twitch of a gray bearded jaw.

"All I'd wanna know is where your jamoke allegedly caught 'em and maybe on what."

With this, God paused like a timberdoodle preparing for a vertical takeoff from a popple stand and started splashing purposefully up the creek.

Some people pray to God while they fish. I get to fish with him and hear him pray to himself. Despite such prayers, I occasionally out-fish him.

"Let's fish," he chanted over his shoulder. "We got us a bunch of water to cover."

Which is what this little book is all about: covered waters.

COVERED WATERS

PART I: THE SIXTIES

". . . We are linked by blood, and blood is memory without language."
—Joyce Carol Oates

BLOOD AND WATER

My first fish was a brass-yellow carp (whistle trout) with scales the size of quarters. I was five or six at the time, and we were fishing in Cole's Pond (which my hometown Rhinecliff, New York, relatives and their neighbors called Coley's). I still remember the tug on the line and resistance against the rod tip. I don't remember actually playing and landing the fish, but somewhere in the family photo graveyard there's a faded Brownie snapshot of a bug-eyed kid tailing a fish as long as his ectomorphic leg. My uncle Harry Heywood was the pathfinder on this outing; my father was not an outdoorsman, but this single carp taken from the still waters of a small pond a quarter-mile above the Hudson River lit the fire for fishing that has been burning ever since.

Though I didn't know it until much later in life, a great deal of my interest in fish probably descended through my mother from my grandfather Atley Hegwood; that surname is *not* a typo. My mom, who was raised in Mize, Mississippi, had only to change one letter of her name when she married my father of Rhinecliff. The fishing gene never surfaced in my younger brothers, Jim and Ed—though all three of us got the gene for wandering and looking around.

Mize is a tiny Mississippi town named after a county sheriff. It was, for a long time, a racist and misanthropic place populated by hard-nosed Scots-Irish who emigrated from the Carolinas and settled into a series of hills and gullies south of town, the area formed by the drainages of Okatona and Cohay Creeks. The hills are covered with long-straw pine and are home to deer, turkey, and black bear. This hill region is called Sullivan's Hollow and was known throughout Mississippi for its lawlessness during and after the Civil War. Outsiders have rarely been welcome, and locals have always done their own thinking, right or wrong.

Few know this, but during the Civil War, this area of Mississippi did not melt into automatic lockstep with the leaders of the Confederacy. Some locals, in fact, seceded from the secessionists and established their own short-lived republic. They had their own pesky army and raided

Confederate stores, generally and specifically disobeying all offensive government orders, much less calls for order. Sullivan's Hollow was a well-known zone for men hiding from the Confederate Conscription Act. A great part of the opposition stemmed largely from the fact that Mississippi men who owned twenty or more slaves were exempt from involuntary military service. The folks in Sullivan's Hollow generally couldn't afford any slaves, and though there is no historical evidence to suggest they were philosophically or morally opposed to slavery, they deeply resented the landed people with money getting an easy out while they would have to risk getting their brains blown out. Some threads of history repeat. A lot of them just flat didn't go. They didn't run to Canada because there was no need. They took to the Hollow.

Denizens of Mize and Sullivan's Hollow did not look to outside authorities to settle disputes; they tended to take care of such things themselves. Shootings and knifings were common. Like many other families in the region, my grandfather Atley's family had trekked west from the Carolinas. My grandfather was one of eight brothers, half of them towering six-three or more, which was pituitary disorder-class in those days; the other half of the litter was of average height. Atley was in the taller half.

I have no memories of my maternal grandfather and few photographs other than a washed-out sepia print of him holding a mule off the ground. He was a physically imposing man, both strong and respected. When trouble brewed, neighbors often turned to him for help before they called the authorities.

He was, by my mother's accounts, a ruggedly handsome and garrulous man, generally easygoing, but with a "temper like a wildcat," which would flare fast and recede just as quickly. He carried no grudges. Atley farmed some and hunted and fished a lot, especially for catfish and "trout" (which in those days meant black bass that lived in local streams or creeks). When he fished, he sometimes took my mother, aunt, and uncles with him. My mother was most often his companion until one day she violated two of his codes.

It was morning and early when Atley settled Mom into a spot on the bank of a creek and went on to find his own hole. This was cottonmouth country and he had always harped on the kids to look closely before they sat down.

Mom was getting no bites and decided she needed to find a fishier place. The rule, however, was that she could not move unless she first cleared this with her father. But this time she moved first and then decided to let him know, so she got up to yell to him and as she stood, noticed a cottonmouth in the bush directly behind her. She dropped her cane pole into the drink and began shrieking.

Atley came running.

"What the hell's wrong?"

She told him about the snake and he said, "Dammit, I told you kids to *look!*"

"I *did* look," she said defiantly. Never one to cower, she added, "It wasn't here when I got here."

He said, "Well, it'll crawl off, it's not bothering nobody. Where's your pole?"

She pointed meekly at the creek. He was flabbergasted.

"You lost your pole over a damn snake?" It was unthinkable.

My grandfather never struck his children, but he laid down laws and expected obedience. He would also listen to them, meaning he treated his kids like people, not objects, which made him somewhat of a modern man in childrearing methods.

As a tall, friendly, and handsome widower, Atley also liked to socialize. In those days, Saturday night parties meant square dances at somebody's home, open to all comers. A room would be cleared of furniture, young kids would be tucked into a back bedroom, and older kids and adults would dance all night to the tunes of a jug band. It was a lot like a *fais do-do* in Cajun country. The area was nominally Baptist with a fair percentage of Holy Rollers, but on Saturday nights, dances got danced, likker got swilled, and wise preachers stayed out of the way.

It was a Saturday night when Atley came home, his head covered in blood. He'd been to a dance at a local house, where the wife, Toni, had somewhat of a reputation for fooling around on her husband, who had somewhat of a reputation for being jealous. Atley was dancing with Toni when the very drunk husband appeared in the doorway with a pistol in hand, declared he had "had enough," and squeezed off a round, the bullet grazing Atley's forehead, over his eye, producing prodigious blood flow but neither permanent nor serious damage. My mother, as the eldest, ministered first aid and demanded to know "What the hell" he was doing at "*that place!*" Always calm in a storm, Mom also sent my Uncle Joe to town to fetch the local doctor who soon arrived and joined moral and aural forces with my mother. What the hell *was* he doing there, especially at *that* damned house?

"Hell," Atley said feebly, "We were *all* dancing with her."

"Yeah," my mother said, "but *you* were the only one that got shot."

She said he stayed home most Saturday nights after that. Atley loved to hunt and fish and roam outdoors, work with his hands, dance, and drink, and he was nonplussed about being sniped. Not a few of my genes flow from Atley.

I said to my mom one morning, "If Atley was hit in the head, Toni's husband was trying to kill him."

She said, "Oh, he was just mad. He didn't know where the bullet was going."

Talk about sanguine.

My grandmother Catherine's death had jolted my mom. It was May and Mom was thirteen and out of school for the summer, set to enter high school the next fall. She was napping across her bed when her mother came in and asked where the Sears catalog was. Mom told her, but it wasn't there, so Mom got up, fetched it, and immediately flopped back on the bed, only to hear a thud and look up to find her mother on the floor, dead. My grandmother had delivered a full-term stillborn baby two months before, and the doctors figured a clot from this birth had found its way to her heart and killed her. I was horrified by the thought of a daughter finding her mother dead, and to suddenly have to shoulder responsibility for four siblings. Mom is a small, gentle woman, but as tough as steel.

My paternal grandfather, Harry Heywood, was a diminutive plumber in Poughkeepsie, New York, and my grandmother Mary worked many years as a dietician at Cardinal Farley Military Academy near Rhinecliff.

In 1933, when my father was twelve, he and some of his pals went down to the Hudson River to swim. My Uncle Joe (I had two Uncle Joes), then ten, was coming off a bout of rheumatic fever amd forbidden by doctors to swim, but he showed up at the river in his bathing suit anyway.

It was a steamy June 21, the first day of summer, 1933, and Joe made all the boys promise not to tell on him if he took a quick dip. As boys will do, they agreed, and Joe took his swim, then climbed out of the river and sat on empty tracks watching a train going by on the other rails, counting cars. My dad and his friends looked up to see a train coming out of a tunnel on the tracks where Joe sat and immediately began screaming at him, but he was engrossed in his counting, never heard the approaching train, and was struck and killed horribly and instantly. It has always seemed ironic that the attraction of a river was a factor in Joe's death.

Eighteen months later, my dad's older sister Clara went into the hospital to have her appendix removed. She had been diagnosed with chronic appendicitis and the family doctor (then barred from practicing at the local hospital because of his problem with booze) recommended that she have it removed. The surgery was successful, but a staph infection set in, and four days after the surgery she died.

My dad, Aunt Marian, and Uncles Harry and Roger survived, and around the Hudson River and throughout Duchess County—from Red Hook down to Poughkeepsie—they were known as scrappers. Like the Hegwoods of Sullivan's Hollow, the "River Rat" Heywoods also had hair-trigger tempers and had seen their share of family tragedies.

My dad always insisted he was "invited" to leave high school, after which he enlisted in the Army Air Corps where he was later selected for Officer Candidate School and made a fine career as a respected officer in the USAF, which became its own branch in 1948. He served in India and Burma during World War II, and was technically a veteran of Korea and Vietnam as well. His youth was wayward; his adulthood was not. When he retired from the Air Force in 1961, we both entered Michigan State, where I avoided classes with him because he single-handedly tended to lift the grade curve beyond my comfort level. Other students used to ask rhetorically who the old fart was, the old fart fucking up the curve. I could never admit the old fart was my dad.

There were always books in our home and a premium put on reading. There was also no censorship; we were expected to decide for ourselves what to read, though there was occasional not-so-subtle pressure to read "the classics."

I have always taken pride in the fiercely independent and scrappy ways of both sides of my family, and I tried to raise my children to question authority in everything. It's a hard road, but you can walk with your head up, which is finally about the best any of us can hope for in life.

I do not believe in imprinting progeny with my passions and obsessions. I've taken my kids fishing, but not all the time. Sandy is not outdoorsy and I figured there was an even genetic chance that some of the kids would side with her, so I have never pressed it.

Our eldest son, Tim, enjoyed ocean fishing and an occasional worm or spinner outing for trout. But one day he took two dunks in the very frigid Spring Brook at age eight, and I think this cooled his passion for trout fishing in densely wooded environments.

My son Troy loves fly fishing but has not yet learned how important it is to make time to do the things you enjoy. He is thirty now and has too many things to do. I once took him on one of my typical day-trips, fishing the Pere Marquette, Rogue, and Gun Rivers all in the same day. He was exhausted by day's end. Before this I was known around the house as the "Old Man." Now I am "that Crazy Old Man." So it goes.

Troy and I drove down to the Dowagiac River once. It has a fast flow and loose cobble bottom. I warned him about the current and bad footing: "It's sort of like walking on the moon. If both feet loose contact, you'll float far and fast."

But you can pass along lessons as much as you want and they are never as useful as the ones learned firsthand. As we waded I warned him about an upcoming hole and the tough current. He waded boldly along and lost his footing. He managed to grab a sweeper as he went downriver, and I managed to hoist him out of his predicament. He had seen a fishy-looking run and was intent on getting to it. He will do fine as a trouter, I think.

The first time we fly-fished together for chinooks, we hooked thirty-one fish and landed only three, but it was a glorious day in mid-October with temperatures in the 70s. We fished with our shirts off and I sat and smiled as he fought several fish for up to forty minutes, leaning almost parallel to the water and laughing out loud with glee.

One spring I took him on his first steelhead outing. After numerous tries I had landed my first steelies only a month or so before, but his first time out he hooked six, getting four to the net, which suggests he has the requisite wiring to handle large fish.

Our youngest children, Tara and Trevor, are sixteen months apart in age and have always been brutally competitive. I used to take them to local lakes and the fishing dialogue would proceed along these lines.

"Why do I have to fish here and Trevor over there?" Tara would inquire.

"So you don't hook each other."

"You always give him the best place!"

"Okay, *switch* places."

They do, and of course, Trev immediately catches a bluegill or a small bass.

And a voice sings out, "You always give *him* the best spot, Daddy!"

The first time I took Trev fishing alone, he caught a nice brown on his first spinner cast in Augusta Creek and then was crushed when there were no more strikes during the remainder of the outing.

I said, "You caught a trout on your first cast."

He shot back, "Yeah, but think how many fish I didn't catch."

He'll do all right as a trouter too.

One time on a brush-choked trail to nearby Hampton Lake, Tara rubbed her arm against some nettles and by the time we got to our fishing spot her arm was inflamed, red, and swollen. No way she could tolerate it, so we headed home.

Sitting in the backseat, I heard Trev tell her, "You did it on purpose because I was going to catch more fish than you."

Kids.

On a family vacation to Holy Island in Lake Charlevoix we had dinner in town. There were dozens of yellowing northern pike heads on the walls of the restaurant.

Tim was seven or eight and kept staring upward. "What are *those*, Dad?"

I said, "That's what we're going to fish for tomorrow."

He was uncharacteristically quiet all evening.

The next morning we rowed over to a weed bed across from Holy Island and began chucking spoons.

I hit a fish almost immediately—a very substantial hammer-handle. When I got it to the boat, I gently squeezed its eyes to momentarily immobilize it and lifted it so Tim could see.

He stared at the barracuda-like teeth through narrowed eyes and said, "Cut the damn thing loose, Dad."

I think parents are obligated to expose kids to all sorts of things, but never to direct their participation. All of my children have tried fishing. If they decide to pursue it as adults, it will be their choice and their passion, not some rote thing dictated by that Crazy Old Man.

· 2 ·

SATAN'S DEMISE

My younger brothers and I grew up in the subcultural species called Brats, referring to the offspring of military, government, and multinational business types. We lived all over the United States and in Italy, and learned through our frequent moves how to cope with losing a place in order to gain a new one. In the process I think we became true children of the world, rather than narrowly focused Americans.

I started high school in Norman while my dad was on a one-year assignment from Uncle Sam to do business administration studies at the University of Oklahoma. We had moved there from San Antonio and predictably, I acquired the nickname of "Tex" from the Boomers and Sooners I befriended. Years later a couple of my high school classmates would show up at Michigan State.

The announcement that we were moving to Michigan's Upper Peninsula (U.P.) did not sit well with anyone. En route, we stopped at my grandparents' place in Rhinecliff. I was fourteen and registered my disapproval by running away from home and living in the woods for a few days. My Aunt Marian coaxed me back by promising I could drive her Jeep.

My act of rebellion wasn't anything personal against the U.P. We had no idea what it was, much less where. We just didn't want to move again. But in the military life, you have no choice.

As we drove north on the two-lane U.S. 2 and reached the road leading to the gate of Kinross AFB, my mother wept. I don't remember her words, only her tears. We were literally in the middle of nowhere.

Lucky for me.

I acclimated so well that I still consider myself to be a Yooper.

I learned about trout on the Little Munoscong River. I fished for perch in the waters around the Les Cheneaux Islands. I got my driver's license and my dad was generous in letting me take the family 1959 Buick Electra. It was white, with a black ragtop, red leather upholstery, and a Wildcat 445 engine that took me to ground speeds adequate to get me airborne, if there had been a better lift surface than the decorative tail fins.

We settled in, began to adapt and to enjoy. We encountered the usual townie-base conflicts, but being a jock quickly dissipated this and allowed me to blend in and become part of the local scene. I played football, basketball, and baseball, and ran track for the Rudyard Bulldogs, as well as bowled and fished and worked as a lifeguard. Though I once held the U.P. and state class C record for the high jump, I played sports with more enthusiasm than skill and spent a great deal of time prowling the woods and waters of the Eastern Upper Peninsula.

One August evening, before official football practices commenced, my friend Ron Kreeger (now a veterinarian) and I headed into the woods to run tote roads, looking for deer and avoiding scat piles.

Near a swamp I saw a black bird flapping around on the ground and kept running, my belief being that pain suffered and endured before the season began would reduce pain later.

When I turned around to look for Ron, he was nowhere in sight, so I backtracked and found him chasing the black bird. Naturally I joined in.

It had fallen from a nest in a very high tree and we tried to figure a way to put the bird back, but the tree was too high and there were no low branches to help us get started upward. After some discussion we decided that if we left the bird flapping around it would soon be a meal for another creature, nature's ways being tidy if not gentle.

We took the bird home.

It turned out to be a baby raven, which stayed two years, alternating between our homes. It was a playful and intelligent creature. It did not talk, but had a bevy of emotional squawks. We named him Satan.

The raven preferred hamburger mashed in milk and loved to untie the laces on our sneakers. He hopped around near the basketball court when we shot hoops, making a lot of noise, and he soared behind us when we rode our bikes.

Summer nights we liked to fish for rainbow trout in Duke's Lake, which was one of those cold, deep, spring-fed U.P. holes reputed to be bottomless. Several times we had lugged huge rocks in a boat out to the middle, grabbed hold of the rocks, and jumped overboard to see if we could hit bottom. We never did. But after dinner on summer nights we would hike down to the lake and flip spoons at the drop-offs, rarely catching trout, but working hard at it. Satan always accompanied us, but when dusk came and night threatened he would squawk and head for home and his roost on a clothesline pole by our houses, and when we got home he did not appreciate social contact. When Satan got up in the morning he expected the world to rise with him.

Every morning during the school year we would walk a couple of blocks through the base housing to the bus stop where our school bus would pick us up and haul us to Rudyard High School, some seven or eight miles from the base. The bird always escorted us.

One morning, an officer came tearing down the street past the bus stop on his bike. He was bald and had his folding blue cap (what airmen called cunt caps) stuck in his web belt.

The ever-vigilant Satan was perched on a rooftop.

We watched as the bird lifted off, set his radar, and dove in on the attack.

He struck the bike rider a grazing blow on his bald pate, knocking him and the bike over. The bird had been counting coup, no harm intended. The victim was the Strategic Air Command Wing Commander and like teenagers everywhere, we played dumb.

The bird was well named.

Satan came to the kitchen window when he was hungry. Mom would open the window and scold him the way she scolded us for always having the refrigerator door open and eating continuously. Like us, she fed him.

The bird was part of two families until his second spring when Ron's dad got a phone call at work.

Most civilians don't know that supersonic fighters have special paints designed to withstand high temperatures and that the aircraft need to be repainted from time to time. By then our F-102s had been replaced by faster and more costly F-106s, a new generation of delta-wing scalded dogs. The base had a special hangar where the birds got their paint treatments.

"You the guy who owns the crow?" the caller asked.

"My son has a raven."

"Yeah, well that sonuvabitch is in our hangar shitting on our fresh paint jobs."

Ron's dad went immediately to the scene of the crime, was put on a rickety, tall ladder and climbed up to the beams above, where Satan pranced about and took umbrage at having his fun interrupted. Every time Ron's dad grabbed for him, the bird would peck at him and raise a ruckus that echoed through the metal cavern. Eventually the bird was recaptured and brought home, and a couple of teenagers got their asses chewed—as if we had any control over what a bird would do. Especially *that* bird.

Not long thereafter, Satan disappeared.

Like some dogs, he liked to have us stop in the car so he could hop in the back seat and be chauffeured home.

We believe that the Air Police (later renamed the Security Police) saw the bird along the street, opened a door, and in he hopped, commencing the same sort of ride and outcome that later erased Jimmy Hoffa.

We were quite sure that a certain two fathers were parties to the conspiracy, but we never confronted them on this. We had learned that the paint for the F-106s went for something like $1,000 a gallon, which meant our bird had cost Uncle Sam a lot of money and we were not about to push the issue.

I always think of Satan when I see ravens, though I have never again been tempted to invite one home.

Oddly enough, the other memory I have of ravens goes back to another set of serendipitous circumstances.

In my junior year of high school the Rudyard Bulldogs were undefeated in the regular basketball season and ranked number one in Class C in the state. The second-ranked team was the Bangor Vikings (a town west of Kalamazoo), led by a pair of brothers named Gent. We lost in the regionals that year and Bangor went on to take the state title.

When I got to Michigan State I met Pete Gent, the elder of the two brothers who had led Bangor to the championship. He was a year ahead of me, a communications major and a varsity basketball player at MSU. We didn't become close friends, but we knew each other and hung out from time to time. His grade point average was a lot higher than mine.

Forward into the late sixties. I am a navigator in the USAF and my crew and I had flown a KC-135 down to Carswell AFB in Ft. Worth to have the vertical stabilizer modified. We had a weekend to kill. We knew that the Packers were playing Dallas. Pete had played basketball throughout his college career, but had been drafted by the Cowboys and made the team as a flanker, an experience that later led to his writing *North Dallas Forty*.

Knowing Pete was with Dallas, I tried to call him at home to see if we could get some passes to the preseason game, but discovered that Tom Landry required his boys to be billeted in a hotel the night before games.

We went over to the Cotton Bowl on game day, hoping to get tickets.

Fate intervened. I went back to the player entrance, which was close to the dressing rooms, and there was the irrepressible Pete hanging over the bottom of a Dutch door, chatting with anybody who would listen.

He laughed when he saw me and got me a Cowboy player pass for the sideline. But one was all he could get, so he told me to go see Herb Adderly in the Packer dressing room to see if he had some passes. Herb had also been a Spartan.

I put on my player pass and walked in like I belonged.

Herb was sitting in the back of the narrow room and I had just spied him when powerful hands spun me around.

"What the hell are *you* doing here?"

"I need to see Adderly," I told the great Vince Lombardi.

He growled and flung me forward. "Get this asshole out of here!"

My crewmates never got in, but I rambled the sidelines during the game, getting my face on camera as often as I could. The guys back in the squadron day room in Michigan saw me and guffawed, wondering how I had pulled it off.

I noticed several large black birds soaring around the top of the Cotton Bowl during the fourth quarter.

I nudged Pete and pointed. "Are those ravens?"

He glanced up. "No man, those are birds of death. The Pack is killing us." He was literary even then.

· 3 ·
THE LITTLE MUNOSCONG ACADEMY

When I was fifteen (before I had a driver's license and a cute blonde girlfriend wearing my class ring on a chain around her neck), I used to ride my black English racer several miles over to the Little Munoscong River, which is in the easternmost extreme of Michigan's Upper Peninsula. The Little M empties into Munoscong Bay of the St. Mary's River, which connects Lakes Superior and Huron. Munoscong is an Ojibwa (Chippewa/Anishnabe) word that means something like "place of the reeds." If you do much reading about the Ojibwas, you'll find a fair amount of waffling on meanings of their language,[1] even among those dwindling few Native Americans who still speak it. Munoscong Bay itself is a low, reedy mess that did and does serve as a northern pike spawning ground, so "place of the reeds" is probably as close as we're likely to get.

The meandering upper reaches of the Little M back then had a sand and gravel bottom and relatively clear tea-colored water, lots of fallen logs, a few rocks, high banks overgrown with tag alder and ironwood thickets, deer runs, bear trails with hairy curls of ursine scat, and the scent of pines and hemlock. There were trout in the Little M, but in those days I had no inkling that there were different kinds of trout. What I knew was that when I crept along the tangled banks, I saw smoky ghosts finning gracefully in the edges of the current and I wanted nothing more than to feel the rod bend to their fight. I had no idea that there were things called waders or fly rods, or that water temperature and alkalinity affected the fish. I knew only that I never saw another fisherman along

---

[1]The most authoritative source on the language is A *Dictionary of the Otchipwe Language* (1878), by RR Bishop Frederick Baraga, a Slovenian priest of noble birth who came to the Upper Peninsula of Michigan and became a legend.

my stretch of the Little M and that the graceful, smoke-colored shadows below were all mine.

My gear consisted of a six-foot, one-piece, no-name metal rod with a bait-casting reel, with what must have been a 1:1 crank and 6:1 backlash to clean-cast ratio. I usually carried two or three small red and white Daredevles; Day-Glo colors hadn't yet been invented, much less applied to the presumed interests of fish or hunter safety. I had never heard of a swivel, a clinch knot, a fisherman's knot, or any other kind of knot, so I improvised, choosing sheer knot volume over technique. If one square or granny knot was good, several must be better. Knots had been my downfall during my scouting career, having fallen one rank short of Eagle. They remain a problem.

Thinking back, it seems to me that the banks must have been undercut, but this is hindsight; most of the time I did well just to get the spoon into water, much less into anything I thought of as a hole or a run. Wet was enough, free-running and unsnagged a bonus. This was trouting at its most basic, and as good an outlet for teenage hormones as could be found until the true functions asserted themselves.

I rarely caught fish at the start of my self-education, but this wasn't really an issue. All that mattered was the chance to try and, in any event, I almost always saw them, usually behind rocks or in little scallops in the sand under sweepers and jams. Once I saw and counted more than two dozen seven- and eight-inch trout near a nice dark hole; they were suspended on the edges of the deeper water, shallow, finning in the bright sun, all of them facing upstream like charcoal-gray torpedoes. I spent an entire afternoon trying to inveigle a strike and got only a half-baked sunburn, which in its own right was an unusual feat at that latitude. This see-em good, no-catch-em pattern has often repeated itself since that day, but now as then, not catching fish is still not a deterrent to spending a few hours in or near moving water.

The Little M was my trouting school and I was its faculty and class of one—its worst and best teacher and student all rolled into a single package—and the lessons were hard learned, but enduring.

Through trout fishing, I came to understand the true meaning of trial and error and more than a little about how to actually see and understand what I was looking at, which is maybe the hardest thing any human ever has to learn in any context. Most of us tend to see only what we want to see. I learned not to repeat my mistakes, to stay focused on the job, and to persist no matter what happened. Probably you can learn these same things in classrooms, but seldom with the same dramatic impact and never with the same scenery. I was not much of a student in the traditional sense, and after having once unsuccessfully tried as a high school freshman to transform an F in Latin to a B, with a pen applied to my report card, I more or less accepted whatever grades my efforts (or lack thereof) brought.

My most vivid memory of School Along the Little M is still with me. I had spotted a single fish at the tail of a small run and was dapping a spoon into a small opening in the foliage. By then I had done a fair amount of experimentation, and had learned to let the spoon flutter down the drop-offs like a maple wing to where the fish were, but this one had a good spot just beyond my drop-and-dap range. So I found a good thick cedar that angled out over the creek bed, balanced my chest against it, and made a sort of swinging, underhanded, circus move under the trunk while I watched the lure's arc increase.

When I got the arc I wanted, I let the cast go, waited for the spoon to sink, and started slowly reeling with my arms still girdling the tree and the rod and reel underneath. The strike surprised me because I could still see the targeted fish finning quietly where I had first seen it. When I jerked the rod tip, the fish jerked back and charged upstream. I knew right off that this was not one of my usual small fish, and I pulled hard to bring him back so that I could slide down one side or the other of my tree; but just as the fish turned and started back, it did a sharp one-eighty, and I had to throw myself firmly and chest-first against the tree trunk for purchase. Which was when I felt a pain in my chest such as I had never before experienced. I let loose a bloodcurdling yelp.

If this story was being told by one of the men or women of the August Anglers Roundtable, you would no doubt hear how they ignored their pain and concentrated on reeling in the fish. What I did was fling the rod away and pitch myself backward, away from the pain.

To no avail.

From a cushion of tag alders I gingerly examined my left pectoral (I had them back then) and saw fresh blood from two of the three points of the treble hook on one of my spare spoons. Jamming myself against the tree had impaled me on my spares, which I always carried loose in my shirt pocket. I had hooked me and hooked me good, pushing the hook points deep into my flesh. The blood was warm and sticky. Bluebottle flies buzzed in anticipation of a summer snack.

All sorts of decisions were pending and pressing. I could still hear my fish flopping and splashing downstream, which was the opposite of where it had been headed when fate and Mister Murphy intervened. I needed the hook out, which meant I had to look at the wound, and I was not sure I wanted to. Had anybody ever died of a treble hook to the heart? Did I dare go home with a hook in my chest when my mom didn't know I had gone off alone to fish? Not a capital idea. What if a wolverine, the dreaded loup-garou, smelled my blood and came to finish me off? It was decades before I learned there are no wolverines in Michigan and probably never were—save a hundred thousand puff-headed, ego-inflated, inebriated two-legged specimens in Ann Arbor on some Saturdays in autumn. I used my pocketknife to slit the shirt; once I got the wound exposed, I simply ripped the hooks loose and got in the cold water to cool the damage. My chest hurt far less than my pride.

Having gotten into the stream, it was relatively easy to retrieve my rod. The Daredevle was still connected, and the flopping fish long gone, but it occurred to me that since I was in the water and already wet, there was no point in getting out; I found that down in the stream I could see better and there was a lot more room to cast, so I resumed fishing upstream.

I had learned early on that the fish seemed to face the current, so it made sense now that I was down in the water with them that coming at them from behind would make me less likely to spook them. Over the next couple of hours I caught and released several small trout with white edges on their fins. Brookies, I know now, are not even trout to an ichthyologist's narrow way of thinking—brookies being char rather than trout on the scientific charts—but back then they were just trout, and that was fine with me. I would add here that before graduating from high school I caught a nineteen-inch brook trout from the Little M and I have not come within six inches of that in the more than forty years since.

I don't remember the story I concocted to cover the torn shirt and I don't think there was any unusual fuss over it, but I recall that day because there is a faded little scar as a reminder, and it sat clear in my mind then as it does now that I had taken a not-so-great moment and turned it into something positive. The implications beyond fishing were evident even then.

· 4 ·

DISCOVERING THE
WEST WITH LESS ÉLAN
THAN LEWIS & CLARK

It was late May or early June 1962 and Big Jon "The Aardvark" Vilhauer and I had his VW Beetle jammed with most of our worldly goods. At MSU, where he was a notoriously reclusive scholar and veterinary medicine student, Jon had nicknamed himself the Aardvark.

We had five or six days to drive from East Lansing to Pierce, Idaho, where we were to spend the summer in the employ of the U.S. Forest Service (USFS). Pierce is not far from Weippe, in case you're disoriented. It's up the hill from Orofino and the Clearwater River, up meaning steeply so, ascending a maze of switchbacks and oxbows of macadam in those days more often than not filled with overloaded, descent-bound logging rigs and homicidal drivers thinking about next Saturday night's bender. As a point of reference, the Weippe sports teams were called the Gorillas; the boys in Pierce played as the Foresters.

Some pals of ours had told us during the school year that the USFS hired college boys for summer work. Jon and I were among several who applied, but we were the only Michigan Staters we knew to be chosen, so we headed West to work and decided to fish along the way; specifically, we decided to try to catch a trout in every state we would pass through. In the west end of the U.P. we each took a nice brown trout from a creek between Trout Creek and Bruce Crossing. We got only one fish in Wisconsin, this from the Bois Brule. Near Valley City, North Dakota, we fished the Sheyanne and had no luck, our first taste of failure. We consoled ourselves with beer. Back in East Lansing you couldn't buy or even get into a bar without a bandolier of ID (fake or legit), but in North Dakota we were served without question.

After several days on the road we were weary and thought we were south of Livingston, Montana. There was a cutoff and it was dark and we were bushed, so we pulled in, set up our pup tents, and fell into deep sleep. At morning twilight, I awoke to foreign sounds and opened my eyes to find the white-striped face of a steer peering into the end of the tent where my feet hung out. Not quite awake and thoroughly surprised, I scrambled away from the imagined intruder, caught a guy rope with my ankle during egress, and pulled down the tent. Bull, steer, cow, all the same to me; I had and have no desire for bovine companionship. By the time I was out I was fully awake, and saw that we had laagered in a grassy pasture of four-leggers; I saw that Vilhauer was outside his tent as well, growling, "Where's my goddamned glasses!" It was a fine scene: A pair of two-hundred-and-thirty-pound college boys in their BVDs surrounded by some Montana rancher's four-legged liquible assets. It looked like a lousy start to the day.

Which, life teaches, is sometimes how great days begin.

By mid-morning we found ourselves on a long macadam road built along a berm beside a large lake. There were a few fishermen standing knee-deep in water along shore so we stopped, changed into the moldy black Converse All-Stars we reserved for wading, and went forth to join our brother anglers. On his first cast, Big Jon's spoon attracted a monster fish (by our standards) with a muted cherry-red jaw. Not much of a fighter, but the rod was bent impressively by sheer weight. When Jon got the thing to within ten feet he handed me his rod, yelled, "Hold this," ran to the VW, started up, rooster-tailed a U-ey onto the gravel on the far shoulder and, crunching his gears, raced away.

Thirty minutes went by before I saw him coming back. He stopped the Beetle mid-road, jumped out, leaving the engine running and the door open, splashed into the lake like a lifeguard after a topless coed in distress, ripped his rod away from me, reeled the exhausted cutthroat in, and scooped it into a huge new hand net.

"Goddamn," he said as he hauled the fish to shore and worked his spoon loose. Jon's crew-cut head turned apple red when he was excited, and at that moment he was the color of a Red Delicious. "I promised myself I'd never buy a net unless I caught a fish big enough to need one," he shouted as he gilled the fish and held it up for inspection. "Today's that damned day!" Vilhauer logic had its own rhythm. I was just glad that we weren't a thousand miles up the Amazon when he struck his landmark fish.

We fished until late afternoon, catching fifteen- to eighteen-inch cutthroats on every second or third cast. I never before or since got into so many nice fish at one time. I have no idea how many fish were along that gravelly shore or why they were there, or why there were so few fishermen, but the half dozen of us lucky enough to have been there along the shores of Yellowstone Lake that day nearly forty years ago had ourselves a memorable time.

We kept six fish. My memory is not entirely clear on what the limit was then—all we knew was that we had more than the two of us could eat—but we couldn't help ourselves. We didn't even know they were cutthroats. We rented a camping site outside the town of West Yellowstone, pitched our pup tents, pan-fried one fish for each of us, and gave the remainder to a family with several kids. Jon and I stayed up late drinking beer and warming ourselves before a blazing campfire, thinking that out there under a star-filled Montana sky we were about the two luckiest college boys in the country.

The next day we drove to Missoula and veered west up to Lolo Pass; when we crossed into Idaho, we stopped along the hard-charging Lochsa River and threw spinners until our arms and backs ached and, when we had expended our energy and had nothing to show for it, we looped back to a tavern we had seen earlier.

The bartender smiled and said, "Lucky?" and we said, "No, they weren't hitting," and he gave us the sort of look reserved for halfwits.

Lucky, we later learned, meant Lucky Lager, a local brew. By the time the summer was over we had personally enriched the brewers and shareholders of Lucky, Olympia, Ranier, and a dozen other brands.

Nowadays the West is a mecca for trouters, but in 1962 we were just dumb college boys on an adventure, and we knew nothing of the legends of the West. We only knew that we had landed somewhere special, and the rest of that summer, when we weren't soaking white pine trees with actidione or scraping tinder out of the path of forest fires, we spent every free moment availing ourselves of what we were sure was the finest trout fishing on Spaceship Earth. Big Jon went on to earn his DVM and an Army commission and we lost track of each other. That's how life was after Vietnam put a half nelson on our culture and society for nearly a decade.

· 5 ·

SHAKY STARTS

I met Sandy Phillips during a "mixer" at Shaw Hall while at Michigan State. She was from East Lansing, going to school at Western Michigan University in Kalamazoo, and was home for the weekend. I asked her out for the next night. When I went to her house I was greeted at the door by her father, who looked me up and down and yelled up the stairs, "Sandy, the biggest sonuvabitch I've ever seen is here to get you." Then he invited me in. We were on our way to becoming a couple.

Years later after we were married, the men at a company picnic were recounting fishing exploits and Sandy leaned close, and whispered, "You fishermen are worse than golfers." This dig gave me pause; my wife had grown up a suburban golf orphan and had always harbored a hard place in her heart for serious duffers who insisted on replaying every shot of every round. Having spent at that time more than two decades in that legal state called marriage, I had often admired her clear thinking and candor. But this comment really bothered me. I had once heard, no offense intended, that golf was invented to keep assholes off trout streams, and I had always endorsed this as containing more than a picogram of truth.

Many years ago there was a craggy old coot named Mort Neff who had a weekly "outdoor" television show syndicated across Michigan. He had one of those squeaky, grandfatherly voices, and a shiny high forehead topped by a pompadour of swept-back white hair. Of *Michigan Outdoors* I remember virtually nothing except for a weekly segment where various Michiganders stood at attention holding frozen dead fish of note for a zoom-in shot, their Warholian moment in the piscatorial spotlight of small-market TV fame.

As I recall it, Mort usually took it upon himself to relate all the relevant details of the Great Deed while his guests stared walleyed into the unblinking eye of the camera, and when the abridged encyclopedic exposition of the take-of-the-hour was done, Mort would ask rhetorically, "You must be real proud?" or "Isn't that right?" And the guests, true to cue, would grunt "Right," or "Yep," or maybe issue a shy and sibilant

"Uh-huh," and then there would be a cut to a commercial break. It was lousy TV on all parameters, but drew a huge audience. Among those of us who considered ourselves "outdoorsmen," Mort was the doddering but beloved high priest of our cause.

A few weeks before we were to be married, Sandy, her brother, Mike Phillips, and I drove up to their Uncle Bob's cottage on Holy Island in Lake Charlevoix. The house was one of several on a small island just south of the Ironton ferry, which you could take across to Horton Bay on Walloon Lake, where Hemingway had spent many of his boyhood summers. The rocky island, which is only a few hundred yards long and shaped like an Ethiopian alewife, has been known alternatively as the Isle of the Pines and Holy Island. The latter dates to a period when local Mormons came by torchlight to the island to do their worshipping; their leader, a man called Strang, later led them over to Beaver Island where they crowded out the preexistent Irish sodbusters and fish-gatherers and took control of the whole shebang.

Eventually Strang proclaimed himself king. I have never been sure if he saw himself as a king or *the* king. Michigan has had a long string of governors, senators, and big-city mayors who acted and lived like kings, but HRH Strang was the only public figure decent enough to overtly declare his intentions. No Mormoms remained on Holy Island, though my wife's uncle was known locally as Saint Bob; near as I could tell, this was a coincidence and a definite misnomer because the Saint was a believer in strong martinis and good times in equal proportions for all, principles neither Mormonly, nor saintly, but greatly admired by islanders and relatives.

We rowed a boat over to a drop-off southwest of the island and anchored. The brother-in-law-to-be and I began casting plugs and spoons for bass. It was a cool evening with a mist settling in, and my wife-to-be, whose blood traces to various equatorial genotypes, was shivering. I know now that this is a sign for me to do something, but we weren't married then and the weather, while not as pleasant as I might have liked, was perfectly adequate for fishing, except that the fish weren't biting. Naturally, Mike and I were undaunted.

Around dusk one of us hooked a small bass, and when it was lipped over the gunwale the WTB suddenly animated. "*This* is what we've been suffering for? You call yourselves *fishermen?*"

It was an ugly moment to be sure, a potential crossroad in the relationship, but we somehow maintained our composure and comportment and kept at it until we were ultimately overwhelmed by the deadly darts of her silent scorn. The wedding went on as planned, although there were some deep second thoughts that weekend on the fringe of Hemingway country. After that Sandy was known for some years in family circles as Mrs. Mort Neff, this the brainchild of Saint Bob. Clearly I was allying myself with a woman who had no soul for fish, yet one does not fall in love on the strength of fact, much less realities. I was committed to Air Force service and she seemed game enough for that; I reasoned that in time she would embrace the fishing part of me.

I suppose grudging acceptance is a form of embrace.

Not that the northern sojourn was a complete loss. She and I were pedaling a paddleboat toward the Saint's place one morning. When we reached shore I found that my line had slipped out and hung up on something, so I reefed it and watched as a marvelous fish rose from the gray surface and smacked loud enough to be heard all the way down to East Jordan. It was a fourteen-inch rock bass, its eyes the color of ripe pumpkins, a specimen such as I had never imagined before, much less seen, and certainly have seen nothing like it since. The catch raised my stature as an angler among the islanders and I rejoiced. We placed the fish in the catch-pond outside the cottage and the next morning it was gone, a late dinner for raccoons or scavenging herons. Sandy might not embrace my ardor for fishing, but she was good luck and no angler passes up a talisman that has proven itself.

Which brings me back to the initial point. We anglers do tend to talk a lot about our endeavors, but whereas golfers seem to focus on success, you're more likely to hear the average angler regaling companions with tales of failure and sheer empty-handedness, because those of us who ply the cricks and rivers and ponds and lakes tend to come home empty-handed far more often than with crammed creels. On the other hand, I have to admit that there are some similarities. Reading a green and a trout stream require practice. Accuracy is more important than power in both pursuits. You need to use the right tool for the situation. Anglers wear funny clothes; so do golfers. We both wear special shoes (both with cleats), and we carry rain and cold-weather gear because on a trout stream or a golf course, you go out in all weather conditions and to hell with what threatens. Some of us sneak out to winter fish and if there is a slight winter thaw, golfers are out there on the frozen links. Most trouters, even the most exalted ones, don't catch fish most of the time or even catch the limit, and few golfers play par golf, this the reason for handicaps. Didn't Lee Wulff travel the world trying to catch Atlantic salmon on Size 28–30 flies? And aren't these about the size of a micro-dot? Surely Lee was handicapping himself, not against others, but against himself, which is where golf and fishing are uncannily similar. Maybe this is true in all human pursuits; sadly enough, if you can hit .220, you can make two million bucks a year in professional baseball these days.

Falling short of goals is the rule rather than the exception, though there aren't many of us who will face this. What I know is that the romance and allure of trouting can't be measured on a pound-of-flesh-per-hour standard. It's nice to actually catch fish, if for no other reason than to remind yourself of the official reason you're out there; but catching and fishing are not synonymous. Some of the more discerning sexologists have pointed out that size counts for nothing, which is a rhetorical statement, not entirely true in reality.

One summer evening on the East Branch of the Paw Paw River I saw a flower the color of a scarlet tanager. It was growing in the lazy frog-water of a side eddy, about six inches from a steep bank. It was a proud, majestic, and lonely thing and I couldn't keep my eyes off it. "Cardinal flower," my friend Slops said as he waded past me.

I can't imagine a golfer stopping to gawk with adoration at one of Nature's smaller wonders or, wanting to, having the time to do it with another foursome pounding up the fairway in his six. That's the difference.

· 6 ·

AN OBSESSIVE-
COMPULSIVE'S
BATH MAT BEAR RUG

There are those who extol the culinary virtues of bear meat, but how something gray, greasy, and often wormy could be relished as a delicacy is beyond me; having tasted the flesh of a bear I can nevertheless attest that the predominant flavor is obsession.

The thing about obsessions is that if you can explain them, they're probably not the genuine article. About all I can do with this one is to sketch a few personal contours and suggest the general shape of the terrain and allow that this one, like many, got started more or less innocently. It is not a complete surprise that bears became the object of my obsession.

In high school I once found a fawn whose mother had been killed by a bear—or had died because of a tough winter and giving birth, and the bear had simply cleaned up the remains. I couldn't tell.

On my way to Idaho with The Aardvark, we stopped briefly at Yellowstone to watch Old Faithful's show, and, eschewing crowds, withdrew to a low-slung ridge nearby, only to discover as the geyser ejaculated majestically that we had a bear sitting about six feet behind us, watching us. Every creature has its own interests. We bailed out: downhill and to hell with altitude or the landing.

During my days with the USFS in Idaho, I had a black bear chase me out of my spray area and consume my lunch, which I had hung on a snag. I had not noticed the claw marks on the tree. With bears, like trout, it is a learn-as-you-go proposition. It was a terrific lunch. I hope the damned animal enjoyed it.

Sandy and I were consigned to K.I. Sawyer AFB in the autumn of 1967, about twenty Yooper miles south of Marquette in the central part of

Michigan's Upper Peninsula. Legend had it that the "Sewer" was four miles short of qualifying for hardship duty under Department of Defense rules—meaning a remote and unaccompanied tour, eighteen months versus three to four years—but it was not a hardship if you liked hunting and fishing and driving most of the time on sand-and-gravel two-tracks, which I did, and Mrs. Mort Neff distinctly did not. The base was named for a former Marquette County drain commish, to give you some sense of local color.

It was summer, after dinner, and I was headed through chopped-up terrain toward a feeder stream that emptied into the East Branch of the Escanaba River north of Gwinn, home of the Model Towners. Some years back a logging company built the town, lock, stock, and barrel, then moved its employees and their families into what was to be a proto-type of the company town for the iron mining industry. By the time I got there the only company left was Uncle Sam, but Model Towners had survived and the houses were holding up pretty well. They still are.

I planned to fish some deep holes where the feeder emptied into the Escanaba and was headed through a half-mile-long tunnel of tag alder, my head down, mosquitoes, chiggers, and no-see-ums swarming, my back bent, rod in hand; as I approached a sharp turn I slowed down and looked up to find myself nose to nose with a good-sized black bear. It was one of those moments when sound dies. I looked at the bear and he/she/it looked at me. There was no room to get by each other and nei-ther of us was spoiling for a confrontation. The bear woofed once and headed away cautiously as I woofed back and headed for my car, slowly at first, then at full tilt. When I walked back into the house and stashed my gear in the spare bedroom that served as a den, Sandy shot me a quizzical look.

"I thought you were fishing?"

"Wasn't in the mood."

It's been my observation that there are certain omens one shouldn't ignore. This is the sort of thing you learn covering water.

While you merely learn some things, other things can take root. I had taken bears deep into my brain and had no idea why.

I wasn't the only one. Nine men, chronological adults, trained at arms, made one of those asinine macho pacts that only men can make and mean, despite minimal words and less thought, the upshot being that we would all hunt bear. Looking back, the pact now sounds as ridiculous as a pact to hunt Chihuahuas or free-range Dutch rabbits. But it was made, and done is done—another male precept.

By the third season, the nine nimrods had dwindled to a lone fanatic with a standing score of no runs, no hits, and no errors, this last category being more important than the other two as it relates to solo hunting. A 30.06 with the clip inserted weighs a hundredfold more than an empty rifle. Or should.

That last fanatic was me.

I sat shivering one morning on a granite ridge south of Marquette keeping watch over a bear trail as well traveled as the Fifty-ninth Street Bridge in Manhattan. Sunrise on the rocks, my feet frozen, my face sweating. Too much hunting takes place with the sun and wind in your eyes. A scraggly red fox came along the ridge that morning, and sat down twenty yards away to share the warm sun. We snuck glances at each other, not certain of protocol. No bear came that day.

For ten consecutive days I dumped fish guts and meat scraps on a promising run, but no bear came. I eventually found that I could not tolerate the stench of rotting flesh and abandoned the bait game as unsportsmanlike (a euphemism for ineffective). I was becoming a sore loser at the game. Obsessions demand results.

Three consecutive autumns I was out an average of three or four times a week. At high exposure levels even a genuine cretin eventually begins to see and learn. Not much had been written back then about black bears, and I had no time to track down people who might know. I was on my own. An obsession often starts you at zero and takes you as far as you dare ride. There were many days when I was tempted to get off the roller coaster. But I couldn't.

I developed a deep fascination for ursine scat.

I would stand blank-faced and mute at cocktail parties until somebody prompted me on the subject of bears, and would then expound at length like an idiot savant, describing the varieties of shape and hue and contents of bear shit, how to tell if it was fresh, or read by its placement what the bear was up to. The Holy Grail was the steamer, one freshly dropped. Raspberries, strawberries, blackberries, huckleberries, chokecherries, thistle berries: shit piles told the story of Upper Peninsula fruit crops, good harvests and bad. After each day in the woods I left my clothes outside the house to let the wind blow away the human scent.

We didn't get invited to many parties.

I scanned the daily Marquette *Mining Journal* for tales of problem bears and went to see landowners interested in removals. There was no shortage of takers. The black bear gets little respect in the U.P., while two-legged omnivores get elected to the state legislature and have handsome expense accounts.

In 1967 I bought a pair of hundred-dollar hunting boots we couldn't afford, each fashioned from a single piece of double leather, guaranteed waterproof and insulated to thirty-below-zero; I walked the tread down to racing slicks. Two resolings and thirty-five years later, I still wear them. Before each season I shot boxes and boxes of 30.06 rounds at targets until the weapon was an extension of my body; I could shoot holes upon holes through paper silhouettes and dig the bullets out of the blocking hill, piled up end to end like cars in a chain-reaction freeway accident. I learned the hard way about layering and dressing to move or sit, and how heat leaches out of the body, how to move silently, how to sit still and let the forest settle around me. I became the commander of details.

Black bears tend to be solitary creatures and habit-bound. Each animal travels a circuit after food. When the berries are in, the animal may hold to the open until the grub runs out; otherwise, it tends to keep moving, traveling and eating by night, napping by day, like hobos. Some days I walked ten miles on what I took to be runs, and once covered nearly twenty miles over twenty-four hours all through relatively heavy cover.

Fortune cookies sometimes provide a line that goes something like, "You shouldn't wish too hard or you might get what you wish for." This has the feel of the sort of vague warning of an aboriginal shaman, designed to deflect our savage sides, but has little weight in the twentieth century. Education and Western culture teach us to set and pursue goals. The obsessed are victims of their own wishes.

Keith, my barber in Gwinn, was snipping away at my whitewalls, wondering if I was still after a bear. An old man in the on-deck chair came to life and said, "Hell, dat's easy." He told me how to find an abandoned homestead built on an island in the middle of a big swamp. It was not fifteen minutes from our house on the base.

"Dey had apples," said the old man, "brung 'em up from down below in da late forties. Bears all over da bloody place dis time a year. Da woman had dark hair and was a bituva tramp and run off wid a peddler, eh?"

Two hours later I had swept the "island" (it was more of a peninsula that jutted into a swamp and was crossed by an old tote road), and found fresh sign everywhere. Most of the apple trees had broken low branches and there were scat piles galore, the ground littered with half-eaten apples. I remember thinking that I should be more elated by the prospects, but felt only a curious aloofness and numbness.

Long before dusk I mashed down a spot in the high grass and waited. One of the apple trees had been untouched. When the sun got flat in the west all sounds died around me. When they resumed I thought it would be just another night in a long string of nothings.

The animal rose up on its hind legs sixty feet away and reached for an apple. It reached for the fruit almost daintily. This occurred to me only in retrospect. At the moment I saw only my obsession and fired without admiration or compassion, much less respect, hitting the animal in the back and the heart with such force that the impact caused him to do a complete somersault; as he reached apogee, I fired again, and a second bullet slammed home less than an inch from the first. After so much preparation I knew without actually thinking it that in less than three seconds I had put two kill-shots into the bear.

It landed with a thump and raised a small mushroom of dust.

Then, this bear with two bullets through its heart, got up and ran like the dickens.

A normal human being might have stood in awe, but the obsessed are not normal. I ran parallel to the bear's route. He headed down into a sand-and-grass bowl at the south end of the island of apples, and I ran the ridge and saw ahead of him a spit of open sand the size of a Cadillac. I knelt, pointed the rifle at the opening, and when the animal emerged I put the crosshairs on his nose and squeezed and he went down, tumbling forward, over and over like a roly-poly VW bug flopped nose-down into a ditch.

When the animal stopped rolling, it lay on its side and began to scream. Not like an animal, but like a human child.

I stood beside the animal and put the fourth bullet into the base of its brain—to silence my guilt and its voice.

I sat on the ground beside the dead animal for a long time. It was small, perhaps one hundred and twenty pounds, a skinny two-year-old, barely off its mama's teats. Be careful what you wish for, warn the cookie-maker seers.

It is disturbing that a skinned bear looks something like a human being, which may be why the Native Americans believed that a powerful spirit (*manitu*) inhabited each bear. When they killed one of the animals, they paid homage to its spirit, apologizing for taking its life and assuring its manitu that there was no other choice, that people needed the meat for food and the fur for clothing, and that they would always honor its spirit for having given itself to them in a time of need. The details of such rituals are well recorded in the *Jesuit Relations*, the missionary priests' letters and reports back to their superiors in Quebec and France. Some priests were appalled by the aboriginals' animistic beliefs; the learned ones were not.

I had no such excuse. I had killed to kill.

I didn't need its meat or pelt or bones or claws. What could I say to appease its manitu and explain *my* behavior? The obsession was gone. All that remained was the carcass of a small bear and my shame.

I have no illusions about the ecological sensitivity of Native Americans in their natural state. It did not exist. This is not a pejorative statement. Consider reality: The Ojibwas, like other hunter-gatherers then and now, were nomadic vacuum cleaners, wiping out everything they could get quickly and easily. When an area lost its easy game, they moved on. It's the same as when miners leave, once the cost of getting an ounce of ore out of the ground starts exceeding the price they can get. A decision based on the principle of diminishing returns. That animals survived in the face of the Native American onslaught had more to do with primitive hunters' lack of technology and lethal throw-weight than any ideological notion of fish and game management. But there was still a genuine respect for the animals, because the Native Americans knew that each one spelled life—and without them, there would be starvation and death. Superstition and theology are often confused in theory and practice. Sometimes ideology gets thrown into the stew as well.

Somewhere in my library I have a scientific paper that explains that hunter-gatherers would need to consume 4,000–5,000 calories a day in order to stay alive. Multiply this by the number of people in an extended family, say ten people, and you begin to understand that since the group has little agriculture, they somehow must produce 40,000–50,000 calories of food a day. Or weaken and die. Such demands and realities don't make for the niceties of conservation. You killed until game got scarce, then moved on; and if you left some animals behind, it was a testament only to your inefficiency as a hunter.

Killing a bear taught me to dream no dreams now that I don't try to sort out first.

My third shot had shattered the bear's left forepaw. I skinned the animal, stretched, scraped, and salted the skin, and shipped it off to a downstate taxidermist. I kept the rug around for more than twenty years as a reminder of the price of obsession. My family called it the bath mat bear rug.

Your demons aren't real until you accept them as your own.

I no longer hunt.

A TALE OF YOUNG TIGERS AND THE COMMUTER WAR

When you are raised in an Air Force family, the accoutrements of aircraft and bases become internalized and form your definition of normal—red tape, BXs, jargon, commissaries, annual immunizations, guards at gates, afterburners popping, klaxons blaring, etc.

Sandy did not grow up in the military, and though her father and uncles had served in World War II, she had lived a stable life of deep roots with a family that owned their own business and called their own shots. She had a huge adjustment to make when we went into the Air Force. Truth be known, I had more adjusting to do than I had anticipated.

Knowing that Vietnam was soon to be on the front burner, and being in a generation where the law required two years of ROTC for all healthy male students attending land grant colleges, I enrolled in AFROTC for two years and then applied for and was accepted into the final two years en route to a commission as a second lieutenant. I was not a stellar ROTC boy and ended my sophomore year as the only enlisted cadet slated for the third year. Everybody else was at least a cadet lieutenant.

This fact alone made me wonder why they had accepted me. The answer: I had warm blood and they were desperate for bodies.

Between my sophomore and junior years I went off to ROTC summer camp at Bunker Hill AFB (later renamed Grissom AFB) in Peru, Indiana, and came back to the fall awards ceremony to have a medal pinned on for outstanding performance in the summer program. My then-ROTC commandant, Lieutenant Colonel Davey, whispered to me as he pinned on the medal, "Who the hell are you?" Having demonstrated some aptitude for performance, my rank steadily increased from that point forward, and all the while Col. Davey and advisors kept wondering where I had been during the first two years. The answer was that I had been enjoying college life—some classes, beer, girls, hunting, fishing, lacrosse.

Sandy and I were married August 21, 1965, and after a brief interlude at St. Bob's, we drove to Yellowstone to spend a week in Old Faithful Inn before continuing to California where I was to report for active duty on September 15. We didn't fish.

I had no interest in being a navigator. I wanted to be a fighter pilot; but when I took the aptitude tests, I failed the pilot portion and passed the navigation section. My ROTC advisors told me I could retake the tests in a few months, which I did. This time I passed the pilot portion and failed the navigation aptitude, which was fine by me. I was on my way to pilot training. But my subsequent physical revealed I was over the limit for sitting height (forty-one inches from tailbone to top of the head is the limit). This meant that if I had to eject I could be seriously injured or killed. In desperation I volunteered for choppers and was told the same standard applied, because chopper pilots had to undergo the same basic flight program before specializing. The advisors told me if I became a navigator and spent some time flying, I could then apply for pilot training and the sitting-height requirement would be waived. I didn't understand how a couple of years of navigation would alleviate a basic physical limitation, but I wanted to fly, so I said yes and got my assignment to navigation training.

We took our sweet time going west and arrived at Mather AFB in Sacramento, California, on the appointed date, only to be informed that this was the day we were supposed to *start* traveling. Naturally, we had exhausted our funds along the way, and if I elected to sign in on the fifteenth, we would receive no travel funds because we were already in Sacramento. I called my father and asked him to wire cash—the only time I ever did this. Sandy was disgusted by the Air Force's initial reception, and her feelings didn't change over the next five years.

That fall wives of student navigators (there were no female navigators or military pilots in those days) were required to attend a reception and officially introduce themselves. Virtually all of the women called themselves Mrs. Lieutenant or Mrs. Captain So and So. But when Sandy reached the general's wife, she said, "I'm Sandy Heywood," and the general's wife grabbed her by the arm and pulled her aside and said,

"Stay with me—you're the only real person I've met this morning." They became friends after that, and though her friend talked up the military as a career, Sandy never bought into it.

During my nine months of Undergraduate Navigation Training School (UNTS), I hit the books and flew and Sandy got a job teaching kindergarten in the Sacramento school district, quickly discovering that the realities of the California educational system, at least in Sacramento, did not measure up to the system's then nationally vaunted reputation. She was reprimanded for teaching her kids their home phone numbers and addresses. Her supervisor informed her that such information was too taxing for children so young. Sandy was thoroughly disgusted.

After UNTS graduation and a two-week leave back in Michigan, I returned alone to California, to Castle AFB near Merced to begin Strategic Air Command Combat Crew Training School (CCTS), a three-month-long program, half of which was in the classroom and the last half pretty much all flying—in a KC-135 Stratotanker. While I was in ground school, Sandy took a teaching position with the new Head Start Program in Lansing to gather a little cash for us. She flew out to join me when my flying phase began and her job had concluded.

When we drew K.I. Sawyer AFB in Michigan's Upper Peninsula for our assignment, she was glad we would be closer to home, but not so sure about facing Yooper winters.

Once there we settled in and began our family. Tim was born in 1967 and Todd in 1970. By 1968 I had been upgraded to a regular commission (I held a reserve commission coming out of MSU), but I also had decided not to make the Air Force a career, and we had a September 14, 1970, discharge date. I figured by then that there was no point to applying for pilot training. I had no doubt I would be accepted, but I also figured unless I finished first in my class, chances were I would end up right back in SAC and I had no desire for that. The Air Force training programs were competitive. Those who finished first in their class could pretty well choose what they wanted. For the rest it was a matter of seeing what was left when your turn to pick came.

Over the next four years I was mostly gone, either on week-long nuclear alert duty, where we sat in a building awaiting the call to Armageddon, or on temporary assignments in Spain, Alaska, Goose Bay in Labrador, Greenland, etc. And, of course, I got a smattering of Southeast Asia (SEA), not on the ground in Vietnam, but from a distance, for two or three months at a time. I became a commuter to war.

I was and remain proud to be a Vietnam veteran, but my pride is tempered because, unlike grunts who lived in the mud, or fighter pilots who spent a solid year in a hostile morass, my war was temporary, relatively safe, and largely vicarious. The Tactical Air Command (TAC), which owned all the fighters and fighter-bombers we refueled, was fully at war with North Vietnam. By contrast, the SAC, to which I belonged, was more of a fence-sitter, loaning us to TAC. SAC's tanker crews would be dispatched to Southeast Asia for sixty to ninety days, to U-Tapao AB, Thailand, to the Young Tiger Task Force, where we would fly every day to provide aerial support to fighters striking North Vietnam, South Vietnam, Laos, and Cambodia. The B-52 Arc Light missions didn't begin until the Young Tiger Program was well entrenched.

Most of us looked forward to these deployments because there we could do a job where results could be seen and measured, rather than training endlessly for a nuclear war we hoped would never happen, and deep down felt certain wouldn't.

I kept a journal during my various tours in SEA, as I have for all my travels, and as is true of the diary form, my views were abbreviated, specific, and not at all comprehensive. My life in SEA was one of moments, fragments, rumors, chaos, and snapshots colored by hopes and personal feelings.

What follows are journal excerpts from 1968–1970. One of the advantages of going in and out of the war over time was to have a perspective on how it was changing, a view those on the ground could not have because they were mired in the reality of staying alive and taking care of each other. What I saw was a deteriorating situation, which left the Air Force robbing Peter to pay Paul, and SAC trying to support the prosecution of a hot war, while it maintained its nuclear forces for the cold one. Over time, replacement parts became difficult to obtain, our equipment began to fall apart, and the Air Force came to be more interested in us not looking like hippies than fighting the war.

I've interspersed the SEA entries with some from my SAC life back in the States, a lifestyle few people knew anything about. There is a lot of jargon in military life and I have not bothered to explain most of it. Some terms are self-explanatory; others I have defined, and the rest provide color and mood.

1968

31 MARCH 68: Tonight LBJ announced a bombing halt over North Vietnam and I soon leave for Southeast Asia, wondering what we will be doing for 60 days. The President also announced that he will not be a candidate for reelection in November.

4 APRIL 68: On the bus out to the aircraft at Castle AFB (Merced, California) we heard on the radio that Martin Luther King was shot and killed in Memphis today. It could be that the real war will be here in the U.S. this summer. We are going to Thailand as passengers with another KC-135 crew, a practice called deadheading. We will slide into the flight rotation after we get to U-Tapao Air Base, about a hundred miles south of Bangkok.

9 APRIL 68: Our first mission of the tour. We handled four Thuds (F-105s) pre- and post-strike and had to go into Laos after the strike to get one of the birds, which was 3,000 pounds low on fuel due to battle damage. Got my first letter from home. Sandy is in East Lansing with her folks while I'm gone.

11 APRIL 68: Day off. I took a *baht-bus* (a local cab in a Japanese-made truck with a set fare of one *baht*, roughly equivalent to a nickel) into Sattahip, the nearest town, which is a deep-water port on the Gulf of Siam and the entry point for all munitions coming in to supply the war effort out of Thailand. The town is poor and stinks and I watched a Buddhist funeral procession. Two monks in saffron robes wanted a handout, "Okay, Yank?" I saw an elderly woman with leprosy—no hands and no nose. There were water buffalo all over the roads on the way into town and even wandering some of the streets. There is a tapioca factory near the base and when the wind is right, we are blanketed by a smell much too close to rotting flesh. Today it was ripe.

17 APRIL 68: We were scheduled to fly at 0430, but got cancelled during the night. The boom operator in the room next door fell asleep while smoking and his mattress caught on fire. He then fell off the bed and it was awhile before anybody woke up to put out the fire. U-Tapao is a Thai Marine base on the Gulf of Siam. To build it, the Thais blew the tops off nearby mountains, hauled the rock down to a huge marsh and created the runways. Much of what is here is still under construction and every morning, double flatbed trucks haul in hundreds of Thai laborers. This morning as we headed for breakfast, one of the double-trucks was stopped and a crowd had gathered and we went over to find out what was going on. A man was pinned under the wheels and naturally we acted as fliers tend to in emergencies and tried to take control of the situation, to get the truck driver to move the truck so we could get the man out. As I reached for the man, I was grabbed by a Thai officer, who pulled me aside and explained that if anybody but the dead man's relatives touched him, that person under law would assume all responsibility for his survivors. Nobody told us about this cultural wrinkle during our various orientation briefings. It seems that an automatic default to Western and American values will not cut it. Having spent some of my time growing up outside the U.S., I know better than to make such a mistake.

18 APRIL 68: Today was a mess. We were scheduled against 12 Phantoms (F-4s), but six birds scheduled for the next tanker showed an hour early and we could only handle four of them, which pissed them off. We were out over the Gulf of Tonkin and left the coast Bingo minus 2,000 pounds. Bingo is the amount of fuel you need in your tanks in order to get home with a safe reserve over your home field. We heard an A-37 get shot down. The pilot was rescued. We flew again in the afternoon, handling four Thuds pre- and post-strike. We logged nine and a half hours in the air today and time is becoming very confused.

19 APRIL 68: We had a 0405 bus time, but the mission was cancelled. No reason given. It rarely is. Bus times are generally two hours before takeoff. The bus picks up each crew and hauls them to the operations building where we fetch our personal equipment (chaps, survival gear, .38s, parachutes, helmets, etc.) and then we are given a weather briefing as part of the mission preparation. Somebody from Intelligence comes in and gives us the latest on what is going on. We assumed on-call status until 1400 and then were released. We were worried in the morning because our pilot was so drunk last night he couldn't fly, and we weren't about to rat on him. This afternoon we moved from the cement barracks into an air-conditioned trailer, No. 69. It is parked on the edge of a banana grove in cobra country and we have dubbed it The Habu Hilton. The Habu is a poisonous snake indigenous to Okinawa, but the word is used generically by aircrews for any poisonous snake.

23 APRIL 68: Four Phantoms pre- and post-. Almost shit my pants on the way home. Prolly the anti-malaria pills we are required to take. Most guys stop taking them because of the diarrhea side effect. Diarrhea and flying do not mix. No more pills for me.

28 APRIL 68: Our 14th mission. Bus at 0305. Hairy takeoff: compass off, rain, crosswind and *mahk-mahk* thunderstorms with lightning. We plugged two Misty Facs (F-100s) over the gulf and gave a Voodoo (RF-101) some unscheduled fuel as we were headed home. The vast majority of our refuelings are scheduled and programmed, but when somebody is low, all tankers will try to help. The fighter pilots have a slogan: No tankers, no targets.

30 APRIL 68: 0630 bus, after we knocked a Russell's viper off our stoop and the other crew on the bus with us got one next to their trailer. Last week I saw a cobra by Crew Control. We are in monsoon season and the rains flush out all the rats and snakes. During takeoff we had a loud thump as the pilot pulled the nose up. One of our engines lost power. We dumped our fuel over the Gulf of Siam, declared an emergency, and landed after forty-five minutes. There were dozens of holes in the flaps and ailerons. One of the engines seized and blew out its metal buckets, which raked us like shrapnel. We were all shaky, but having aborted, we were consigned to spare status and at 1125 got launched in a new bird to handle two F-100s. We also took care of an EB-66, who was running short. We drank a lot when we got home.

3 MAY 68: 0715 bus, but we are Rescap today. When we went out to our truck, somebody had wrapped a dead Russell's viper around the steering wheel. The AC and I nearly destroyed the truck to scramble out. I have a good idea who put the snake there. A major next door killed two of them yesterday. Our job today is Cover, meaning if some sort of rescue mission becomes necessary, we will launch and orbit to keep the covering fighters gassed while they fly close cover over the downed crew and to protect the Jolly Green rescue helicopters coming in. The cost of the bombs the B-52s drop, we have been told, is $3 a pound. Each B-52 drops 60 seven-hundred-and-fifty pounders and there are about thirty B-52 bombing sorties a day, which equates to $4 million and change a day, just for BUF bombs. B-52s here are almost always called BUFs (Big Ugly Fuckers). I wonder if the Pentagon has economists looking at all this.

6 MAY 68: 1315 bus. Our two receivers did not make it back from their strike today. Both sustained battle damage and diverted into Da Nang. Intelligence says we have lost 17 aircraft in the past 36 hours and times are grim. We flew again later, bus at 2250, more bad weather all over the subcontinent. We watched a BUF strike from a distance. Their bombs lit the sky like a fierce electrical storm. There was a huge secondary explosion, prolly an ammo dump. Our 20th and 21st missions. I am tired and horny.

10 MAY 68: 1030 bus. At the briefing we were informed that all refuelings over northern Laos, adjacent to the North Vietnam border, are being stopped today. MiGs are ranging all over the place. They chased two tankers off the Tonkin Gulf yesterday and shot down a Thud this morning. Peace talks are getting under way in Paris, and both sides seem to be jockeying for negotiating position. It has been raining every day for weeks, but this morning we had the most yet, and 3–4 inches left standing on the ramp in an hour. We hit Phantoms over South Vietnam's Central Highlands.

12 MAY 68: Mother's Day and of course I never sent anything to Sandy, my mom, or Sandy's mom, but I know Sandy will handle it. 0850 bus. Our plane is tail number 3139. It came off the Boeing production line in 1955. Thirteen years old and looks it. Worse, it behaves like it. Lost a generator after takeoff, and shut down #4 engine during flight because of low oil pressure, but we completed the mission.

14 MAY 68: Another two-mission day. 0520 bus. Intelligence claims we are "kicking hell out of them," but no specifics. We handled four Thuds and had MiGs at 120 miles and all sorts of warnings screamed over Guard channel, the one frequency we can all hear, but which is reserved for emergency communication. We had to crosswire our #1 to get it started. 1405 bus to take care of four more Phantoms. Today we also heard somebody call out, "This is God on Guard. You people piss me off." The humor here is weird and dark.

26 MAY 68: Our son Tim's first birthday and I am 15,000 miles away. This is not a life for families. 0230 bus, Thuds, smooth mission, our 38th of this tour.

29 MAY 68: 0745 bus. Our aircraft commander came in drunk last night, so the copilot took over and handled the mission like a pro. We put the AC in a cold shower in his clothes, and then got him into his flight suit and loaded him on the bus. At the mission briefing he dropped a can of Snappy Tom on the tile floor and it sounded like a gunshot and scared hell out of everybody, but he didn't even notice. In the bus I rode in seat across from him with my boot against him to keep him from falling over when we made turns. At the aircraft we laid him on our equipment bags and did the pre-flight, then strapped him into the cargo area in back and let him sleep it off. He awoke after our pre-strike refuelings and I went back and let him loose. He slid into the left seat and tried to act sober and said, "Pre-refueling checklist." The copilot said, "They're on the target right now. We're waiting for them to come back." The AC was silent the remainder of the flight but as the copilot made the approach to the runway, the rudder suddenly jerked hard and he had to fight to recover it. The AC looked over at him and said, "You're not hot shit yet." He had jammed the rudder to catch the copilot by surprise. At conclusion of flight we were told we are grounded because we have flown too many hours this month. The AC promised to never go on another bender. We'll see.

30 MAY 68:   So much for edicts and regs. Another crew was sick, so we were tapped for duty at 2 A.M., spent nearly six hours in the air, and all of us are exhausted.

1 JUNE 68:   0155 bus. Four Thuds pre- and post-, bad weather everywhere, and fighters screaming for fuel all over the place. We offloaded 73,000 pounds and left the area Bingo minus 5,000 pounds and had to use tail jacks again after we parked, only this time we had the ground crew scramble up the crew ladder and stand in the cockpit to keep weight forward while others put the jacks in place. As we landed, the Command Post was launching the sixth tanker spare since midnight. Our 43rd mission since April 9. We're supposed to head for home tomorrow. Forty-three missions is the most a YT crew has ever logged during a 60-day deployment.

4 JUNE 68:   Got back to Lansing on the Blue Goose at 10:30 and Sandy and I hustled off to the Holiday Inn which had paper-thin walls. We didn't much care.

5 JUNE 68:   Bobby Kennedy was assassinated today in LA. The killer was caught, a Jordanian named Sirhan-Sirhan. No motive known yet. Bookends for my deployment: Martin Luther King as I left, Bobby Kennedy upon my return. Are we fighting a war halfway around the world so people can be assassinated back home?

1 AUGUST 68:   My monthly net pay is $622.20.

5 AUGUST 68:   A tanker crashed at Castle AFB today, killing nine crewmen. Appears to have spun-in inverted. We are speculating it was vertical stabilizer failure of some kind. As result we are now prohibited from making any steep turns (to prevent Dutch Roll) and make only one landing per mission. Later in the day we heard that the escape hatch was open, meaning the crew tried to bail out, but didn't make it. No surprise. Only two people have been able to safely parachute from a KC-135 in its 13 years of military service. Our tankers do not have ejection seats. We have to unstrap from our positions, stand, and drop down an escape chute to be free of the bird. If the plane is in an unusual attitude, the G-forces keep you pinned in place and there is no way out. We all know that bailing out of a tanker is a poor option, but nobody talks about it.

21 OCTOBER 68:   Operation Coronet West. We are escorting fighters to Vietnam. As combat planes need to be replaced, the replacements have to be flown across the pond to the war zone. We left 15 Oct and the next day took two Phantoms from California to Honolulu. On the tarmac that night, someone banged into a pitot tube of one of the F-4s and it was grounded until it could be fixed. On my birthday, 18 Oct, we escorted an

F-105 to Guam, a 7.5 hour flight, spent the night, and took him on to Da Nang in South Vietnam the next day, then returned to Guam all that day, a trip of about 5,000 miles. Today we took four F-100s over to the Philippines and a bad typhoon moving onto Guam forced us to land at Clark AFB, north of Manila. We are not allowed off base because there have been 17 murders this month in Angeles City, the town outside the base gates. We will remain here until the typhoon moves away from Guam.

27 **OCTOBER 68:**   We returned from the Pacific yesterday, were given 12 hours crew rest, and went on Alert this morning.

13 **DECEMBER 68:**   One of our former copilots, Charlie Griffin, has been killed in Vietnam in an F-100. He was married with three daughters, and an Air Force Academy graduate. One of our lieutenant colonel navigators today made a comment about there being cheating among navigators. He's a West Pointer in a non-career and bitter that the younger guys do better than him. The Wing Deputy Commander (DCO) asked me about it and I told him it seemed like sour grapes, something without substance. Our Squadron Commander called together all the flight crews and gave us a lecture on integrity, professionalism, and morale—all the while our crew chiefs were waiting outside in minus-ten cold and snow waiting for us to come out and do our morning pre-flight checks of Alert birds.

15 **DECEMBER 68:**   The Board of Navigators met today. I served as recorder. We found nothing awry. Our ring-knocking bitcher will have to find another excuse.

1969

1 **JANUARY 69:**   Our next-door neighbor crashed his F-101 Voodoo at Wurtsmuth AFB last night. The aircraft was a complete loss, but he and his GIB (Guy in Back, or Radar Intercept Officer, RIO) were uninjured. He landed short of runway because there were unreported obscured landing lights (I assume snow accumulation). They tore off the nose gear and the aircraft proceeded to disintegrate. Lucky it didn't ignite. The pilot is the Air Defense Squadron's officer in charge of making sure that all birds coming out of maintenance work properly. His squadron is very short of navigators, so I sometimes ride along in the backseat of his 101. He is from North Carolina and has ice water in his veins. His wife is from Puerto Rico and they have a life-size painting of her in the nude over the couch in the living room—a real attention-getter.

6 **JAN 69:**   Tim took a nosedive off the couch today trying to dive for a football. Three stitches. He cried but tried to be brave. Our babysitter quit

today and Sandy's doctor is transferring. We also found out she isn't ovulating. Not a good day.

15 JANUARY 69: I caught a penetrator inside the alert facility today. He had a badge that looked legit, until I turned it around and the back was blank. Per security rules, I threw him down the stairs where other crewmen grabbed him, hustled him outside, and pinned him in a snowbank. The idea of all this is to make everyone responsible for security. As a result, we all have bad attitudes for the imposition of another game, and the poor bastards who get sent in are there because they have screwed up and this is their punishment.

9 FEBRUARY 69: We are in Spain for three weeks (Torrejon AB, Madrid) flying support for airborne B-52s carrying nukes. The U.S. has armed birds aloft at all times and always within striking distance of the Soviet Union. Today we have spare duty, and were in the plane waiting to see if the primary tanker could get off, and he finally did. Out over the Atlantic there was a B-52 who wasn't sure he could lower his landing gear. The job was to fill him up so he could fly back to Seymour Johnson AFB in North Carolina and make a crash landing there if it became necessary. The government can't afford a nuke accident here in Europe, so I understand the order, but I can't imagine what goes through the minds of the crew as they spend several hours crossing the pond in anticipation of a crash landing. There is a lot of Mickey Mouse in this business, but it is first and foremost a deadly undertaking. Spain is a Fascist country with Franco still at the helm.

16 FEBRUARY 69: Talked to Sandy and Tim via phone from the CP. Clear connection. She and Tim are leaving tomorrow for her grandparents' place in Florida.

28 FEBRUARY 69: We are still in Spain, flying today as #2 in a two-ship cell against two BUFs. Our aircraft was not ready to go when we did the pre-flight and I lost my radar during the takeoff roll. After liftoff, the AC called for flaps up but we continued to sort of lumber along, our altitude not increasing and the foothills climbing with us. Suddenly it dawned on me. My hand shot out to the flap lever at the same time as the AC's and we retracted the flaps and the aircraft lurched into a climb. AC then punched the copilot in the helmet. This is the kind of mistake that can kill us. The refuelings were uneventful.

8 APRIL 69: We are en route to Thailand by the indirect route. Today we flew from Honolulu to Guam. We left Hickam AFB before midnight in thunderstorms, and Honolulu Control vectored us 60 miles off course because of commercial traffic and weather, and then it was catch-up for me after that. We had turbulence and high cloud cover all the way to Wake Island. Every time I got up to use the sextant, the clouds blocked my shot, so I had to dead-reckon my way across. At Anderson AFB in Guam we met a bunch of cocky BUF-drivers wearing pins on their hats that read, "Kill a Commie for Christ."

13 APRIL 69: U-Tapao, the usual briefing. Each time we get treated like chummies (combine cherry and dummy). New facts today. Thai house-girls work for 16 cents a day. Thailand taxes all imports 1,000 percent. The dollar is currently worth 20.67 *baht*. GIs on R&R in Bangkok average spending $70 a day. U-Tapao was having stray dog problems, so the U.S. Wing CO hired the Thais to exterminate the animals for so much per dog. Business was good, but the supply soon ran out, so the Thai Marines sub-contracted relatives in Bangkok to round up strays there and bring them to U-Tapao, so they could shoot them and collect the bounties. Most of the whore-houses have moved away from the main gate and are now housed in a walled compound called Newland, which is government sanctioned. The prostitutes are checked for VD every Wednesday by U.S. medical personnel. Each working girl carries a red ID card with a number. After the med tests, the numbers of the girls who have tested positive are announced on AFTN radio so the guys can get over to the dispensary for treatment. The ritual of the numbers is called U-Tapao Bingo, a game you don't want to win. I wonder what the mothers of Americans would think if they knew that their government runs buses from the barracks to Newland.

14 APRIL 69: First mission of this tour and good weather. Fourteen receivers. We had evaluators on board who said we were the best of 11 crews they rode with over past two days. We have now been recommended to lead big gaggles. Our Wing Commander, a one-star general, landed short this morning and clipped a row of landing lights.

15 APRIL 69: This morning, when I went to my personal equipment locker, I found that my knife had disappeared from my survival vest. No idea where it is, so I'll prolly get docked for it. We went way up in northern Laos, near Dien Bien Phu, only 120 miles from downtown Hanoi, which is as close as we care to get. We had Thuds pre- and post-strike, and during pre-strike they were up tight over heavy flak and surface-to-air missiles (SAMs) they would be facing. No electronic ground aids for navigation this far north and no nearby GCI. I had to use radar and map-reading to find the refueling area, and then brought the fighters in on radar. The receivers were supposed to take 54,000 pounds, but took only 10,000 and cancelled their post-strike. No idea where they went, or even if they went.

16 APRIL 69: Over South Vietnam, plugging six Phantoms and two Thuds. Weather relatively clear. An F-4 crashed near Nakhon Phanom (NKP or Naked Fanny). Both guys punched out and were picked up safely. Last night an EC-121 was shot down over Korea and 30 people lost. They were 60 nautical miles off the coast so the North Korean MiGs had to come out after them. The EC-121s fly the coasts of various nations doing electronic eavesdropping.

17 APRIL 69: We are on a station providing forward air controller support for a pair of F-4s who shuttle back and forth from searching their patrol areas for targets. I need new combat boots but can't get them through regular supply channels. My boom operator says if I get him a bottle of booze he can trade it for boots. I did. The microphone was out on the nose-wheel steering so I had to call out the 80-knot check today.

20 APRIL 69: Seventh mission of the tour. Our bus time changed to 1810. We taxied out and CP told us we were on a one-hour delay, no reason given. When we finally took off, nine receivers cancelled and three were substituted along with 2.5-hour hang-time in the refueling area. Our #1 engine flamed out twenty minutes after we reached our station and we had to RTB. We moved to another aircraft and sat spare until 0300. The media are now quoting Nixon as saying if there is one more incident with North Korea, we will retaliate violently and without warning. Yeah, yeah.

25 APRIL 69: One of our crews left for home today with 54 missions in 60 days, a new record, eclipsing our 43 of last year.

27 APRIL 69: Supported two FACs and listened to two Thuds going against a 37-mm site built into a box canyon. Their only ordnance was 20-mm cannons so they decided it was a poor match and went home. No mail in several days. Sometimes Sandy and I trade cassette tapes. Her voice doesn't sound like her and I don't think she likes using the machine.

30 APRIL 69: 0250 bus. We lost our ground power unit and air-conditioning and sweltered for two hours in the cockpit. We worked with two Thuds who knocked out a 37-mm AAA site, and damaged another. We took off again midday in another bird and covered a passel of Phantoms. My radar malfunctioned and I had to crawl down into the hell hole to try to fix it. The hell hole is an area under the cockpit that contains racks of black boxes and electronic equipment. I have to crawl down the vertical crew tunnel, then squeeze into another horizontal shaft about 2.5 feet wide. To work on the equipment I have to sit on the nose-wheel, which is disconcerting. Ended up driving my combat boot into a metal rack and the radar popped back on: Brogan maintenance. One of the Lion Control

(GCI) people at Ubon said he'd never seen a refueling, so we took our four Phantoms down to the deck and did a fly-by in refueling position so the ground-pounders could see. We'll prolly get our asses reprimanded.

4 MAY 69: Nice short mission. An F-100 was shot down and we could hear the search and rescue (SAR) effort. No voice contact with the pilot, only his beeper. He was down in Laos so it could have been a Pathet Lao flak trap. The NVA and Pathet Lao sometimes kill pilots and leave them in their chutes with their emergency beacons on and place guns around them. When the Jolly Green choppers come to get the guy, the guns open up. Found out later that the PJs found the pilot dead in his harness, his neck broken during ejection.

10 MAY 69: We covered some F-4s bombing trucks and doing ground interdiction along the tri-border area. I was in the right seat most of the way and the copilot was in back doing the refueling for the boomer. Our AC believes in cross-training in case we take casualties (or if he over-indulges). Both the boomer and I make takeoffs and landings and we can all do all the jobs, at least in part. It is against the regs to do this, but it also makes sense. A B-52 went down at Guam today. Hurrying to make an on-time takeoff, they set the wrong trim, went down in 16,000 feet of water on the edge of the Marianas Trench, the deepest hole in the Pacific Ocean. No remains found yet. We heard that one helmet washed onto the beach. All crewmen are presumed dead.

13 MAY 69: 2135 bus, Mission No. 27, and we flew for just under six hours. We've been here about 30 days and 20 aircraft have been lost in this time, not tankers, but throughout the zone—about two losses every three days. We worked with Thuds today and a nearby o-2 Birdog FAC called and asked if we could give him a thousand pounds of fuel. The AC asked what kind of bird and he said, a "Mini-motor." The AC said, "No prob, we'll just *pour* a thou on you." Our AC was drunk again last night and prior to takeoff puked out the window. The pitot tube had beans caked on it and some of our instrument readings were screwy.

17 MAY 69: Today was Young Tiger Day. We invited units from all over SEA to send people to U-Tapao. Hundreds of cases of beer were loaded on flatbed trucks and trailers and hauled out to the runway, where we all sat and drank as the visitors arrived and showed us their stuff. If the FAA or civilians saw this, they would faint. Got drunk and went over to Grunt's Grove, a little cafeteria by the flight line where we eat moldy hot dogs we call green weinies. There is a huge python in a cage at the Grove. We got the python out of his cage, and posed for a snapshot. I talked to a Forward Air Controller (FAC) about interdiction packages. Usually the package consists of one huge mine, but to keep the enemy from exploding it prematurely, they seed the area with tiny antipersonnel mines. The enemy uses a rock tied to a string, throwing it ahead of him, then dragging it back to explode the CBUs. After he clears a path, he pulls an ox in front of the main mine. With a rope the ox then pulls a plow or metal object like a garbage can lid by the big one, exploding it. The process, which takes us a day to put in place, and many thousands of dollars, is cleared by the enemy in 2–4 hours with a rock, a string, an ox, and a piece of metal. Simplicity can always best complexity.

18 MAY 69: Bad day yesterday. Three Phantoms and a Navy KC-130 were lost. One of the F-4s took a flak hit, which caused the GIB to be ejected through the canopy. He broke both legs and an arm during egress. Radio contact was established with him on the ground, then lost. The Jolly Greens found him shot to death in the jungle. The pilot managed to land the bird at Naked Fanny. The other accident was a midair. An F-4 was on the boom of a Navy tanker when the collision took place. Both pilots ejected, but were killed by sharks before the choppers got to them. One of our crews witnessed the midair.

24 MAY 69: The most beautiful air refueling I have ever witnessed. Both Phantoms were about fifty feet below us, and under them there was a mist and in it a rainbow, which moved right along with the fighters, like it was following them. The sun, which had dipped just below the horizon, filtered its rays to reflect off the aircraft canopies and the camo paint on the birds shone a bright green. Naturally I didn't have a camera. When you see things like this you understand why man must fly machines into the skies. The speed, silence, and beauty are overwhelming. The AC missed the 80-knot check on takeoff.

25 MAY 69: Our copilot today was notified that he is being sent to Vietnam for a year as the pilot in o-2s, dropping propaganda leaflets on the enemy—what we call a bullshit bomber. He's not happy about it. Our bus was supposed to go at 1950, but got delayed three hours. After we got to the briefing, we found out the takeoff was delayed until after 0130. They could have called and gotten another bus and let us rest, but nobody thought of that. An AC-130 took hits in Laos tonight and limped into Ubon AB (Thailand) for a belly landing. Seven guys bailed out okay. The gear collapsed on landing and the aircraft slid off the runway and exploded. Three men were okay, the crew chief was killed, another crewman died from flak wounds en route to the landing, and one man is missing.

26 MAY 69: Tim's second birthday and here I am again, 15,000 miles away. Mission No. 34. This was a fucked-up night. Our mission was changed as we started engines, from a pair of receivers to three. Our aircraft had no autopilot, an engine using eleven quarts of oil per flight, a screwed-up fuel pump, and they tell us to make sure we fly safely. Our receivers showed up an hour early. I am nervous these days, but not sure why, and not sleeping worth a damn. So far this year I have slept in the same bed with Sandy only 33 of 150 nights.

29 MAY 69: Day off. I got drunk at the Club with a Thud pilot who punched out ten days ago and has a cut the length of his face with stitches still hanging out. He is on his way to meet his wife in Honolulu tomorrow for R&R. We traded patches.

30 MAY 69: It is Buddha's birthday. Our copilot is sick so we had a sub. I didn't feel red hot either. Mission No. 36. An F-4 went down today. Both pilots rescued. We stuck Thuds again up near the North Vietnamese border. Grunt's Grove today has a new snake, a mean bastard about eight feet long with a little head and nasty disposition. He strikes at anyone and anything.

3 JUNE 69: Our 40th mission of this tour. The bird we're supposed to fly home is grounded. Boeing is sending a fix-it kit, but it will take two weeks for the kit to get here, and 500 man-hours to fix it once the kit arrives. We will deadhead to Kadena, and still be home on June 9. Last night the Cascades entertained at the club. One lyric sticks in my mind: "Send me a blonde because I'm tired of squeezing blackheads." I'm in a foul mood.

4 JUNE 69: Supposed to have the day off, but we got tapped to fly an unscheduled mission. We had a hydraulic leak on engine start. CP added two more receivers who had late takeoffs. We flew the mission as fragged, Phantoms, three and a half hours. One of our tankers aborted a takeoff today and burned out eight tires and eight brakes. Speed approx. 120 knots when he put on the binders. Lucky there was no fire. We had a crew party at the Swan Lake Hotel off-base. Met the Third officer of the *Pacific Victory*, an old Liberty ship hauling napalm. He was at the bar after a month at sea and begging to talk, so we talked. The copilot and I bought him a hooker for the night and missed the 0100 base curfew. We crawled under the security fence, then swam and waded through the swamps to get to hard ground.

10 JUNE 69: We carried a B-52 crew home with us. They've been gone six months. When we pulled onto the parking ramp at K.I. Sawyer, the BUF crew was met by a brass band, flags, lights, wives, children, cheering

Boy Scouts, etc. It looked like something out of a B movie. While they were feted, we shut down, buttoned up our bird, grabbed our gear, and the bus dropped us at our houses. Sandy is in Lansing, so I still have to go down there and get her. I am scheduled for 0610 flight.

11 JUNE 69: The Blue Goose is temporarily operating off the runways at the base, but I have to get to Marquette, then take a bus back here. Sandy has the car in EL, so I tried to get my AC up, but couldn't, so I walked out to the main gate with my B-4 bag and hitchhiked a ride down to Sands. I stood there until 0610 but couldn't catch another ride, and I missed the bus and the flight. As it turned out, I was confirmed on the 0655 flight and standby only for Grand Rapids at noon, so I took the late flight to GR and Lansing. Bumpy flight. Sandy not at the airport. The airline had given her wrong arrival time by an hour. Tim jumped and grinned from ear to ear when he saw me, stood between Sandy and me in front seat, patting my shoulder, saying, "My Daddy home!"

22 JUNE 69: This is Day 203 of the year. I have been home 40 nights, spent 33 on Alert, and 107 flying or on TDY.

26 JUNE 69: I called Sandy and told her I have to remain on Alert until Saturday. Almost lost her. We decided to meet at the base golf club for dinner, but it was reserved by a group so we went to the O Club, ordered 2 burgers and Mexican special, and waited 90 minutes to get food.

3 JULY 69: We are in a bit of a shell game. We have eight birds sitting alert, but only five crews and soon we will reduce to four crews. We are so short of flying personnel that we cannot meet our flying commitments and our alert needs. To the outside world all looks fine, but it is far from that. Another cost of Vietnam, which is siphoning flight crews and resources into that mess.

9 JULY 69: Yesterday at March AFB in California a 14-year-old boy snuck under two security fences in broad daylight and climbed up into a B-52 loaded with nuclear weapons. The boy then rifled classified documents and stole two handguns. He was in the bird nine hours and observed security guards bouncing a golf ball back and forth to keep from being bored. When he tried to leave, he was caught between the two fences, but was released. This morning the bomber crew went out for their daily check and discovered the plane had been entered and called a Four-Skin security breach. All the guards and security personnel have been arrested and all classified documents have been changed throughout SAC. The kid? They'll prolly make his folks live off-base.

10 JULY 69: Two POWs were interviewed by a *Look* reporter. They answered all questions with identical phrases and directed their answers to the guards. We all fear being POWs of the North Vietnamese and we worry that those who have been will come back as veggies. I took Tim for a haircut today. He was great. Afterward we went to Presque Isle Park in Marquette, took off our shoes, and sat with our feet in Lake Superior.

13 JULY 69: Tim, Sandy, and I had a picnic in the car at the Alert facility.

31 JULY 69: We had a squadron awards ceremony this morning. The AC, the copilot, and I each received four Air Medals for our YT missions. Sandy and Tim attended and Tim jabbered and commented through the ceremonies, making all of us laugh. I hope he'll grow up to be always amused by bullshit.

26 AUGUST 69: Sandy went to the doctor today to find out if she's pregnant. She's not. Instead, the doctor says she has an ovarian cyst or tumor, and a cyst in her breast.

3 SEPTEMBER 69: Sandy didn't believe the first doctor, so we arranged for her to see the Flight Surgeon who told her the other doctor is loony. He did pregnancy test, which the other guy did not think to do. The test was positive and we're happy and relieved.

6 SEPTEMBER 69: Dinner with Sandy to celebrate. Confirmed reservations for 2000, but didn't get in till 2030. Tim raised hell when we left. We don't leave him with sitters enough.

25 SEPTEMBER 69: Our Squadron CO caught two of us leaving the Club not wearing our red ascots and threw a tantrum. He called us "rinky dink."

30 SEPTEMBER 69: Sandy got a telephone call today warning her we'll get a ticket if our lawn doesn't get mowed. She went ballistic.

12 OCTOBER 69: We're on alert and staff weenies suddenly began showing up and huddling. We've learned that the Command Post has gotten an order to get eight crews on alert ASAP. All training flights are canx. We are told this will be a "test" lasting from 48 hours to two weeks for the entire Strategic Air Command. Nobody knows why, but it seems a harbinger of a higher Defcon (Defense Condition), and this usually means serious trouble is brewing.

17 OCTOBER 69: A Top Secret message instructs us to maintain our posture for two more weeks. No flying except for missions designated by higher headquarters—until further notice. Also possibility of higher Defcon in this period. 62nd Air Defense Squadron here is also mobilized and on full alert. The whole thing is still being called a test, but now it's not just SAC.

18 OCTOBER 69: My 25th birthday and we are still on alert. Much of the time we live in the airplanes and food is brought out to us. Today two aircraft carriers hurriedly departed the States, jumping off unannounced and so fast that they left crew members behind on the beach. Another carrier departed the Netherlands. We are told that we will fly now only to maintain pilots' proficiency. Last night one of our tanker crews was sent on two hours' notice to Carswell AFB (Ft. Worth, Texas), spent the night, and then to Castle AFB (Merced, Calif.) and right back home to K.I. Sawyer today. Nobody knows why. Four American GIs were detained in the Korean DMZ today and murdered by the North Koreans. Nixon warned the Koreans after the EC-121 incident that he would retaliate if they did something else. Now what? My guess is he'll do nothing.

20 OCTOBER 69: Rumors are circulating today that Nixon will start pulling troops out of Vietnam at a rate of 20,000 a month.

23 OCTOBER 69: Today we generated five new alert birds. We've been told that we will soon go to 18: beds, etc., are being placed in the facility to handle all 18 tanker crews. This deal still being called a test. The Wing Commander says that his intelligence sources say there is nothing awry in the world that might cause this.

25 OCTOBER 69: We have to fly a SNO-TIME mission next Tuesday night, an exercise designed to mimic a nuclear mission (EWO or Emergency War Order). We will refuel B-58 Hustlers in a two-ship cell with me leading, land at Goose, de-brief, refuel, and head back home. 26 tankers, 80 bombers and countless fighters are participating. The B-58s will simulate the enemy. (Soviets)

28 OCTOBER 69: One of our B-58s aborted and we offloaded only half of our planned amount to the other. We landed at Goose Bay and were whisked into a quick debriefing, went back out to our bird, refueled, and sat for 4.5 hours. We were told we could not de-plane because we were in an EWO simulation. I pointed out that in an actual EWO situation, Goose would be cinders and none of us would be sitting there. My observation was not taken kindly.

29 OCTOBER 69: As of 2100 tonight, the "test" was terminated, no explanation offered. It lasted 17 days.

31 OCTOBER 69: The Wing Commander is pissed off because of people "crashing" the Officers Club (not paying dues, etc.). Interestingly, his civilian cronies play poker at the club every Tuesday night, even when he's not here. RHIP.

3 NOVEMBER 69: Televised Nixon speech tonight. We are transferring military responsibility for Vietnam to the South Vietnamese. We will pull troops out at a rate commensurate with the "war mood." He rejected a full pullout because it would fall down on a commitment to our allies and cause them and citizens to lose confidence. *What* confidence? What a fool.

8 NOVEMBER 69: After our flight on Wednesday the Scheduler and Bomb-Nav planner changed my paperwork to reflect an integrated mission when I had flown a basic nav-leg. By changing the paperwork the mission result was out of tolerance. I called them and chewed ass, told them they illegally changed official paperwork not only without consultation but without bothering to tell me at all. They changed it back.

1 DECEMBER 69: The first draft lottery since WW2 was held today. Winning dates: Sept 14, April 21, Dec 30, Feb 14, Oct 18, Sept 6, Oct 26, Sept 7, Nov 22, Dec 6. My brother Ed, my brother-in-law Mike, and I all had our dates pulled. I'm already in, so it's moot.

12 DECEMBER 69: Our Squadron CO gave us a speech because he caught a tanker navigator at the club last Friday with long sideburns. He told us, "Any man with sideburns below halfway down his ears will get a letter of reprimand and so will his Aircraft Commander." Another fine example of leadership. I pointed out that his order supposes that ACs will keep their hair in tolerance and asked if an AC was the one whose sideburns were too long, would he, the Sq CO, also get the letter of reprimand, and if so, would he write it to himself? He didn't like the question. Neither did he answer it.

19 DECEMBER 69: We were on Alert and the klaxon sounded. The pilot and copilot were at the photo lab and got to the aircraft five minutes late. The cartridge wouldn't fire to turn the engine over because the battery was dead, but our quick-thinking boomer started a ground power unit and used that to ignite the cartridge. Then our #4 engine wouldn't start due to a frozen fuel control valve. The ground crew said it was our fault. The Wing DCO came over and told the boomer and me to tell Maintenance that the pilot and copilot were only 2–3 minutes late to plane. We passed the whole deal on to the Command Post and by tonight the story was that the pilot and copilot were late and the boomer and I never showed at all! I shake my head.

1970

7 JANUARY 70: We had a briefing at the base theater on "Dissension and Demonstrations: How Not to Speak Out in the Military." We were told it is unlawful for a military man to make derisive comments about the President, his cabinet, or the governor of the state where the base is located. It was also announced that because gambling is illegal in Michigan, Bingo is being terminated at the O-Club. Meanwhile the Wing CO and others shoot craps at the club for hundreds of dollars.

18 JANUARY 70: One of our birds was at Guam and witnessed an accident. Four tankers ready to roll. Lead went but an F-4 had pulled onto the runway. He had all his lights on for takeoff, but with all the lights and leading edges and him on the base side where there was more light, the tanker never saw him. The Phantom exploded and burned. The pilot ejected but his chute didn't open. The RIO burned up in the wreckage. The right side of the tanker caught fire as it dragged the burning wreckage down the runway, and its inboard engine tore off. The Task Force Commander said they were not approved to launch. The copilot insists they were. The fighter pilots were in a unit returning from a year in Vietnam and the two men were their last casualties. You never know when your number will come up.

24 JANUARY 70: We had a klaxon-out alert, which took us all by surprise. First-ever alert of any kind on a Saturday. We raced out to our birds, our radios wouldn't work, and our #1 engine had a frozen starter-control valve. Our Bravo time (time ready to taxi) was a terrible 14 minutes. Met Sandy at the club tonight for dinner. Tim was extremely rambunctious, talking to anyone who would listen.

3 FEBRUARY 70: We are on alert. The temperature today is minus-26 and the chill factor minus-75. At our morning briefing the Command Post called and told us to breathe slowly and not expose any skin because it will freeze in 15 seconds or less, and then they added, "Take your time with aircraft checks." Tonight one of our pilots aborted when ice froze his controls. He would have been able to rotate but not level off. The bird had just come off alert and we wonder how many of the others are in the same shape. The abort was charged to weather.

15 FEBRUARY 70: Our furnace went out last night, fourth time this winter. We awoke at 0500 and the temperature was 52 in the house.

19 MARCH 70: Sandy went to the doctor—same idiot who first diagnosed the baby as a tumor. She asked about having the baby induced because I am leaving for SEA for 90 days and had missed the first birth. He said, "You don't need him to have a baby. Who's having it, you or your husband?" She said, "Both of us," and walked out. The military does as little as it can for spouses and dependents.

23 MARCH 70: Our Squadron CO briefed us today on the "Misuse and Abuse of Drugs in Southeast Asia." We had to wait from 12:45 until 1500 so he could do this. He said drugs could cost us fines, prison and even ruin our military careers. No mention of addictions or health risks. He also asked if we had completed our quarterly 5BX aerobics testing. After the meeting the boomer asked me what the "Old Man" was talking about.

25 MARCH 70: On our way to Southeast Asia. We flew to Westover AFB in Chicopee, Mass. Met by my dad and Uncles Roger and Harry. We drove over to Rhinecliff and joined family, including my mom, for my grandfather's 81st birthday. Pop still smokes cigars and has nightly shot of whiskey. The AC made the best crosswind landing I have ever seen. Wind was 70 degrees off the runway, 20 knots gusting to 38, and then shifted to 90 degrees off at 8 knots, gusting to 10. He had to crib the nose 20–30 degrees off runway heading to make it to the concrete, but we hardly felt the touchdown. We spent the night. This deployment is to be 90 days.

30 MARCH 70: Kadena, Okinawa, and here I am again, different crew this time. We will fly some Combat Apple missions out of here before deploying to Thailand. At our Scat briefing we were told that the Pathet Lao are no longer taking prisoners. All downed U.S. flyers are being shot on the spot. We were issued Navy-type flights suits—called Nomex. Supposed to be more flame-retardant than what we have been using. Feels a little warm for tropics, but no choice—as usual.

31 MARCH 70: We flew Combat Apple, refueling an RC-135 in the Gulf of Tonkin. Mission lasted 7+20. On the way down to the refueling the boom operator wrote letters to his ladies. They all begin, "My Dearest Darling." He writes them all at once, then spaces out the mailings and replenishes as time permits. If he hits slack in return mail, he has a standard letter that says to the effect, "Look honey, I can't fight a war and worry about you, so get on the stick." He is a piece of work.

5 APRIL 70: Still in Okinawa. Today we took off at 0307, leading a cell of three B-52s and topped them off just north of the Philippines. At our briefing a chaplain came in to bless the BUF souls and told the Lord, "They'll be busy in a short time and might forget You, but please don't forget them." I had to choke back a belly laugh. Chaplains don't bless tanker crews; fighter pilots do that.

11 APRIL 70: We are back at U-Tapao and the word here is that the new wing commander is a psycho about haircuts. We were each given a diagram of the sideburn-ear ratio, and told there are to be no mustaches below the mouth or more than 1/4-inch outside mouth corners. We were told this by a colonel, a lieutenant colonel, a major, and a first lieutenant. I immediately went down to Sattahip and had red-and-white polka dot railroad hats made up with a patch that says, "Some Fucking Railroad." The AC doesn't think we should wear them. I'm wearing mine. Besides, my hair passes. There aren't any regs on hats yet. It used to be that we came here and did our jobs. Now all the stateside chickenshit is creeping in. When the focus is on haircuts, you have to wonder where the war sits in priorities.

12 APRIL 70: We went out to the Gulf and refueled F-100 Misty Facs, lingering while they scooted back and forth trying to find targets along the North Vietnamese coast. As we orbited I calculated that Thuds cost us $3.5 million and enemy trucks an estimated $10 thousand, so for every Thud they knock down we have to kill 350 enemy trucks to have a push. Again I ask. Is anybody looking at the economics? Never mind the suffering and death. Last night at the club a Jolly Green pilot told me they are using CBU-13 gas. They drop it on downed flyers and it makes everybody in half-mile radius sick. PJs then drop in, wade through the enemy in masks, fetch the crewman. To abide by the Geneva Convention, the PJs are not allowed to kill any of the enemy while they are disabled. How very nice of us. 0535 bus. All of our receivers showed up at once and it was a mess.

13 APRIL 70: 0525 bus. Heavy rain for takeoff and clouds all day. Last night was the start of the Thai festival called *Songkran*, sort of a Thai Mardi Gras. Everybody in the club was drenched by waitresses wielding pitchers of water. This will go on for the next two weeks. We handled two four-ship flights of F4Es. We listened to an air strike that killed nine road workers. A tenth man escaped despite multiple strafing runs. Only two bodies remained after a bomb was dropped. Sandy is a week overdue with the baby. I was on alert at Goose Bay (Labrador) when Tim was born. I worry about her.

14 APRIL 70: 0300 bus. Original takeoff was 0510, but we caught a hold of 1+35. Ground weather over the targets was marginal to bad and the weather aloft in Thailand and in the refueling areas was terrible. We came back fat on fuel. I took a *baht* bus up to Pattaya beach and the driver kept veering into traffic and I told him to stay to the side and he said if we crashed it would be Buddha's will and I told him I don't believe in Buddha, so drive on the fucking side! He did.

16 APRIL 70: We had eight Thuds post-strike in Orange Anchor. We lost our left hydraulic system when our receivers were 30 miles out and sucking wind. We got the offload made and headed back to BUT, dumped our remaining fuel, cranked the gear down by hand, and landed. Flight only 2+35.

17 APRIL 70: Went through Intelligence and mission briefings and out to the bird and learned that the Command Post had been trying to reach me. When I called on the radio, they said, "Go cipher." This is a machine called a ciphony into which I have to position hundreds of rods to set the day's code. So I encoded it and got on-line and they informed me that our son Todd was born today (16 April back home). He and Sandy doing well. She'll be in the hospital until Sunday and will leave for East Lansing with her mom on the following Friday. Having gotten this information in code, the CP then changed our mission—receivers, location times, etc., in the clear. Then they cancelled the mission entirely and reverted to spare. I got a call in to Sandy through the command post. Said she had a pretty easy time of it, which could mean anything because she never gives in to pain. We stayed on spare rest of the day and night, but never launched.

22 APRIL 70: Wrote horny letter to Sandy today. We lost eight airplanes today, 1 F-4, 1 C-130, 2 OV-10s, 2 A-1Hs, 1 D-2, and a Goony Bird (C-47). We are at Takhli AB for 7–10 days. This is a Thud base that has suffered heavy losses for years. Taking a shower here is interesting proposition. No curtains. While you shower, house girls troop in and out of the johns to "make water." The shower house is separate building and it is filled with lizards, toads, frogs, gekkos, and half the ant population of Asia. The postal strike that went on back home for months has created an 8.1-percent raise in base pay for all military personnel, retroactive to 1 Jan.

24 APRIL 70: 1620 bus. On station with night bombers again. Our take-off was delayed by thunderstorms and we were soaked as we went out to our bird in a downpour, then put on 30-minute delay to allow weather to pass. The runway here is 9,600 feet and takeoff distance is 7,600—with no allowance for hydroplaning because of standing water. The last time this bird flew its gear wouldn't retract. If that happened tonight we were or-dered to go to U-Tapao and orbit until the field opens at 2200 hours. (U-Tapao is closed until this time each day while the runways and taxiways are being redone with new concrete.) Talk about weird days. There was Thai boxing (feet included) at the club tonight. Hoped we'd get back to see some of it. We didn't.

25 APRIL 70: We had a troupe of go-go girls at the O-club tonight, round-eyes from home. I had a drink with one who called herself Philly ("like the town?" she said). After a couple of salty dogs she said she'd blow me for $20. I said, "How many already tonight?" "Four," she said, "but I'm shooting for ten!" I told her I liked my fifths out of a bottle and she said I was funny, and moved to an alternate target. We had a pressure bar tonight. This means drinks are on the club until one person leaves—for any reason. Guys keep drinking and piss in the corners. I love this place! Philly corralled the copilot tonight and I watched him kissing her. Later I asked her if she got her ten, and she said, "Plus two," and laughed. On way to our hooch I asked the copilot how Philly tasted, and he said, "Fine, why?"

5 MAY 70:   Heard today that Andy Anderson, who used to be a navigator in the 46th ARS at K.I. Sawyer, was killed April 29 in South Vietnam. His AC-119 crashed during takeoff at Ton Son Nhut in Saigon. Word is that it was loaded beyond capacity, which may or may not be the case. There is so much rumor in the military that it's often hard to sort out facts. Andy leaves a wife and two or three kids.

6 MAY 70:   We were originally scheduled for an 0625 bus. We went to bed at 2300 but got a call at 0140 telling us a bus would pick us up in an hour. First we knew of it and we were beat. I spent most of mission in right seat. Copilot was in back on his air-donut. When we got back we were told we wouldn't fly again until tomorrow night, but then we saw sked and it says 0605 bus. Big screw-up today. The King of Thailand decided to visit Takhli today, which closed the base for security reasons, so we had to scramble 14 additional sorties out of here.

11 MAY 70:   After a few days on Guam we have moved up to Okinawa. Went to the stag bar at the club to get a beer, but were informed that we could not be served wearing our flight suits. What the fuck is going on? Apparently Higher Hdqts has declared that personnel in flight suits will not be allowed in areas of clubs serving liquor. We're here for 10 days, then down to Taiwan for 18 days, then back to U-Tapao for a week. These will all be long missions.

15 MAY 70:   We lost two SR-71 Blackbirds today, one in Thailand and one near here. All four crewmen ejected safely. We now have two crews in tankers here prior to the recovery of a single BUF. Talk about mismanagement. Most Americans know nothing bout SR-71s, which replaced the U-2s for high-altitude recon around the world. Even we don't know much about the birds, but the AC and I spent a night with a couple of SR-71 drivers at Kadena last year and learned the following: The Blackbirds are called Habus by their crews and the rest of us. Cost is $8–10 million per bird. Flies at 80,000 feet plus and mach 3+, and has an escape capsule.

Two Buick V-8s are used as engine starters. The ultra-fast T-38 is used as a chase plane. The navigation system is computerized and if the bird were to get 300 feet off course (it never has), all sorts of warning lights come on in the cockpit. The turn radius at mach 3 is 210 nautical miles. There is a moving map tied into inertial guidance that provides real-time picture of where the craft is at all times. Cockpit temp is 900 degrees (which seems improbable to me) and outside air is 2,200 degrees. The pilot and navigator wear NASA spacesuits. A 32-man team pre-flights each bird for 36 hours before it flies. The bird takes off at 220 knots and lifts like an elevator. Landing speed is 150 k, plus one knot for every 10,000 pounds of fuel. Ejection is o/o m, meaning the two-man crew can punch out as they sit on the runway. The birds use a special fuel and there are very few places in the world where they can land. Their home base is Beale AFB in Northern California. The flight from there to Okinawa takes 5+00, which is slowed down by two air refuelings en route. Two men have ejected safely from above 80,000 feet. Flaps and all control surfaces are all computer-driven. In mach flight the cockpit lifts three feet. We talked to our pals at U-Tapao and learned what happened to the Habu that went down there. Apparently he got refueled over northern Laos, but the new fuel was contaminated and the pilot began to have immediate problems and headed deadstick south for U-Tapao. The engines flamed out about 10 miles north of touchdown, and the pilots had to eject, landing in a rice paddy. The pilot left the navigator to secure the wreckage, hiked through the swamps to a road, and flagged down a *baht* bus and got a lift to the base. The pilot was wearing a NASA spacesuit and the guards demanded to see identification, which the pilot didn't have—per regulation. The colonel ended up taking the gun away from the guard and getting the draw on him and demanding to see the wing commander, who came running, saw the space man, and just about passed out. The events of Air Force life sometimes are far more interesting than fiction.

26 MAY 70: Today is Tim's third birthday and once again, I am here and he is there with Sandy. I will not be home with him until his fourth birthday.

3 JUNE 70: Got to our aircraft and discovered no MD-1 pack survival kits on board, so I called the Command Post and Personal Equipment and they said, "Sorry, we just don't have any more." What this means is that we would be operating without rafts. We have parachutes, but little for survival once we are in the water other than the tiny butt-boats in our seat kits. Mission cancelled. Over the last three years I have seen shortages of equipment and parts everywhere, a result of the long war and budget problems back home. It will get worse.

7 JUNE 70: Flew 3+45. Our boom operator got caught butterflying last night—screwing somebody other than his regular bar girl—and she has put out a contract on him. He is living with us for the moment. At the briefing this morning some asshole lieutenant colonel got up and said missions are going smoothly, but we need to work on our taxi interval—what I call the SAC Tidy-Taxi Plan. What a jerk. He's a sure bet to get a squadron somewhere.

11 JUNE 70: We were told today to not mention offload amounts while airborne because EB-66s are flying electronic interference for B-52s and their refuelings (based on fuel offload quantities) are tip-offs to the enemy of impending BUF raids. Sandy will be at Sawyer when I get back, a first. Usually I have to go collect her.

13 JUNE 70: We are Cover bird today. When we got in the truck, the gear shift broke off, so we jerked our way to the motor pool in first gear to have it repaired. Everything is falling apart here.

16 JUNE 70: We had to switch aircraft due to a bad fuel pump. The new bird also had a bad one and that had to be fixed. We got to Laos–SVN border and Lion changed us to Cherry Anchor because our original flight, Bobbin, cancelled airborne. We headed for Cherry and five minutes later we were changed to Yellow Anchor, so we turned east. Five minutes later, changed back to Cherry and we turned west and finally Bobbin flight showed up, four Phantoms. The flight leader said it was a bad month, six ground cancellations, three airborne, and we are only halfway through the month. We hit some bad overhang from thunderstorms on the way back to BUT and got a major burble. We had a flight surgeon and the hospital commander riding along and both puked.

19 JUNE 70: A BUF took off today and had control surface problems, slid into 20-degree bank, and couldn't get it out. The gunner blew his pod and bailed out. The pilot finally regained control and flew for three more hours to burn off fuel so he could land. He could turn the plane only using full aileron. On the ground it was discovered that some wires had been installed backwards and others not installed at all. Yea, Maintenance. We did not have to fly today.

21 JUNE 70: 0440 bus. Went to briefing, then to plane, then to an ops hold. The mission was cancelled at 0830. One of my copilot friends told me the formula for figuring max tailwind for an EWO (Emergency War Order—meaning nuke war) takeoff. First, get the basic figure based on wind and direction, then half it, then half it again, and if it's still over five knots, make it under five knots and go fly. Roger that.

24 JUNE 70: Flew from Kadena, Okinawa, to Eilson AFB, Fairbanks, Alaska, today, 9+15. Actually, it was a pretty quick crossing. Fucked up systems. Drift read half of what it actually was, showing everything in the green. In 2.5 hours we got 45 miles off-course. On next leg ended up 30 miles off after 50 minutes. I used long-range radar to get a good fix heading into the Aleutians, hoping we weren't too far off. When we landed, our compass was 10 degrees off the runway heading. All of these aircraft are falling apart.

25 JUNE 70: I slept 14 hours last night. On takeoff out of Eilson we flew through a flock of ducks, one so close it filled up the AC's windscreen. This was our second attempt. At end of runway on first try we were told to hold due to an execution problem, no explanation of what that meant. We were supposed to go to Westover, but winds were too bad there, so they sent us home. Our beloved Squadron CO met us thirty minutes after landing and wanted to "chat"—while Sandy and the kids sat in the car waiting. He asked if we had landed yet, and I said, "No, you stupid SOB, we're still in the penetration," and walked away.

15 AUGUST 70: The three-year-old son of one of our pilots got into the family auto and released the brake. The car rolled down the driveway and T-boned another car. Kid okay. The Security Police gave the 3-year-old a ticket for driving without a license and careless driving. The guy with the other car got three tickets: parking on wrong side of the street, no windshield wiper, and no current base inspection sticker. The cop then tore up the kid's tickets. This is unreal and I am reminded of a Charlie Brown quote: "Semi-fully manned at 50-percent efficiency."

2 SEPTEMBER 70: Twelve days until I am a civilian and we flew. FD-109 problems prior to takeoff. Weather called for a few thunderstorms. Turned out to be numerous and huge, a line 100 miles thick. Our F-106s had to climb to 40,000 feet to get over them and come down to us for gas. Back at K.I. Sawyer the weather was 300 feet and 2 miles, fog, rain, and wind gusting to eight knots. Thunderstorms had knocked out the ILS and we were instructed to make practice approaches. We descended to 200 feet above the trees, spotted the runway, and made the go-arounds. We had to get within a mile to see concrete.

5 SEPTEMBER 70: Tim has been waking up every night about 2 A.M., crying and carrying on. One night a "monster" chased him out of his room and we couldn't get him to go back in. He was so afraid of the monster that he threw up a dozen times, claimed the monster was reaching down his throat and making him "spit up."

14 SEPTEMBER 70: Maintenance inspected our house at 0915 and we left the base. When we reached the Mackinac Bridge, Sandy announced, "I am never coming back to the U.P." She means it. After five years, we are civilians again. Meanwhile, the war goes on. Part of me feels like I am abandoning the troops, but a larger part says I have a family to take care of.

Almost thirty-one years after Sandy and I drove out the gate of K.I. Sawyer AFB, I went to Marquette for a reunion of the 46th Air Refueling Squadron (410th Bomb Wing-H). Our former top enlisted man, Senior Master Sergeant Ed Caldwell, was there, looking not much different than he had three decades before.

Ed came up to me during the cocktail hour with a grin on his face. "You remember Miss Thailand of 1969, Cap'n?"

Remembering the remarkable beauty of Thai women, I doubted I would forget such a meeting. "Nope," I said.

"The painting," Ed said.

I stood there like an idiot.

"The hag nursing the baby," Ed added.

That brought it back. In 1969 while in a gloomy mood, I had painted a beleaguered Asian woman nursing a baby and entitled it "Miss Thailand, 1969." When we finished our Young Tiger tour, I passed the painting to the next 46 ARS crew coming in and asked them to pass it along to their relief. So the chain began, forgotten by me.

Ed smiled. "It was passed along crew to crew until 1975 when the final tankers departed. Our last crew fetched it back to the squadron at K.I., where it hung until the 1990s. When the squadron was deactivated, the boom operators had a party and raffled off non-government stuff from the squadron building, and I got the painting. It's got hundreds of signatures on the back."

I was speechless. The painting had circulated among crews in the war for six years and stayed part of the squadron for more than two decades. It was a reminder of how small gestures can take on lives of their own, and things like books and paintings can come to mean something more than they started as, something more than their creator imagined (much less hoped for).

My war was pretty mild compared to what many experienced. Serving in the military is part of the tradition of both sides of my family. My father and my uncles served in World War II, my dad in India-Burma, and my Uncle J. N. Hegwood with Patton, all the way from Africa to the link-up with the Soviets. My Uncle Willard Hegwood was a Marine in Korea, at Inchon, was wounded and frozen, but survived. My brother Jim spent a year in Vietnam as an intelligence officer with an Air Force A-37 fighter unit. We all did our duty the best we could. And now none of my children or nephews and nieces have had to serve, and I couldn't be happier about it. The world remains a violent place, but at least in the United States we no longer have entire generations being pitched into the meat grinder of war.

· 8 ·

MISSIONS NOT MISSED: ADIEU TO WARS, HOT AND COLD

To Vikings Ultima Thule was the name of the northernmost point of earth where people could survive, which semantically was stretching the point, as proven by the demise of Leif Ericsson and lesser Nordic lights who wandered too far off the grid.

In 1951 the USAF opened a base at the end of the Thule Fjord in Greenland with permission from the Danes, alert to the possibility of high-tech, high-velocity assaults from the USSR or the Arc of Capella; you can never be certain where your real enemies lurk.

Paranoia was the primary fuel of the Cold War.

I don't know if the Thule base is still there, but in the late 1960s all of the utility pipes were above ground; during the White Nights they served as sidewalks for besotted aviators trying to find their beds. There were blue-green icebergs in the gunmetal gray waters in July. Suntans among the few local Danes were rare. Hungry polar bears, cut off from pack ice and their preferred diet of seal fat, wandered the island in summer. Pleasantly plump flyboys stuck to the pipe trails.

One day a B-52 Stratofortress, an infamous BUF, tried to make an emergency landing at Thule, came up short, and pranged (it's bad form to say "crashed") a few miles short of the runway, leaving a trail of debris, including the crew and a number of multiple-megaton thermonuclear devices (bad form to say "bombs"). Some of the crewmen bought it (we don't say "died"). The devices survived, bent and dinged, but otherwise fissionably able.

The survivors all suffered frostbite. If you leave a hot dog on the grill for two or three hours it turns a brittle black. If you expose flesh to extremely cold temperatures it looks pretty much the same. We were never taught this in high school or college. The survivors, for reasons never clear to any of us who read the post-prang reports, apparently were unaware that the hard packs under their butts in their ejection seats contained survival kits, and that inside each one was a sleeping bag designed especially for arctic use.

The casualties were judged to have resulted from "collective crew failure."

The Air Force solution was to require all SAC crew members with polar missions to demonstrate that they knew where the survival kit was, how to open it—blindfolded, and to be able to do this with socks on their hands to simulate the loss of sensation and flexibility in fingers that comes with exposure to extremely cold temperatures. Thus outfitted, each crew member had to identify every item in the survival kit and find and wriggle into the sleeping bag, all of this to be done in three minutes or less. Fool me twice, goes the aphorism. Bureaucracies and their minions loathe critical and negative news coverage. My dresser drawer of socks still reminds me. While taking one such test during an Operational Readiness Inspection (ORI), one of my zany squadron mates dropped a glass ashtray into my kit as I was pawing through it with the time clock running. Only a less-than-tight blindfold allowed me to pass.

Presumably, the thermonuclear devices were all found and refurbished.

As a former Cold Warrior, I have never before revealed the details of my nuclear mission; but now that the Soviet Union has dissolved and Russia is on an economic par with Brazil, I feel there's no more reason to hide the facts of what we were tasked to do.

The premise of the Cold War, to recount it briefly, was as follows: They had bombs and missiles; we had bombs and missiles. They were bad people and might drop their bombs on us; therefore, we tried to have more bombs to drop on them than they could drop on us. We believed that by having more bombs than them we would make them think twice about bombing us first. The balance achieved by the margin between our numbers and their evil intent (presumed by strategy-makers to be tempered by Slavic pragmatism) would dissuade them from striking first. This algorhythm was called nuclear deterrence. Overlaying all this was the notion that it made no sense for either side to shoot first because both sides, regardless of who took the first shot, would be annihilated. This was referred to as Mutual Assured Destruction, or MAD, the penultimate acronym. In some ways this was the *real* World Series of Poker. Through a blend of luck and cooler heads prevailing, this insane formula worked.

In the event of a nuclear attack, here's what our jobs would have been. The klaxon (a siren with laryngitis) sounds. We jump into our AF-blue double-cab Ford truck and race out to our aircraft. We use explosive cartridges to simultaneously gang-start all four Pratt & Whitney J-57 jet engines. While one of the pilots is gang-starting the engines and the ground crew is standing clear of the intakes to keep from being ingested or toasted, the rest of us turn on our radios and hear a voice that says something like this: "Sky King, Sky King, this is Looking Glass with a Red Dot One. India, Delta, Lima, Yankee, Sierra, Mike." I-D-L-Y-S-M.

"Red Dot" tells us that this is the real thing and not just another drill.

"One" lets us know that a shooting war had already begun: America is under attack. Probably missiles have been launched at us but have not yet struck. They will arrive shortly.

The six follow-up letters in the message are authentication codes. We have sealed envelopes in a locked box in our bird, which each of us now opens. If the broadcast letters match the letters in our envelopes, it means we should get off the ground fast and fly our mission. This is a six-card deck with no wild cards. If we win, it means we lose. You have to love the irony. What all this would mean was that the whole world was in deep shit.

Let's assume that the cards match the radio transmission. We immediately make a high-speed taxi to the runway and take off. Around us there are seven other KC-135 tankers also trying to get off the ground, and probably the last of eight B-52Hs lifting off in a pall of blue-black exhaust smoke as the first of our lot gets to the runway and rolls. Once airborne, we nudge our heading a little to one side or the other to avoid the violent eddies of jet wash roiling from the aircraft ahead of us, retract the gear and flaps, and fly north out of the Upper Peninsula into Canada. Our predetermined destination is the ice pack beyond the northernmost tip of Greenland; we've been briefed on this beforehand.

As soon as we're off the ground we insert flash protector plugs in all of our windows. These plugs have handles on their backs for ease of installation; the exterior skins are covered with a sort of aluminum foil and designed to keep all external light out of the cockpit. The plugs are to keep us from being flash-blinded by the few odd mushroom clouds we are likely to encounter on our journey to the Far North. There are not many significant military targets along our route to the north, but these were the early days of primitive multiple warheads, or MIRVs, sort of nuclear buckshot fired by solid fuel scatterguns seven thousand miles away.

As any bird hunter can attest, your pellets don't all go where you hope they will. This description will not satisfy the technically reverent, but it gives the rest of us a picture we can hold on to. Accidents happen.

Not that Uncle Sam doesn't care about us. When possible we are to avoid the nuclear mushrooms along our route; nuke bursts, they assure us, will show up on our radar screens as bright yellow balls. But if we happen to fly into one (assuming it doesn't melt or disintegrate us), we are supposed to take out a styrette (a combination eye dropper-syringe) of adrenaline and jam the needles into the tops of our thighs, through the fabric of our flight suits. The drug will keep us going.

Our job is not to drop bombs. Our job is to provide fuel to those who will go on to the USSR and drop bombs on our collective behalf. We have no weapons, but we are critical to the outcome of the retaliation. No tankers, no targets. Back then, most B-52s couldn't fly that far without getting gas en route.

Our receivers will drop their bombs on targets in and around Moscow. It seems odd to write about this now, but this is what I lived with for four years. And all that time, I never told Sandy about any of it.

Upon reaching our refueling area, which is a collection of map coordinates rather than a place with discernible landmarks (or even land below us, for that matter), we orbit to await our B-52s, which are loaded for Soviet bear. Under the normal war plan, we will give gas in midair to our receivers, then land at Thule, but under other conditions we could be ordered to pump all of our fuel into our receiver, saving only enough for us to "clear track," meaning we should get the hell out of the way of the B-52s headed for enemy lands.

Having cleared track and depleted what remains of our own fuel, our engines will stall. We are then to parachute onto the Arctic pack ice five to seven miles below us and make our way on foot back to our reconstitution point, which is Billy Mitchell Field in Milwaukee, Wisconsin. How we get there is up to us. A downed aircrew is supposed to improvise. Optimism won't hurt the group effort.

There are a few fishhooks and some line in our survival packs.

The Strategic Air Command's motto was Peace Is Our Profession. What the aircrews said was, "I'd rather have a sister in a whorehouse than a brother in SAC."

Our individual survival kits each contain an over-under firearm with a foldout tubular steel stock. One barrel holds .410 shotgun rounds; the other is for .22 Hornet ammo. There are thirty rounds for each barrel, each of which is about eighteen inches long. As the only certified bear killer and small-arms expert on my crew, I am elected to the quasi-official position of crew hunter and shooter; it is to be my job to dispatch any polar bears or Russian paratroopers blocking our several-thousand-mile hike back to Wisconsin. Knowing this, I lobby hard for focusing on fish before bears.

Nobody was happier to have an end to the Cold War than SAC crews, especially those flying tankers. It was going to be a long, chilly walk back to Billy Mitchell Field.

Stanley Kubrick did not have to embellish reality to make *Dr. Strangelove*. SAC crews saw it as a documentary, not a farce.

In those days we used to say, "I shit you not."

This meant you were hearing the truth.

My sphincter still pulsates when I hear a siren.

The Cold War was one thing, but a hot one is much different.

With apologies to Tim O'Brien who came closest with *Going after Cacciato*, the great Vietnam story has yet to find life. Coppola, for all his genius, concentrated only on the fun parts in *Apocalypse Now*. The trouble with explicating that particular brouhaha was not that the Xs and Os were unknown, but that the war existed in a cocoon of impenetrable irony. To have a widely accepted Great Cause is to have a conceptual structure to work with; Vietnam was notably deficient in this regard.

It's no wonder that some vets still flash back and imagine setting Claymores around their hunting blinds. During the Gulf War, "Hanoi Jane" Fonda's most recent husband gave us around-the-clock, "Live, It's Baghdad Burning!" Two wars twenty years apart, and Jane-the-Pain found a way into the revenue stream both times. Jane Fonda was and remains uniformly loathed by Vietnam vets; I once heard some vets in a theater, watching her film, *Cat Ballou*, shouting, "Forget the bitch, Shaleen! Side with the railroad!"

Coppola had one thing right: Vietnam was a comedy in the classic sense. There are only so many tears in our glands; after a certain point, we can only laugh at the sheer absurdity of life, even when we're in it.

A saffron-robed monk in Sattahip, Thailand, chastised me roundly one day for killing Vietnamese. "You ought to kill Cambodians," he added. "*They're* the evil ones." Viewpoint is all.

Some of our Thai "house girls" traded blow jobs for boxes of Tide and Ivory Snow. In the 1990s some Russian girls did the same thing for packs of Marlboros, which were to become the early post–Cold War's preferred international currency.

Westover AFB in Chicopee, Massachusetts, was reputed to have the highest divorce rate in the U.S. in the late 1960s. If true, this was no accident. It was inescapable collateral damage.

The Westover boys flew the oldest model B-52s. When it became clear that there was a need for carpet bombing in Vietnam, the old-model BUFs were retrofitted to iron bombs, meaning the same kind we dropped from B-17s, B-24s, B-26s, and B-29s on the Nazis and Japanese. Once the old planes were modified, the crews flew them over to Guam or Thailand and from there began a campaign of bombing monkey colonies in South Vietnam, Laos, and Cambodia. Details are unimportant; we all know about the bombs. The BUFs did do the work.

Before some B-52 missions, leaflets were often dropped on enemy positions (or suspected positions, which was more often the case) by O-2 Birddogs, which we called Bullshit Bombers. These said: "*Chieu Hoi.* Surrender now. The B-52s are coming. You will not see them. You will not hear them. They will kill you." This is called psychological warfare. Sometimes it worked and the enemy troops gave up; more often, they simply dug in, tightened their chin straps, and died.

Here's something you probably don't know: Air Force regulations stipulated that anybody who served one hundred and eighty days or more outside the U.S. in a twelve-month period had to get credit for a full foreign tour, which made the individual ineligible for a Permanent Change of Station, or PCS, for several years. Ergo, anybody who spent more than one hundred and eighty days on temporary duty outside the U.S. in a twelve-month period could not be transferred to another base; the implications for Pentagon and Air Force personnel weenies were horrendous. What the Pentagon did to get around this was to take the Westover gang (later, there were other units) and send them en masse to Southeast Asia for one hundred and seventy-nine days, then rotate them home for a little over that amount, and send them back again. The Air Force called this an operational plan; the crews called it a crock.

The military had responsibility for a lot of families in those days, but often seemed oblivious to their needs. A colonel once told me, "If the Air Force wanted you to have a wife, they would have issued you one." He wasn't smiling.

Say you were assigned to Westover AFB in Massachusetts; under a normal PCS you could expect to be there three or four years before you uprooted the family for your next assignment. But by rotating the wing as previously described, you would spend eighteen months of your three years in the combat zone and then be eligible for a separate and additional one-year PCS in Vietnam. By the end of four years you would have spent thirty of your forty-eight months at war and away from your family, assuming you still had one. Luckily this didn't happen to me, but it happened to enough families to give one pause about government decision-making.

A high divorce rate under such conditions is not particularly surprising; that any marriages survived was the true marvel. Whoever writes the great epic of SAC and Vietnam, please work this in.

My first copilot was Terry Daugherty, against whom I had played college lacrosse (I was a crease attackman for Michigan State and he was a goalie for Ohio Wesleyan). Terry had been a copilot in B-47s before his assignment to tankers. B-47s were the forerunners of B-52s. Years later I learned that 100 percent of the B-47s were not expected to complete their missions.

When he left the Air Force Terry became a Pan Am (and later a Saudi Air) pilot, and I once asked him if he knew that none of the B-47s were expected to survive. He just grinned and shrugged.

The crazy part of all this is that if the klaxon had sounded and our go-code had been authenticated, we would have gone and that would have been the end of the world as we knew it.

I shit you not.

PART II: THE SEVENTIES & EIGHTIES

"If you rest, you rust."
—Helen Hayes

"If you obey all the rules you miss all the fun"
—Katharine Hepburn

· 9 ·

HUNTING FOR
SOMETHING

Obsessions aside, I was never much of a hunter, though I thoroughly loved the Grand Company of Deer Camp and the fellowship that was at the heart of it.

An effective hunter is essentially an effective killer. Killing is the bottom line, and hunters who deny this are idiots, or self-delusional. Killing is not wrong; we eat meat every day. Most of us just don't kill for ourselves.

I have always believed that the ability to kill quickly and efficiently boils down to cerebral circuitry that enables some people to see, compute, and fire, all in short order. I lack the requisite wiring and do not feel denied. I have killed, but am not a killer, a lesson learned the hard way.

The essence of deer hunting is suffering: getting up before daylight, stumbling blindly through a dark forest, air so cold that snow snaps under your boots like Styrofoam peanuts and turns nose hairs to straw, numbness crawling up your legs into your groin, the distant report of rifles, trying to stay awake, the adrenaline rush when an animal approaches, the disgusting mess of cleaning a carcass, and the exhausting work of dragging the thing back to camp. This last bit gives you a better fix on the term, "dead weight."

As in trouting, where seeing the rises can be most difficult, the hardest part of deer hunting is The Seeing of the Horns. Most of my companions could put eight-inch spikes on a deer running full tilt and head down at thirty mph, two hundred yards away, ten minutes after sunset. I couldn't see a Boone and Crockett rack at the other end of the cribbage board. My companions will bear witness to this shortcoming.

I never much worried, hunting in the U.P., because there were more deer than hunters (and not many of either), which left plenty of time to be certain of all the technical aspects. Is it a buck? Is it alone or are there others nearby? Where are my pals? What's my line of fire look like? Is it safe to shoot? How far back to camp will I have to drag the sonuvabitch?

After years of hunting the Upper Peninsula, my first hunt BTB (Below the Bridge) was terrifying.

To hunt with heavily armed and aggressive flatlanders leaves a Yooper's mind reeling. One fall in the late 1970s, some friends and I bow-hunted the ridges and creek bottoms on the eastern periphery of Yankee Springs; we had put in a lot of hours, eventually concluding that there were three, maybe four bucks in our favorite square, which was privately owned. That November, when gun season commenced, there were no doe permits for that area. At our latitude it is shotguns-only (you have to hunt farther north to use a rifle). Starting an hour before I could see and continuing until two hours after respectable and measurable daylight, I counted more than three hundred shots, often in sputtering, anxious flurries, none from our bunch.

It was like having a seat one arroyo over from the Alamo.

Near Cadillac one morning, an old softball teammate's teenage son was on his first hunt and knocked down a nice eight-point, which stumbled up to the shoulder of the U.S. 131 Bypass, collapsed, and died. As the boy made his way across a wide swale toward the deer, a sedan screamed to a halt. Two men got out, hurriedly opened their trunk, pitched the dead buck in, slammed the lid, and sped off. Sportsmanship in the Winter Water Wonderland.

East of Trout Lake in the U.P., I shuffled out of the bush at noon one day to wait for my friend. After a few minutes a buck with no right front foreleg hopped onto the macadam and flopped around in agony. I finished what somebody else had started with a single round, gutted the deer, and sat down to wait. Two middle-aged men in need of shaves came along later, looked at the deer, and leveled their rifles at me.

"*Our* deer," one of them growled. I told them that if I had wanted to make off with the meat, I would have been long gone. They dragged the animal back down into the swamp and disappeared. Another lesson in sportsmanship.

The general rule among hunters is that first hit takes the meat, which makes the kill-shot moot.

A bullet alone and out of context is not a frightening thing until you think about how it does what it does, and what sort of effect it is designed to exert. A bullet that goes through the trees just over your head makes a clicking sound, like a cricket on crack cocaine, before you hear the actual report. This is a microcosmic example of the sound barrier. Several rounds in close proximity sound like bees and leave your knees weak. Movie characters look for immediate justice after a close call; real people try to crawl down into the ground, get as flat as an amoeba, and remain there until the deer season is over.

North of Baldwin a neighbor of mine passed a fellow in a red snowmobile suit one snowy morning and, a few minutes later, heard a shot and frantic screams. He backtracked and found the man on the ground, shot in the leg with a two-hundred-grain round out of a 30.06. Here's what happened: He had bought the rifle the day before. When it began to snow he wanted to protect the barrel from rusting; in the process of pushing the rifle business-end first down into his snowmobile suit, it discharged. Its first shot drew blood: his own. Thanks to my neighbor the man kept his leg. For what it's worth, the man was from Indiana, but Michiganders do equally stupid things.

One of my former high school basketball teammates was dressed in red one Thanksgiving weekend during his first week of college, and hunting near his house in the eastern U.P. He came up out of a cedar swamp and saw a hunter on the hill above him and waved to make sure he had been seen.

He had.

The first round struck him in the hip. The other two flew high. The shooter left without coming down to gut his prize. My friend crawled out to get help. He still has the bullet in his hip and a limp to prove it. He played no more basketball.

Surgeons can't fix everything, especially intent. Laws on paper don't mean much to the illiterate or homicidal.

Some years back two deer hunters near Kalamazoo were killed while hunting thirty yards apart in the same state-owned woodlot. Neither man knew the other. Apparently, neither man knew the other was there. State Police forensics experts concluded that a third party, or parties, had shot them both. With no motive and no suspects, the case remains glaringly open. Pray for prey, Pogo might have said. They are we and we are they. It took something like a decade, but the case was solved just last year. The accused is alleged to have taken umbrage at the two hunters who were using public land he considered his own.

One year, I think it was in upstate western New York, a farmer painted "COW" on the side of one of his dairy animals. The photograph was picked up by a wire service and appeared nationwide. It's not recorded whether the animal survived the hunting season.

Conservation officers in Michigan and elsewhere have in recent years started using lifelike mechanical deer decoys. Some COs call the device *Blambi*. They set these things conspicuously in fields along side roads. More often than you would think, drive-by hunters buzz down their electric windows and unlawfully squeeze off rounds from their vehicles. We have drive-by shootings in our cities, but as far as I know the police there have not yet resorted to the same sort of traps. Maybe the deer are more important. Who can say?

The Department of Natural Resources (DNR) has deer inspection stations set up along the state's main highways. Hunters who kill deer are asked to stop at the stations so that measurements can be taken; biologists use these data to get a fix on the general health and well-being (ignoring the obvious state of the animal being checked) of the state's deer herd. Each hunter who reported in got a "Successful Deer Hunter Patch." I have seen guys wearing these merit badges on their churchgoing duds.

Hunters in Michigan have, for as long as I can remember, carried their dead deer strapped to the fenders or roofs of their cars. Every November we used to count how many we saw. For a while in South Vietnam our GIs strapped the bodies of dead Viet Cong or NVA troops to their trucks and Jeeps and APCs. The photos did not play well back home. Some habits are difficult to break.

The last buck I saw while I was carrying a shotgun walked up to my beech tree blind and began pawing the ground, ten feet away. It was a nice buck, with a tight eight-point rack. I lifted the gun, aimed, and whispered, "Pow." Then I put the gun down, made sure the safety was on, and poured myself some more coffee.

All the years I hunted, I was looking for something: me. That morning near Hastings I found a pretty good part of myself.

My shotgun and rifle are now quietly pitting in their padded cases.

My killing days have ended.

· 10 ·

LIFE FORCES:
SEX AND RIVERS

etaphorically there is something to the notion of human repro-
duction being akin to anadromous fish battling their way upstream. For trout, the womb of life *is* the river. Pacific salmon
spawn once and die. Talk about a wicked price for genetic transfer.

I'm not sure why, but rivers seem to encourage human mating rituals. Could it be the abundance of natural music and wild flowers? In
Michigan, I always look for forget-me-nots along streams and rivers and
nearly always hook fish where the delicate and beautiful flowers grow.
It's even better if the flowers are adjacent to a riffle where the river bois-
terously and unabashedly sings its songs.

Most of the time I try to find forget-me-nots, but not other trouters.

Sometimes you can't avoid other anglers, and this creates interesting
moments.

There is, as an example, a hairpin turn near the Green Cabin access
on the Pere Marquette. One day around noon I waded downstream and
cut across a narrow, swampy peninsula, wanting to sneak up on a spot
where the water narrows down to the shape of a venturi tube and trout
stack up behind rocks along the edges. Big fish dwell in this place, and
have for the quarter-century I have been going there. Despite their
finicky appetites and eating customs, I occasionally hook into one more
focused on food drive than the instinct for cover.

It's somewhat the same with some humans.

I was in a prison of tag alders, trying to figure out how to situate my
bulk for a sneaky cast, when I heard a soft woofing sound, and looked up to
see a couple at the top of the embankment on the far side of the bend. Neither young, nor geezers. Mature folks. Like me. At least chronologically.

The woman had her hands pressed against the trunk of a great oak
tree and her companion was behind her. Neither was clad from the waist

down. I vaguely recall the sex manuals—sorry, marital instruction materials—calling this "doggie." They took a remarkably long time, trapping me where I was. I could not bring myself to be the cause of *coitus interruptus*, and by my watch they lasted just short of thirty minutes (not including the time elapsed before I happened upon the scene), which made them world-class in such endeavors. In a world-class blue-ribbon trout stream, such a performance seemed quite appropriate.

In camp that afternoon I related my tale to my fishing pals and ever since then, when one of us passes the spot, we look up at that oak and say, "Woof, woof." It's part salute and part incantation, but I doubt the lads are trying to conjure fish. As a prayer we are entitled to keep private that which we pray for.

A guide who works the Pere Marquette River system told me of the time he had a couple down near Walhalla one hot summer afternoon.

The man was a fly-fishing aficionado (we do not say addict). It was his wife's first time out and she was clearly bored and not "getting it."

As the drift boat slid around a bend, the guide spied a couple on shore below a cottage. The woman was on her back on a picnic table, her legs around her man. Their clothes were in a heap on the ground. You can fill in the rest of the details.

The noble guide immediately tried to draw the couple's attention to the less carnal side of the river, but the wife was not interested in anything he had to say and instead looked directly at the picnic table.

"Now *that*," she said wistfully, a wide smile sweeping her face, "is my idea of a great day on the river!"

The husband, of course, never looked. He was too busy casting.

We all have different passions at different times. It's nice when they can coincide.

It was also on the Pere Marquette River that I cut across another peninsula to get to a long run where I knew there would be fish. Above me I saw a bright blue rubber raft beached on gravel and sand, snugged against the shoreline.

It was a blistering hot day with a white sun and a clear sky.

I paid no attention to the raft, tied on a hare's ear nymph dropper, and began working the run with singleness of purpose.

As I fished, I kept hearing a dull slapping sound, steady and muffled. But I could not peg the source, and on a river if you have to identify the source of every new sound you hear, you'd never get any fishing done.

But the sound did not recede. It grew louder, almost frenzied.

Which is when I noticed that the beached raft was animating, flapping up and down and squishing in the low water. It was basically out of the current, mostly on pea gravel, and there was no breeze to animate it so. The movement was clearly suggestive of some form of carnal conjoining.

Not long after my discovery, a couple stood up in the raft. They were dressed like Adam and Eve. When the woman saw me, she gave off a squeak and both of them jumped unceremoniously toward the bushes and tag alders.

Minutes later they were dressed and launched the raft. When they passed me, they looked the other way.

I offer these vignettes because there are some aspects of rivers that rarely see the light of print.

Forget-me-nots, bright sun, a river's music, and the songs of birds: hell, I'd join the Curled Toes River Club too, if opportunity presented itself, which it hasn't. Who wouldn't? Making whoopee in a beautiful natural place certainly beats hell out of the backseat of a Subaru.

Mankind has been fishing for a long time. We've been doing other things even longer. In the novel *The Late Mr. Shakespeare*, Robert Nye's narrator tells readers, "There's not a lot to suggest that Mr. Shakespeare liked fishing. I think he preferred to stare at the waters, without disturbing them with his own ambition." To be a writer is to learn from contemplation, which is a form of doing. Amen.

A HYMN FOR SHRINKING WATERS

Now, well past my half-century birthday and more than half a life lived, if actuarial tables can be believed (and because large fortunes ride on them, they probably can be), I have come back to that which has always been in my mind, kept neat and dry in an airtight box in my swampy unconscious. Once 50 percent over my so-called ideal weight and addicted to smokes (a habit not acquired until I was free of military obligation), I stalked my cricks and rivers under the prophylactic healing powers of 800-milligram Motrin tablets and mid-outing cans of tepid beer. Fishing breakfast, pre-strokes, and when I bothered, comprised a Moon Pie or two (the ultimate in trouting soul food) and a chilled Diet Pepsi from the cooler of the local Stop-and-Rob. Lunches consisted of a warm beer, another Moon Pie, and kielbasa or pickle loaf and raw onions on rye bread smeared with hot mustard and horseradish.

My kind of trouter uses a truck for an inn and his gustatory taste runs to foods grabbed for a few bucks from jars on the checkout counters of country stores.

I met a young man one Sunday morning on Campbell Creek near Kalamazoo. He drove up in a rusted truck and got out a small spinning rod with a gob of worms on the end, took his daughter down to the bank by the culvert, and let her drop it in. His clothes were ratty and soiled, her dress threadbare. The back of one of her sneakers was torn out—not designed that way, but torn out. I watched him show her what to do, then sit back and let her do it, let her learn and feel and see.

"We used to catch our limit like this every Sunday morning," he said wistfully, "but there aren't so many fish left nowadays, and no place to take a kid." After awhile they packed up and drove a mile or so up to the next place where a creek crossed under the road.

(In 2002 a law was passed in our legislature that allows kids to kill one 8–12-inch fish a day in no-kill waters. I never knew a kid interested in killing a fish. The focus was on catching, so one must wonder what the logic in this law is. Kids don't have problems following the rules — especially when what they are doing is something that catches their fancy.)

You don't have to have a lot of assets, a DAR (Daughters of the American Revolution) pedigree, or a Ph.D. to be a trouter. Most trouters, in fact, are more like that young man and his daughter than those of us outfitted by Orvis, Simms, and Patagonia. Some of the moneyed folk would like to reserve the rivers for themselves; historically, some have bought up huge tracts of river property and made entry and access impossible or difficult. To be fair, a lot of people of means have also turned over huge tracts to the state for all of us to enjoy, but usually after they were done with the property. We have a riparian law in Michigan that says citizens can go anywhere in navigable water (a term stemming from our state's logging days, and meaning water that will float a log), and that the water belongs to all of us. But the number of times I've been on rivers where somebody's dug it out to form a pond or put in a barrier that makes passage impossible would be tough to recount. There's a club along the Pere Marquette, not far below the M-37 bridge, where the club's caretaker comes out to pitch rocks into the water to spook the fish for passing waders.

I have a message for the landed gentry: There are lots of people like me who grew up prowling rivers and learned how to fish the hard way. We learned because we don't give up.

Draw your own conclusions.

· 12 ·

LAMPREYS AND OTHER NOMADS

I loathe snakes, and because of this I also must confess to less than a solid attraction for eels. I was born in Rhinebeck, New York, and grew up off and on among the River Rats of nearby Rhinecliff. This was before various bridges were constructed upstream and down, and ferryboats used to cross the Hudson River from Kingston to Rhinecliff, connecting the east bank to the Catskills on the other side. In those days there were still some men in the village who put their nets out for the annual shad runs. Some of them also caught and smoked or salted great quantities of river eels. People in town thought of eels as a delicacy; I classified them as water snakes. So it was a long time after this, during a trip to Amsterdam, that I grudgingly ate my first genuine eels in a green sauce. Didn't like them one bit.

In Barcelona many years after the Amsterdam experience I consumed my first baby eels, smothered in garlic. Heartburn aside, I could eat baby eels several times a month with a nice bottle of Rioja and be quite happy. Years after Barcelona, during a visit to Madrid, I ordered baby eels, and my Spanish host lunged across the table and hugged me with great ardor, proclaiming that I was the first American he had ever met who had actually asked for eels. I would add at this juncture that I've also eaten snake, which was described pre-meal as chicken-like. An Australian who used to live in my neighborhood, a man with an international job that put him on the global circuit most of every month, always insisted that any time a traveler heard, "tastes like chicken," he should take the next plane home. Write this down if you suffer food aversion.

But the point of this is that eels—lampreys, to be more precise—are considered by our European brothers and sisters to be a fine delicacy, while we trouters see them as archenemies.

One summer during the eighties I slid into the Little South Branch of the Pere Marquette River, where last century the first German browns were first planted in Michigan. My friend Al VanDenBerg told me to anticipate a five-hour wade up the late Little Red Bridge (since removed), where he would be waiting with the car and a six-pack of cold beer. Anticipating our usual luck, we had already planned to grill some steaks that evening, so I entered the water with no pressure to produce. Not that I'm much on keeping trout; I think I've kept two dozen fish, all for the camp skillet, over the course of the last twenty-five years. (Some might argue that this represents my total take over that same period, but they would probably be wrong. I claim the Fifth on the degree of deviation.)

My plan was to fly-fish with a trusty Adams (Sizes 16–18) and I was in a wonderful mood. I came; I saw nothing and caught nothing. The river was as dead as the Salton Sea, and after an hour or so I noticed that parts of the bottom were covered with some sort of foot-long blades of fat, flat grass the color of sun-ripened limes. In some places the river resembled the Great Sargasso Sea, and I was alarmed that the sandy, gravelly river bottom was suddenly being consumed by these strange weeds, which looked like mutated kudzu.

By the end of the second hour, I decided to examine some of the weeds, and nursed some of them upward with my rod tip. I held a handful for a while before it registered what I actually held: lampreys. Out of water they were a pale ocher and had the texture of wet sawgrass, but there was no mistaking the circular, teeth-filled mouths. It was like discovering severed fingers floating in the river.

The Pere Marquette had been poisoned with rotenone, and the bottom was littered with wads of pale green corpses bumping their way downstream.

Lampreys are nomads, and first came into the Great Lakes and connecting waters some time around the midpoint of Prohibition. They weren't noted until the late 1940s, and by the end of the Korean Conflict they had nearly decimated the entire lake trout population of Lake Michigan and done serious damage to the population of Superior's slower-growing stock.

Subsequent federal and multistate wars against lampreys were fought, with no less emotional commitment than the government's various non-military wars (against cancer, against drugs, against illiteracy, against smoking, against violence in schools, against fill-in-the-blank), and with about the same result—meaning commendable progress, not eradication. Whereas 90 percent of lakers showed lamprey wounds in the 1950s, only 5 percent had them by the 1980s. Of course, there were a lot fewer lakers by then as well. Now there's some concern that our stumbling national productivity will reduce government resources, which could mean reduced antilamprey programs, and consequently, there are renewed fears that we may suffer major losses of Great Lakes lakers and salmon.

A Lake Superior laker takes a decade to reach seven or eight pounds. The average catch for many years in our era has become a three- or four-pounder; before lampreys came and overfishing was recognized as a contributing factor to the fishery's downfall, lakers lived twenty-eight to thirty-two years, and often reached weights of up to forty pounds. There's one report somewhere in the literature of a seventy-pounder caught in a commercial net in Minnesota or Wisconsin, but I don't put much stock in such tales; the anglers in those two states, both sporting and commercial, are well documented for their tendencies toward prevarication when it comes to the size of fish or cheese wheels.

When lampreys found their way into the Great Lakes they found no natural predators (there being no restaurant-going Europeans here), and copious natural food. An adult lamprey grows to a couple of feet long and lives less than two years, but in that short lifespan will—on average—kill forty pounds of gamefish. Each. They use their mouths and pointy teeth to grind holes into the host laker's flesh, lock on like remoras on sharks, and drain blood out of the fish. Vampire eels would be a better name for them, and knowing this you have some semblance of what it felt like to be in a small river with millions of them, much less clutching a handful.

That day on the Little South was a washout. The rotenone used to kill lampreys reportedly does not kill other living creatures, but it does affect other things, which is why the Department of Natural Resources waited until the dog days of summer (after the major hatches) to treat the river. A sure sign of poisoning that affects nothing other than lampreys is dead frogs along the bank. I guess they don't count. The chemicals whack the eels outright and put the trout down "till next spring's my guess," one DNR fish biologist told me later. Ordinarily a fishless afternoon would not dampen my spirits, but when I met Al at the bridge, we were both crestfallen over the plague of lampreys and the continuing need to control them.

Since then it has occurred to me that we have all sorts of unforeseen imbalances and problems visiting our flora and fauna, and that most of these travails we've brought down upon ourselves.

The Michigan salmon frenzy started back in the late 1960s. A few years after it began, my dad went off with a friend to northern Lake Michigan to give firsthand witness to one of the early coho runs. My dad wasn't an angler, but he was cursed with curiosity (which he passed on to his three sons), and this particular time he came home shaking his head, an expression that was some part wonderment and a greater part anger over sheer human stupidity.

My old man was a career Air Force man. In India during the big war, one of his men had once brought him a human hand, fetched fresh from a C-47 crash, all that they had found of remains in the wreckage; the man plopped it on the old man's desk and asked what they should do with it. His answer was lost to history.

So he had seen some shit in his day, but his trip to the coho carnival had left him speechless. What he described was an army of anglers shoulder to shoulder along the beach and surf, and farther out, afloat on the big lake, cruised the navy from Hell: V-bottomed rowboats, leaky wooden prams, dented aluminum canoes, sailboats, rigs of all sizes and descriptions, engine-powered and arm-powered, rigs with no power, and all of them drifting or cutting across each others' bows in four- to six-foot Lake Michigan waves for a try at Big Fish. People drowned that day and numerous boats were lost. My dad had no good words for such lunacy. The state chamber of commerce calls it tourism.

Salmon aren't native. They were transplanted by the Michigan DNR, whose job it is to regulate the state's fisheries and wildlife assets. In England (and other countries) the fish still belong to the owners of various properties along the rivers where they live, but in America we the people own the animals. Ostensibly, this is a sort of communist philosophy—everything belongs to everybody—but like the former Soviet Union, we replaced blood aristocracy with Party hacks, and another caste system replaced them and began to think they were the true owners of the country's assets.

The DNR, as it's known hereabouts (some wags claim this stands for Damn Near Russian because of the department's sometimes officious ways), is officially charged with managing our state's natural resources, and individual employees' interests aside, the purpose of this endeavor, no matter its label, is to generate resources for the state coffers. When you're charged with producing revenue and the current product line won't cut it, you find new products. Think: Capitalism in action. America got income tax this way back in the early part of the twentieth century. New revenue sometimes entails creative thinking, which can lead to unnatural acts, which produce unanticipated and often unnatural results.

Thus came salmon to the Great Lakes as finned revenue, a new draw for tourists (meaning more sales taxes), and of course, increased license sales, more boats (more sales taxes, registration fees), and so on. Michigan has for many years had more registered boats than any other state. The multiplier effect is a much-revered deity in Lansing and other state capitals.

The salmon prospered for a while, and fishermen came from all over the country to try their luck with coho, kings, Atlantics, pinks, and drowning. We had people hauling back boatloads of piscatory torpedoes. Our better taxidermists had to shelter their profits in golf-and-ski condos in Traverse City and Petoskey. At one point the annual business generated by all this reportedly reached an estimated two to four billion greenbacks. The big fish, led by the salmon, chomped their way through alewives and then turned to smelt, which cut into another segment of the angling sport as well as a small but healthy commercial fishery. Michigan smelt get shipped to Japan, where they get made into sauce.

All the while, of course, we've been trying to undo three hundred years of polluting our Great Lakes. In Lake Ontario the smelt populations suddenly declined in recent years, as did the salmon that needed the smelt for chow. Cleaner water, speculated learned fish biologists, meant less nutrients for the smelt. Since the salmon depended on the smelt, a decline in party of the first part brought a perfectly connected decline in party of the second part. Now you see 'em, now you don't. Clean up your water, lose your fish. Good-bye billions. Can you spell disaster?

This greatly simplifies things and that's not all bad. With apologies to my friends in academe, let us proceed in this line.

Action, reaction—and all of it unnatural. What we see are the direct and indirect consequences of choices. Or maybe it's mostly to be attributed to the law of unintended consequences.

Alewives, the herring-like baitfish that once died by the millions on Great Lakes beaches because there were insufficient predators to keep them in trim, were themselves accidentally introduced to area waters in the late nineteenth century, whereupon they immediately decimated walleye and yellow perch populations. Smelt, which were stocked in Crystal Lake in Michigan's northwestern Benzie County in 1912, had found their way into Lake Michigan and from there swam into the other Great Lakes, where they proliferated unchecked and displaced other species.

Each time one of these events occurs it takes decades to see the result. It's like betting on a horse in 1992 that won't hit the tape until 2010, or hitting a flyball in 1946 and having it caught in 1964.

The central tenet of fish biology is biomass. Think of the aquarium in your den. You take the surface area, average depth, and mean temperature and get a figure in pounds of fish these inputs can support. Mostly it comes down to oxygen. You can push this envelope, but not much.

If your biomass is five hundred pounds, you can have two thousand quarter-pound fish or one five-hundred-pound behemoth, but no matter how you slice it, five hundred pounds is all the biomass your ecosystem will support. If you put a bunch of minnows in this five-hundred-pound system and one five-hundred-pound fish, it's going to eat them all before they can reproduce. These are extremes, of course, offered here in scientific naïveté for purposes of illustration, but the bottom line is that nature has its limits and what we've done here in the Great Lakes is to play around with the constitution of our biomass; calculations made in the security of our math many years ago often don't play out as calculated.

An old fishing pal of mine likes to say, "In practice the theory is different."

If the choices are left to sportsmen I think we can expect fairly sensible decisions. The success of no-kill trophy trout fishing is an example of a biomass decision that anglers are embracing, and even those who work warmer water species are not keeping the numbers they once kept, sensing that the resource is not endless. In a presidential election I can remember ole Poster-Toter Ross Perot talking about doing something so that our kids would have the American Dream to shoot for. It's been one hell of a long time since politicians realized that the sporting side of the out-of-doors is also part of that dream and the heritage that created it. I wouldn't vote for old Ross for dogcatcher, but I had to concede this point.

It's a sad thing to see a fine trout stream littered with the sorry carcasses of dead lampreys, but I expect there will be much stranger sights down the road as the DNR keeps trying to balance revenue generation with good biology, the natural limits of biomass, and the legitimate interests of sportsmen. It's not a job I would want.

I offer a prayer in this regard: May there never come a day when we look down at a plate of lampreys and garlic, lift a glass of Sancerre, and chant, "Bon appétit."

Nomadism is inherent in nature, and mankind keeps exerting its influence on nature, which then modifies its ways.

Newton's Third Law is a dynamic trouters must live with every time they venture out. Stumble too clumsily into a hole and you kick the fish up or down the river in a sort of violent physical chain reaction that extends far beyond where you are when you commit the original sin. It's like one of those desk gewgaws with suspended stainless steel ball bearings; when you lift one end and let it strike the main pile, a near perpetual chain reaction commences. For trouting purposes it pays to remember that like the invisibility of microdrag to the human eye, this action-reaction takes a long time to recede to normal.

Most of us have heard endless variations of the hydrocarbon debate and theorized depletion of the ozone layer, meaning the earth may be warming and the icecaps melting; as the protective layer of ozone oozes into space, the more dangerous rays of the sun knife through to us, elevating rates of skin cancers. If this keeps up we'll all have to live underground like Dulutholians and Minneapolistians.

Thoreau wrote, "My desire for knowledge is intermittent; but my desire to bathe my head in the atmospheres unknown to my feet is perennial and constant. The highest we can attain is not Knowledge, but Sympathy with Intelligence." This is a high goal to shoot for. Given the choice, I'd take one of Izaak Walton's clean alehouses as a preferred venue.

Species of flora and fauna (I've heard there were twin exotic dancers by these names in Toledo) once native to Michigan aren't here anymore, not because they have become extinct, but because they have moved north in search of colder climes. Examples cited in this regard include the woodland deer mouse, red-back vole, finescale dace, grayling, ebony spleenwort, and *Calypso bulbosa* orchid, none of which I have actually seen. All these living things are gone from Michigan, having relocated themselves north of where they once were. Some species, experts tell us, are hiking north at a brisk clip of sixteen kilometers a year.

If you live in Michigan's eastern Upper Peninsula, you could see a species cross into Canada in seven years, which is fast by any measure. This sort of migration apparently is due to the earth's current thermic ups and downs, but it's not unprecedented. Fossil studies show that trees and plants have migrated in past eras, some trees at rates of six to 125 miles a century, and some plants, whose spores were moved largely by migratory birds, at twenty miles a year.

As the polar caps melt they draw certain cold-weather things north.

I have a mental picture of the possible ultimate playout of all this: four scrawny polar bears, their backs against the North Pole, watching the earth and water below them cooking to a Venusian parboil. This is the problem with pushing scientific observations all the way to their maximum theoretical outcome.

Still, such thoughts should give us pause.

Supporting evidence of ozone depletion consists of the alleged fact that the ten warmest years on record have come since 1973. But 1997 also went into the books as the coldest and most overcast summer in the past century; for the moment, I take consolation in the anomaly and have given up worrying about how to fortify my southern Michigan property with gator traps.

Still, it's hard not to marvel at nature and its patterns, both natural and those that have occurred as reactions to man's actions.

Canada has, by one count, seventy-four kinds of mosquito, one hundred and ten varieties of blackfly, one hundred and thirty-two flavors of deer fly, and one hundred and eighty strains of no-see-ums. Not all of these insects are carnivorous, but enough strains are that only a fool or a thick-skinned rhino would challenge them. There's a good reason why they don't sell a lot of bikinis in hockeyland, and temperature's only one part of the answer.

In the past six summers I had to dope myself only thrice despite the fact that we had a prodigious amount of rain and most of my favorite trout waters run through thick, wet swamps.

I live in very southern Michigan and we aren't known to have black-flies, but they are advancing south as inexorably as African killer bees are trooping north. It would make for a great Hollywood B movie: The Killer Bees versus the Pestilential Blackflies. The truth is that blackflies won't kill you, but they can make you wish you were having a long look at the lid, as the Irish so delicately describe death. The killer bees are coming north from sheer mean-mindedness; but the blackflies' southern migration has a different genesis. In May 2000 I was walking in the Al Sabo Preserve and felt a bite on the back of my arm; I reached back and killed an insect and then found the palm of my hand covered with blood. The blackflies had arrived in Kalamazoo.

Mosquitoes breed in slow, often dirty and turbid water, whereas blackflies procreate only in clean, fast-moving water . . . trout water. Over the past twenty-five years we've put a lot of effort into cleaning up our state's water, and a lot of marginal streams are now as clean as grandma's drawers. Twenty years ago we didn't have blackflies below the Mackinac Straits and I don't remember them as much of a problem back on the Little M in the late 1950s and early 1960s in the Upper Peninsula; now they've jumped the Straits and are moving south as our water gets cleaner. Call this the good news, bad news aspect of the pollution war.

Before leaving this subject, let me ease your concerns.

Only female blackflies bite. They need the nutrients of our blood to mature their eggs. The pain of a blackfly bite is difficult to capture in words, but think of a hatpin shoved through your eyeball like a pearl onion on a shish kebab skewer and you'll get the general idea. The thing is that they come in silently like Tomahawk missiles. Nothing will keep them permanently at bay other than your absence from the field of battle. I remember a sequence on CNN during the war with Iraq. The pictures showed a cruise missile flying down a street in Baghdad as a lone Iraqi soldier stood in the street firing at the thing with his pistol. Forget DEET, use your feet. When the blackflies hit, split. Fast.

Sometime in the early eighties my friend and fellow fish-nomad Reg Bernard and I were in a marshy area west of Whitefish Point in the Upper Peninsula, next to a dam on the Shelldrake River. It was late June or early July as I remember it. I had just gotten out of the Camaro (my fishcar in those days) when he shouted, "Look up," which I did, just in time to see the point of an arrowhead cloud of blackflies closing on my head. By the time I reached my car, which was no more than twenty feet away, I was covered with them. I threw myself into the car and slammed the door and Reg and I began slapping; hundreds of them had gotten in with us. The swarm had been so massive that some of the blackflies had gotten into my shirt, so I took it off and started knocking them away. When it was all over, we had blood spatters all over the glass and upholstery and I had welts upon my welts, a hundred or more, all over my body, but concentrated mainly on my head and neck.

Welts aside, the bites didn't aggravate later the way deer-fly digs, mosquito nips, or no-see-um nibbles do, but the moment of the assault was a lot tougher to bear. It was interesting to observe that the blackflies fluttering around the interior of the Camaro showed no interest in attacking; we killed them anyway. It occurred to us later that maybe those in the car were all males, or perhaps they were females shocked at the stupidity of letting themselves be trapped. Whatever the reason, once they were inside they seemed to lose interest in human meat, which jibes with what I heard years before: that blackflies in a house won't bite. Go figure.

A month after the Shelldrake blackfly attack I was back in the same area at the same time of day under almost identical conditions. I walked around shirtless and in shorts, and nary a bug bothered me. Timing is everything, my high school basketball coach, Ed Jarvie, used to insist, and he was right. Ontario researchers once counted something of the magnitude of thirty-three thousand blackflies produced by a one-square-meter stretch of water, but once they've hatched and had their flings, they go away and in later summer in the Yoop, trouters can get back to business and not worry.

Some final thoughts: Carbon dioxide attracts most carnivorous insects. And blackflies and mosquitoes love humid days. If you exert yourself too strenuously on muggy days you sweat sooner or harder. Sweat, of course, exudes carbon dioxide, which attracts insects. When old-timers tell you to fish slow and don't work up a sweat, there's more in the advice than quaint aesthetics. Slow and easy does it in biting weather. Trust the old farts on this.

If you're prone to wander the nomadic road, it pays to take advice where you find it.

MICHIGAN TRIBES:
INGRIDS AND MILITIAS

I have stumbled across a place colonized by a tribe of Viking women. I'm not going to reveal the location, except to say it's in Michigan and, before lurid imaginations run amok, let me add that these are not the svelte Viking wench-warriors of Hollywood; rather, these are NFL-size women with translucent, muscular flesh, and hair whitish-blonde trimmed short in bowl-style, as fine and diaphanous as angel hair. They move effortlessly and make no sounds. Lovely ghosts in plus sizes. I stared at them as if they were white tigers.

The Sisters of Valhalla run a restaurant near a famous blue-ribbon trout stream. It's an immaculately clean establishment with blue-and-white gingham tablecloths and curtains, and their food is served in generous portions with no-nonsense seasoning. You can have salt or pepper or pepper and salt, your choice; the cash customer is always right.

The proprietresses seem to span three or four generations and look enough alike structurally to have been produced on some high-tech Aryan brood farm. They wear loose, white, ironed T-shirts, loose, white skirts hemmed modestly below their knees, whitewashed, squeakless tennis shoes, no makeup, no nail polish, no smiles. The business of business is business. They also don't shave their armpits or legs and the hair in these locations is as pale as that on their heads. They have high-pitched, estrogenic voices, nearly melodic in tone and with academically precise diction to boot.

Except for customers, there are no men around the place and no sign of men. Clothes get hung out to dry in the sun on taut rope clotheslines; everything's white and large. I confess: I've looked.

I have imagined more than once that the restaurant, satisfactory as it is, may be a mere front, and that these Viking femmes, these massive blonde Valkyries, use it solely to select potential Aryan breeding stock. Somewhere out in the forest swales and drumlins behind the restaurant there may well be a fenced-in compound, the Cyclone fence topped with curls of gleaming concertina wire; inside, there are one or two or even three captive studs silently serving their pale captors in the hope of propagating this isolated and magnificent human strain, and in the process, earning their freedom. Jim Jones was real in an unreal way. Why not this?

"Damn you, Joe, you've been gone the better part of the year. Where've you been?"

"Held captive by Viking women. Swear to God! They nearly killed me. I was lucky to get out alive."

Such discoveries and imaginings are regular companions of this particular trouter. Certainly there is a point where fact and fiction part company, but I see no reason to look for it.

The women wear white plastic nametags with black letters proclaiming that they are all named Ingrid.

Before my most recent visit to the Vikings I stopped at Fredericks of Hollywood and bought several fancy size 16 garter belts and nylons all in black, and after finishing my meal I left the package on the bench seat with a note that said, "From Odin the Admirer."

Next time I'm up that way I'll be checking the clothesline.

While I will happily cruise the periphery of the Ingrids, I will give wide berth to our Michigan militias. There is a place not far from the Pere Marquette where the resident (I assume) has painstakingly painted a huge billboard outlining survivalist and militia philosophies. I always took my foreign friends to view this, just to show them the stuff about our eccentrics and loonies they get off CNN is not completely baloney. The sign is in black and red letters and starts:

OKLAHOMA BOMBING: That killed babes! Other innocent people. Senator Key from OKLA gives evidence that bombs were inside the buildings. ATF and FBI and their children were removed from the building, when the bombs went off and they passed terrorist legislation. Remember WACO! ATF and FBI agents with support of Janet Reno and Bill Clinton burned babies at Waco.

One humid summer evening Godfrey Grant and I crawled sweating out of Dowagiac Creek and drove into a nearby village for a cold beer. I was at the time writing a novel about some militia whackos who took over the U.P. and declared their own country. God had a hard time understanding that people can simultaneously love their country and hate their government, so I asked him to listen, sidled up to the bar and made a few remarks about Washington, D.C., and within fifteen minutes the entire bar was in an uproar of seditious talk. God walked out shaking his head in serious mentumentation. "What the hell's wrong with those people?" he asked. Random House turned down my novel on the subject. My editor called one day and declared, "It couldn't happen in this country." The next day the Federal Center in Oklahoma City was blown up and my editor called again and said, "Okay, you're right and we're wrong." But the book never got sold and the manuscript sits gathering dust.

If the Ingrids opened a gun shop annex, they would pull in the gungaloots. In my studies of the militias and similar groups, I have always been struck by how many militia leaders own gun shops. An acquaintance, retired as a special agent from the BATF, has confirmed my suspicions. Fiscal self-interest appears to be a primary fuel of militias, who too often couch their self-interest under the label of patriotism.

· 14 ·

TRACKING
NATTY BUMPPO

S pring Brook is a cold and narrow winding creek that flips and flops and tumbles from a lip of high ground on the northeastern wall of the Kalamazoo valley. It meanders politely through a semi-suburban housing plat north of the Paper City of Parchment, and farther west dumps itself into the Kalamazoo River, less than two miles from where James Fenimore Cooper is alleged to have written his novel *Oak Openings*.

Cooper is to American literature what Jerry Lewis is to comedy: an outcast and a reject, often ridiculed in his own country. In France both men are honored as bona fide geniuses. I have no way of knowing Cooper's personal qualities, but I have read that he came out to Kalamazoo to visit his niece and to write. Quite often he hitched up a buggy and drove to a lovely area that now includes our local nature center and a stretch of forest called, in his honor, Cooper's Glen.

Cooper picnicked there and probably, being a writer, he did some thinking and took some soothing naps in the summer shade. A couple of small streams that feed into the big river have their headwaters up where James Fenimore rooted around for ideas. There are brookies in the feeders, but back then they were undoubtedly larger and easier to catch. I sometimes think of James Fenimore and imagine him lofting a catgut line into a quiet pool and laughing out loud when a trout took hold, his laugh echoing through the wooded glen. Private pleasures often are the sweetest.

Possibly the brookies were more abundant then and of a more cooperative strain than those available to us now. Surely James Fenimore's fish weren't overworked; up there west of Cooper's Glen settled raw-boned, no-nonsense Calvinists, Dutchmen who tamed the land with raw strength and determination and had no time to waste on small fish too hard to get at.

Nowadays the brookies across the Kalamazoo River in Spring Brook have an affinity for tight cover, and to have any chance at all with them, you have to flip your spinner or fly under tag alder overhangs and shoot it through narrow windows in sagging wild vines. Fly fishing was not possible for mortals until the local Trout Unlimited Chapter bushhogged a section of river to open it up. If you can get close enough, the Spring Brookies will give you a dance, but more often than not casts go awry and you spend most of your time retrieving hang-ups and clambering over deadfalls. It is an unexpectedly wild place and more than once I have imagined myself fishing along in the company of Natty Bumppo with Indians trying to drop out of the trees along the bank into my imaginary canoe. Spring Brook is hardly as wide as a canoe is long.

Cooper, his critics rail, had faults. Who among us doesn't? His plots, they complain, don't add up: A character speaking with a Dutch accent early in a novel might have a Finnish or Italian accent a few chapters further on. *Deus ex machina*, too. Cooper had a tendency to help his stories and characters along by plucking unlikely solutions and helpmates out of the forest like a ham-handed prestidigitator.

What I remember most about Cooper's work is a cast of characters who were peculiarly American: odd, fiercely independent, doctrinaire, instinctive, courageous—doers. Cooper was one of the first of our authors to begin framing who and what we imagined we were; Europeans recognized this in his work and clucked with sincere admiration, while our scholarly critics berated his mechanics, the craft of his work, and ignored the fact that the works *worked*, which is the ultimate test. People also said Picasso couldn't draw.

Most American kids of my generation had more than a passing familiarity with *The Deerslayer* and *The Last of the Mohicans*. We knew about Natty Bumppo long before we knew Dan'l Boone or Davy Crockett. We crept the good creep (to twist better words) and put a premium on quiet feet in the woods. We watched for unbroken spiderwebs on the trails and we knew to pay attention when birds flushed ahead of us in the forest or suddenly went silent. I'm certain that Natty and James Fenimore would be pleased.

Maybe James Fenimore Cooper awakened this in us because my friends and I first read him when we were only ten or so, read him as pure and delicious adventure, and the stories were fine. I didn't know from literature then and probably still don't, but I know a good yarn when one gets spun. Cooper wrote good yarns. About Americans. About us.

Spring Brook always takes me back to Natty and Chingachgook and the other grand figments of Cooper's imagination. The trout stream and its proximity to Cooper's spirit are linked in my mind. Sometimes when I reel in a fat brookie I imagine I can hear the peal of his laughter.

Cooper, the late Ralph Miller used to teach at Western Michigan University, wrote his stories straight through, meaning he didn't go back and revise and edit and adjust tempo or polish. He just scribbled them down and moved on to what was next.

Not a bad credo for trouting. Or life.

15

TROUTING CONUNDRUMS: THE NAME GAME

One afternoon decades after I caught my first trout, and after hours of traipsing the flat, visually unimpressive battlefield at Waterloo, my Upjohn colleague Leigh Bailey and I stopped for a late lunch at a tourist restaurant. We sat down, and each ordered a Stella Artois beer. Leigh studied the menu as I surveyed the premises decorated with faux battle memorabilia. Along one wall I saw a long aquarium and my eyes naturally locked onto the fish swimming in greenish water. Trout! But with markings I didn't recognize.

I urged Leigh to ask the waiter what kinds of trout were in the tank.

The waiter looked perplexed, pondered the question, snapped his head back officiously, stuck out his jaw, and declared with a dismissive tone, "*Ce sont des truites normales.*" Translation: "They're regular trout, you dolt!"

Regular for him but not for me, and though we did not order the fish, not recognizing the markings disturbed my gustatorial pleasure that day.

Names are personal things, and once we get attached to one, it is hard to surrender it.

There is no base fix to mark my embarkation into the fly-fishing world. Once upon a time it happened and now I do it. I suspect it dates back to the early 1970s when Bob Phillip of Scientific Anglers asked my bassing pal Charlie Snoek (aka The Snooker) to host the group Three Dog Night for bass fishing. Charlie invited me to go along as boat ballast. Al Ciner and Cory Wells were into bass fishing in a major way, and were good at it. We took them out to nearby Lake Doster, and as I remember it, one of them got the biggest largemouth (more than seven pounds) he had ever caught in the U.S. The band was *the* band in the period 1969–1974—with twenty-one consecutive top-40 hits, eighteen straight in the top 20, eleven in the top 10, and seven number-one hits. The guys had so much fun that for several years they booked trips to play Kalamazoo so they could go fishing. After that trip, Bob Phillip and SA sent fly rods and reels rigged for bass, and Charlie and I began to play with fly rods. For me, the real attraction of fly fishing is less the quarry than the method. I prefer trout, but I will catch suckers, any bass, panfish, walleye, pike, and just about anything that swims as long as I can use one of my fly rods.

What attracts me to trout, I think, is their colors and their infinite and delicate beauty. They have scales so small that their skins look like microfiber garments.

To catch a trout is to be reminded of species differences. Humans acquire color in the sun and lose it in the water; out of water, a trout almost instantly loses its color. They are creatures meant to be immersed in water, and we who are mostly composed of water are not normally meant to be water creatures. Choosing trout is a sort of unconscious search for primordial identity, or whatever trendy psychobabblers are calling such things these days. There may even be a bit of cachet in trout. An old associate of mine, M. J. Wyatt, once wrote skits for *Saturday Night Live,* and authored the one about the sick and famous "Bass-o-matic." The skit never could have succeeded with trout.

A friend once tried with a heroic and obnoxious effort to lure me south to the Florida Keys to hunt bonefish. I resolutely refused and had no qualms in doing so. It would be a criminal act for me to catch a bonefish or tarpon on a fly. If one chooses to reach the fly-fishing hierarchy, I believe one must earn one's way upward, as with upper echelons of all endeavors. I remain at fifty-eight, a hopeless flapslasher, flaying rivers mindlessly and happily, and only occasionally with measurable effect. Besides, the glories of bonefish and tarpon aside, I prefer trout.

An early version of the Peter Principle (from the book of the same name by Dr. Laurence J. Peter, theorizing that people in organizations get promoted up to their level of incompetence) might have been the expression of meeting one's Waterloo. I had never much thought about this until I toured the actual battlefield. It was a nondescript and pitiful place for Napoleon to have taken his fall, but as I learned later, Napoleon was sick when his deputies decided to take on Wellington in the rye, and by the time Bonaparte saw the field, it was too late; the dice had been thrown and the French failed to make their number. In Flanders in the *smoor*

(Flemish for a palpably thick fog), I found a small graveyard filled with the bodies of the Irish Rifles, a unit of soldiers all killed on the same day during World War I, not thirty minutes from Waterloo. Seeing killing fields has led me to understand how micromanagement evolved. Details count, and if ignored, can unravel the most brilliant stratagems.

My entry into the fly-fishing world brought both a fascination with the jargon and not a little intimidation over what people termed "technical fishing." Details count nearly as much in fly fishing as they do in war, though I will grant that the stakes are different. If you fish with flies, details are everything—none too small to look past, none insignificant—and each time a poor knot slips loose and a good fish with it, I think of Waterloo.

Other details and arcana aside, the most basic detail of trout fishing is being able to identify what you are catching. This seems like it ought to be a simple enough task, but the inability to know what you have can create quandaries.

To wit: My friend Buck Berger and I were standing a few yards apart on a sandy spit in the lickety-quick Pine River west of Cadillac. There were riffles to the right and a deep run along the outside bank, and we were feeling at least a thousand miles away from the rest of the world. Buck (who is now Ph.D. Berger) had been a Ranger in Vietnam, half his tour spent with long-range recon patrols in Indian country, and half a tour in graves registration, which by my accounting amounted to a portion-and-a-half of nightmares. He hails from Centreville, Michigan, got his B.A. from Central Michigan before Vietnam, and added an M.A. from Western Michigan afterward. We met as grad students at WMU. His Ph.D. is from Kentucky. He's spent a good deal of his life sneaking away from the real world to chase trout. He's secretive as hell about the places, too.

Sometimes, after a few beers, he would tell me of trout-rich environments along the Michiana border, where creeks were overgrown, long casts went less than ten feet, half your throws got hung in wild grapes or tag alder, and there were rocky walls from old homesteads crawling with small rattlesnakes. No names or directions and no major landmarks, just vague mentions of generic places and specific past events. Buck plays things close to the vest, but he's the sort of friend you can see after a ten-year interlude and feel like the time apart has been nothing at all. In the nearly thirty years we've known each other, we've gotten away to fish with each other just once.

As trout are wont to do, they eluded us for a couple of hours. And then in less than sixty minutes, we had five nice fish on the bank, three browns and two rainbows, which tasted great that night. What I remember now was that we disagreed about the identity of a couple of the trout, which were ten or eleven inches long and thick. Buck thought that they were brookies because they had reddish-orange spots, but I held for browns because there was no white piping on the edge of the fins. Neither of us carried a microscope to count gill rakers (assuming we'd know what they were in the first place) or the presence of mind or ichthyologic moxie to count fin rays, so we agreed to disagree and ate the take with no prejudice for species; truth told, any fish dumb enough to fall to us deserved to be put into a remedial class all its own. Sometimes when I've released a fish, I've imagined all his sniggering buddies asking, "You got caught by *that* dork?"

Back on the Little M, I rarely paid attention to such things as species distinctions; trout were trout and knowing this was enough. But there lingers the question, When is a trout a trout? For the majority of us who catch nothing at all most of the time, this is not exactly a burning issue, but there are places and times when a mixed creel of the wrong complexion can put you in legal jeopardy. Ignorance of the law is no better an excuse to a fish cop than it is to a street cop.

The thing is that there are lots of kinds of trout, plus some trout that aren't really trout at all, either by biologic or taxonomic standards (what we call them notwithstanding), and some species that have a lot of different names, depending on where you are and who you are, and other species whose classifications are still changing. With apologies to various sources not to be named in the interests of protecting their guilt or innocence, and at the risk of raising the ire of the Bunsen-burner-and-test-tube-set, I've gleaned what follows somewhat in the manner that a laker sucks up a smelt: helter skelter and what's next on the menu?

Trout, char, and salmon all belong to the family Salmonidae. The Atlantic salmon, *Salmo salar*, is called a Sebago salmon in Argentina. In Maine, *Salmo salar* is also called a Sebago, as is at least one line of outdoor shoes, though I can't speak for connectedness. Unlike Pacific salmon (and the occasional biblical personage), Atlantics can spawn more than once, which may help explain why I prefer them to salmon who do it once and die, which turns don't-want-no-trouble-just-out-for-a-good-time into a suicidal activity. Spawning ought to be about life, not death, pragmatically and metaphysically speaking.

The brown trout (*Salmo trutta*) is not indigenous to the New World. The first eggs came to Massachusetts either from England in 1882 or to New York State from Germany's Black Forest in 1883. Trout historians tend to favor different permutations of the same facts. A third strain, called Loch Levins, from Scotland, also have been planted in the U.S. The Loch Levins are silvery with black spots—like Atlantic salmon— and lack the buttery yellows of the German browns we love so much in Michigan. Browns, you may know, can tolerate a wider and warmer range of water temperatures than brookies or rainbows, our native American trout.

So far, so good; but now it starts to get interesting. Europeans referred to their home-bred brown trout as brook trout, which means after ocean voyages in 1882 or 1883, depending on the version in your fish bible, we once had the condition of having *our* brookies (*Salvelinus fontinalis*) and *their* brookies (*our* browns) side by side. Stay with me here. The first pioneers into the West sometimes called the rainbow and cutthroat trout they found out there brook trout, another iteration of our brookies and theirs.

Time eventually combined with regional, ethnic, and national pride to sort of sort out all of this.

The brook trout found out West (*Salmo gairdneri*) eventually got tagged California brook trout, then California trout, and eventually some perceptive soul, possibly sensing the cultural hell California was bound for, rainbow trout, which is good because rainbows (at the time I started writing this) were still trout; technically, our brookies are actually a kind of char. In Canada the natives call brookies speckled char or speckled trout, meaning our northern neighbors' brookies are as the Thais say in pidgin English, "same-same as ours," scientifically speaking. Canadians also call them squaretail trout, but let's forget that I said that.

Browns, as previously noted, are hardy fish, and it didn't take long for them to move in on our brookies. When foreigners fished our waters for browns, they often referred to them as brook trout, which right as it was for them, was wrong for us, so our locals started calling brookies "natives" as a way to differentiate them and still maintain a respectable international tourist trade. By natives they did not mean *Homo canucki* who call brookies "specs." Some Americans probably still call brookies natives in some locales, but in Michigan when we say native, we refer to browns, brooks, or rainbows which have established themselves in streams and are reproducing in an admirable display of natural genetic single-mindedness. We also often vote for creeps in national elections, so don't be swayed by our practices.

I would add to this murky stew that what we now call brown trout initially were planted in the state as German brown trout, but around World War I, when anything German was presumably pejorative, this name seems to have been shortened to brown trout. You probably couldn't order Kaiser rolls during or for a long time after that war either.

While we're on the subject, you ought to know that a lake trout (*Salvelinus namaycush*) is often called a toque out East, a mackinaw out West, a laker at Mackinac (which we in Michigan capitalize and pronounce *Mackinaw*), and a grey trout in Canada (where the normal Anglicized spelling of the color is grey rather than gray). The marvelous part of all this is that a lake trout is not a trout at all; it's a char, which is why you can crossbreed a speckled trout/char (our brook trout) with a laker (which is also a char) and call the result a splake. Not being a fish biologist, I tend to get pretty confused by all this. But here's more to ponder while we're mired in this swamp: Cross a female brown trout (Europe's old-time brookies, our brown) with a male brook trout (our native trout, which is a char) and you produce a tiger trout.

California trout, as previously noted, were rainbows waiting for a name to take. Ergo, there are no more California trout, but there is a rainbow subspecies, or strain, called *Salmo g. aquilarum* that lives almost exclusively in Eagle Lake, California. It's a trout, the experts claim, but misnomers have passed this way before. I have read one source that calls these California things "specs," which only adds to the confusion.

If one strain of rainbow trout spawns in a creek or river, but moves out into large lakes or oceans to live and then returns to the stream to spawn, it's called a steelhead; you'll sometimes hear steelhead and lake trout used interchangeably, which won't do. They often live in the same big waters, but so, too, do alewife and zebra mussels, and nobody confuses them on the sheer basis of geography. I would add here (God knows why) that a form of lake trout, called *Salvelinus siscowet*, lives at depths of three hundred to six hundred feet in Lake Superior and it never gets confused with anything, except maybe the occasional sunken ore boat.

Arctic char, a relative of the brook and lake trout, is called *Salvelinus alpinus* and has another close relative called the Dolly Varden, *Salvelinus malma*, or bull trout, and that's no bull. If an arctic char is landlocked, it's *Salvelinus aureolus*. Blueback trout are not trout, but are actually the char *Salvenlinus oquassa*. This helps explain why they look a lot like Arctic char, which makes one wonder why they're not called Arctic/blueback trout or char, take your pick.

Why is consistency in labeling such a difficult thing for people?

It gets worse.

The landlocked salmon (*Salmo salar*) is called by those who can pronounce it *ouananiche* in Canada and Sebago in Maine and Argentina. Knowing this and a buck-fifty may get you a cup of hot coffee in a decreasing number of establishments on the American continent.

Cutthroat trout (*Salmo clarki*, which should not be confused with the fictional reporter *Clarkus kenti*, whose working colors were suspiciously similar) is a trout in its own right and with its own naming conundrum. Cutthroats apparently exist in various strains, all of which thrive, like certain sweet melons, only in their own unique ecosystems and minihabitats, which accounts then for what we know as Colorado, Lahontan, Paiute, Rio Grande, Utah, and Yellowstone cutts, to name some that I've heard of. Try to transplant Paiutes to Yellowstone waters and you end up with fertilizer for the garden. Where they are is where they is, say the experts, which suggests they've done some tinkering along these lines. So be it. I don't intend to lose any sleep over it.

In Arizona there's an Apache trout, called *Salmo apache*, which sometimes gets called an Arizona trout. Not a problem, except that Arizona also has the native Gila trout, *Salmo gilae*, which also gets lumped under the catchall term, Arizona trout. This is not really a problem for most of us, and probably not for wiser Arizonians either, but *Salmo apache* is a protected species and *Salmo gilae* is not. Probably the Arizona Fish and Game people make some money off this, revenue—like love—being where you find it.

The most beautiful trout in the world (other than the one on the end of your line) is said to be the golden trout, *Salmo chrysogaster* (a native of northern California with transplants living at high elevations in a few other states). Given all the misinformation and plain disinformation about Salmonidae, I'll leave it to you to agree or disagree. I've never seen one and don't expect to.

To close this out let me add that fish biologists are tinkerers at heart. Some years ago I heard that in a hatchery in New York's Catskill Mountains there were brown trout fry called Zeeforellen which I think translates roughly to lake trout, but technically means lake-dwelling brown trout (*Salmo trutta lacustris*) versus the browns already here (*Salmo trutta fario*). What I fear is that *our browns* are about to be confused with *their lakers,* and this will no doubt take us down that same damned slippery slope that turned a speckled char into a brook trout into a native. History, after all, does sometimes repeat itself.

For most of us, all these names are pointless except in certain board games. Salmonidae all look somewhat alike, so when you catch one, which isn't all that often for 95 percent of us, the simple word "trout" seems more than adequate. Anything more than this I'll leave to those of you suffering from obsessive-compulsive disorder.

A few days before this was written I learned from a newspaper article that scientists had tentatively decided that the rainbow trout is actually a char. I hesitate to bring this up, but there it is; do with it what you "will."

When is a trout a trout? When you've got it in your net, partner. Until then it's nothing more than a happy obsession.

16

ROAD-RANGER RAMBLE

It was near the end of the trout season and I was on my way to a conference of book lovers in Alpena on the shores of *Mer Douce* (Lake Huron); the conference didn't start officially until Thursday morning, but would kick off unofficially with a cocktail party for speakers the night before. I also had a Tuesday night commitment. Despite all the gotta-be-theres-at-a-given-time I was determined that before, between, and after all this, I would squeeze in some exploratory fishing.

On Tuesday afternoon I slipped away to the Kellogg Forest, which is a hair north of a line between Battle Creek and Kalamazoo. The forest is an experimental station for Michigan State University; Augusta Creek, which runs through it, has a population of small-planted browns. It was September, when our air and land start the annual cool-down for the coming winter, the time when trout fishing revives for a couple of weeks before the season closes. I parked along the road in late afternoon, caught four browns in less than two hours, and had a fifth fish on. All of the strikes came on hare's-ear wets high-sticked slow along the bottom, almost like jigs. I took two fish on consecutive casts from the tail of the same pool above a sand trap.

Having temporarily sated my hunger for catching trout, I repaired to the company's conference center where I made a presentation to science and medical writers from twenty-eight countries. My speech was entitled "Ruminations of an Old Family Doctor with Empty Bag and Parakeet." My message was that medicine had come a long way in my lifetime; and that our family doctor in 1952, a Hungarian educated in Canada, used to walk around his Jackson Heights, Long Island, office with a parakeet on his bald head—this to capture the interest of the children he treated. The reality then was that he didn't have much in the way of medical tricks in his bag and if he could calm a child, well, that might be all he could do.

After the presentation we had dinner and attended a staged "Fifties Party" on a ten-by-ten dance floor.

By 6 A.M. Wednesday morning I was headed north. Alpena was a hard five hours away, but it was my plan to fish along the way. The point was not so much to catch fish as to have a look at the water I had never sampled before. By evening I had fished the Clam River near Cadillac, the Rifle River near Selkirk, the Au Sable where a feeder creek runs in from O'Brien Lake, Brush Creek near Hillman, and the headwaters of the Thunder Bay River, west of Alpena. I got two browns out of the same run in the Rifle, another brown from the Au Sable, and a dink small-mouth from the Thunder Bay. I also had seen more than a hundred deer in broad daylight and a couple of hundred wild turkeys. Twenty years ago turkeys were extinct in the state; now they are as common as blondes in red convertibles on Telegraph in Detroit.

After the two-day conference in Alpena I drove west to sample other waters. My first stop was Canada Creek, where I caught no fish, but got a nearly full look at the range of Michigan's fall weather. Above me floated fat, yellow-gray clouds against a clear blue background. In fall in upper Michigan the light goes flat and white as if all the heat's been sucked out of it. I started fishing in cold sunlight, but thicker slate-blue clouds soon drifted in and a cool drizzle settled over the landscape. This turned to a harder and inexplicably warmer rain, which eventually gave way to a fran-tic storm of micro-hailstones, which churned up the creek like a bubble bath. When the hail had run its course, the sky turned dark and it began to snow huge wet flakes, which came down for nearly twenty minutes. After this the sun came out again and I waded back downriver to my truck, marveling at the show I had witnessed.

It was midnight when I got home. I had not only worked Canada Creek; I had stopped to fish the upper Manistee River near DeWard and my favorite stretch of the Little South Branch of the Pere Marquette. Re-sult: zero fish on the homeward leg, but I had seen a lot of new water.

The whole thing was a pointless stunt that often overcomes trouters, to use any excuse to go see new water. What I had gotten from the trip, beyond the satisfaction of naked curiosity, was an idea that I might under-take the writing of a book about Michigan trouting waters—not the big and popular rivers of trouting legend, but the little jungle creeks in out-of-the-way places that are usually dismissed in guidebooks with the boiler-plate statement, "There are some brook trout in the feeder streams."

When I proposed this idea to Sandy, she growled, "Sounds boring," and rolled back to sleep.

Some of my trouting pals have wives who make five-course break-fasts for them at 4 A.M. These wives pack gourmet lunches, rich in the basic food groups, covering, of course, the RDA of various vitamins and minerals. One wife I know includes a linen napkin and a place setting of their for-guests-only silverware. These women are exceptions and I men-tion them only to illustrate the diversity of human behavior.

At my place I'm on my own.

I would add that another friend of mine has a lover of long standing who always slips a pair of her finest French-made panties into his fishing vest before he goes off for an extended trout jaunt. These garments are marvels of space-age fabricology, so light and dainty that they can be scrunched into a wad small enough to fit into a matchbox from a five-star hotel. My friend's girlfriend insists that these delicacies are there to remind him that there's more to life than trouting. Indeed. But there's timing to be considered and that old action-reaction bugaboo thing to be accounted for.

My friend, who shall remain anonymous, uses his girlfriend's panties to mark the spot where we get into the river, and presumably will egress. More often than not, however, my friend gets out somewhere else and it falls to me to fetch the dainties back to the truck. I always worried that one day I'd arrive at the house with these unmentionables in my vest and as I hauled my gear into the house they would flutter floorward like a diminutive parachute and there would be an immense silence as Sandy stared at the incriminating evidence, the smoking silk gun as it were, and I would frantically search for the right words, and would weakly bleat, "They're trail markers."

"I bet," she'd say on her way to see the lawyer.

In the late eighties I was invited to participate in a writer's confer-ence at a community college near Ludington. It was October and the Chinook salmon were in. I thought, what the heck, acquired an eight-weight rig, and accepted the invite.

Though I had never fished for salmon with flies, I knew right where the salmon would be and sure enough, they were there, a huge pod of a dozen or more fish.

I tied on a yarn egg, pink with an orange spot, waded in, and began casting.

I immediately caught a foot-long rainbow, which leaped to eye-level with me.

In the next thirty minutes, I caught two king salmon, both around seven or eight pounds, neither showing the sort of fight I had anticipated. Three fish in thirty minutes is pretty exciting, for me not so much for what had been done, but for what it portended, the Mother of all fishing days.

During the next eight hours, I had exactly zero strikes and no more fish.

I had caught a nice rainbow and my first two salmon on a fly and left disappointed. This is what can happen to you if you catch nice fish too easily. You begin to think of them as an entitlement rather than a gift.

Three winters ago, God and I co-taught a graduate professional writing course at Western Michigan University. One of our students had been at the Ludington writer's conference I spoke at years before.

She said, "You used a lot of sports metaphors in your presentation."

"Did I say anything about the foolhardiness of chasing big fish?"

"I don't think so."

"I should have."

If you grow up in some semblance of jockdom, you get programmed to chase championships and trophies and gewgaws and strive to be the fastest, strongest, toughest, and so forth.

Then you grow up and spend the rest of your life trying to become a human being.

I'm still trying.

17

CATS:
NOT THE MUSICAL

I met Deb Tabart through my company's Australian subsidiary, where our marketing manager Nick Maas had worked out a deal to promote our vitamins and over-the-counter products through the Australian Koala Foundation. It was the kind of program that made sense to me, a corporation and an environmental group cooperating for mutual benefit. Later I met Deb and helped her to set up The Friends of the Australian Koala, a related special interest group in the U.S. I still serve on the board of the U.S. group.

To travel with the Koala Queen is to ride a wave of psychic and righteous energy that engulfs everything in its path. Debbie Tabart, The Tasmanian-born Savior of a Species, believes in "the Gods" and facing the world jaw-first.

She claims clairvoyance and has been known to stop total strangers dead in their tracks.

"You're from Poughkeepsie," she once announced to a man at O'Hare.

"How do you know?"

"Dunno, but the bloody word's been flapping about in me mind all morning."

It had, and he was.

Witches used to get torched or dunked for less.

Sometime back, one of Deb's good friends died of cancer and the Queen was at her side, her friend having stubbornly clung to what was left of life for six weeks while the Queen traveled America strong-arming deep pockets for money to save koalas.

"Godfather," says the Queen. "She vomited food that had been in her stomach for six weeks. By the end her whole body was blue, except for her face and a small patch of pink flesh around her heart. I told her, 'It's time to go, Dear.' Which she did."

You get the picture. The Koala Queen is a force who tells it the way it is.

She's swum underwater with giant rays in Tahiti, been made to sit in the kitchen in Singapore while the menfolk were served first, pressured government ministers to mend their views on ecology, and helped develop a satellite-tracking system for koalas and their habitat. She defies time and space, and is obsessed by geraniums.

The Queen believes that all wild animals should be left that way, meaning out there, habitats intact, unhindered and unpressured by people. Many of us who consider ourselves natural wanderers share the Queen's feelings, but most of us mere mortals tend to talk the talk while the Koala Queen is one of the very few who walks the walk.

I was in New York one summer for company business and for a Koala board meeting. It was the cocktail hour at the Algonquin Hotel, where local fauna and hominids gather; I was bushed. I had been up before 6 A.M., and it had taken me twelve hours to get to the hotel; I could have driven from Michigan in about the same amount of time. The journey included a bus ride from Allentown, Pennsylvania, to LaGuardia Airport. Along the way we passed gutted Volvos in the speed lanes of Manhattan's northwestern DMZ. Having crossed Manhattan by bus, I had to spend another hour in line at the airport waiting for a cab to take me back into the city.

I asked if I could smoke, which was against the posted rules.

My cabbie was named Jesus. He told me, "Chure, Man, go-hed an' smoge. I don' like no laws."

What I needed was a Bombay martini up with three olives, green not black, but the Queen sashayed into the Algonquin bar and promptly announced that we were going to the Mayflower Hotel on Central Park West. Outside it was as humid as a mangrove swamp in Australia's Northern Territory. Who was I to argue with a queen?

We barged into the dining room at the Mayflower; Deb guided us to a round table, around which were gathered several attractive ladies and two men, one of them America's TV zoo personality, a younger Marlin Perkins, a Montana boy (and trouter by the way), eternally young, who talks like the cowboy who might say after a tussle with a wild beast, "It sure weren't no picnic." Indeed. Or at sixty below it would be, "A might chilly." You've seen him on TV—"Jungle Jack" Hannah.

The Queen put the gentle bite on Jack for a cash donation to the Australian Koala Foundation and then a lovely young woman led us up to a rambling suite on the fourteenth floor of the hotel. As soon as the elevator door slid open we were overwhelmed by stable-smell and I heard birds whistling, which turned out to be a good lesson in the potential dangers of ignorance.

The whistlers had fur and long tails: two eighteen-month-old mountain lions, a brother and a sister. I once spent an evening with several girls in an after-hours establishment on the banks of the North Fork of the Clearwater River in Idaho. There was a mountain lion there that night, too, "fully growed," and sort of knocking folding chairs around and growling to have its ears scratched while we humans danced the two-step and put back shooters of rye whiskey; I didn't remember any leonine whistling from that time. It occurred to me that a man who doesn't know that cougars whistle could possibly make some serious miscalculations out on the trail.

What we had on the fourteenth floor was a sort of felinagerie: two mountain lions, a Canadian lynx with paws the size of tea saucers, a curmudgeon bobcat, a tall and regal orange servil that found a scrap of towel and adopted it, a two-year-old snow leopard, a hairy rabbit, and a lizard that lived in a Hostess cupcake box. There also was an owl in the closet.

The Mayflower, you may recall, was once associated with a famous Park Avenue madam, the establishment serving as a high-class flophouse for bluenose trollops, a leased cat house of sorts—so the change was not so great, bipedal cats having been replaced by four-leggers.

I surveyed the regal cats and said, "Shit."

Not missing a beat, the Queen asked our guide, "Whatever do you *do* with their poo?"

Never at a loss, always questioning the basics.

Some of the zoo crew had in mind to invade the Hard Rock Café that night, though a pre-6 A.M. pick-up for *Good Morning America* lay ahead, and this tempered their enthusiasm. I had no desire for full-body immersion in a high-decibel Manhattan sweat shop, and opted for a quiet snort in the paneled peace of the Algonquin, where Matilda, the hotel cat, was on station inspecting guests taking the lift to their rooms. It's said that hotels with cats are happy places. If so, the Mayflower that night had to be one of the happiest on earth.

If one is lucky one can come upon snow leopards in the Mayflower, but it requires a connection to the Koala Queen.

Decades before, I was hunting deer near Trout Lake in the eastern Yoop of Michigan one Thanksgiving weekend, walking along a tote road, which ended at a huge blue spruce. Nothing on my mind, not even deer. I was pleasantly tired, at peace, just walking and happy to be outside, when an indescribable shriek cracked through the icy air like a sonic boom. I unceremoniously dumped my Model 90 Winchester barrel-down in the snow and mud. I thought, when my faculties returned, that a child had been quartered alive on the other side of the spruce, and I made my way around it nervously to find the body.

"Lynx," my friend's father said that night after listening to my story. "Get your attention?" As far as I know there are no lynx left in the U.P.

Meow, Your Highness. Or is it *Grrrrr?* The koalas are in good hands, and those who will not cooperate in protecting habitat are going to have a huge load on theirs.

I sometimes wonder if she'd like to take on the cause of trout. When I fish I usually head upstream—in honor of the Koala Queen and the battles she fights.

There is an Orvis shop in Manhattan. I always find it mildly disturbing to consider that city people appreciate fly fishing, but take comfort in thinking that those who like trout and live in the city are probably prisoners of war. Why else would they live there?

I was in the Orvis shop one morning while a Chilean man and his twelve-year-old son were stocking up on flies, line, and $900 reels for steelhead under the Southern Cross. A blonde woman, I assumed to be the mom-wife, sat with a shapely, bouncing leg reading *Elle* in front of a case of folded neoprene waders. Her high heels were covered with leopard skin, which led me to believe that she was not an adherent of catch-and-release. I hoped she didn't know about the Mayflower mob.

Some presentation flies in glass-covered frames cost more than my last used car. The Chilean said the steelhead down his way were *mucho grande.* I had no reason to doubt him.

On Forty-fifth Street there was a barefoot man asleep on a subway grate; his feet were faded indigo. Fifty feet away, a greeter from the Roosevelt Hotel whistled for cabs in a Foreign Legion uniform and new red Reeboks. New York and other great cities are great places to collect characters, which is a passable pastime if there are no trout readily available.

Around the corner, in front of Brentano's bookstore, there was what I have come to think of as an Inca band, meaning three small men, a guitar, a drum, and some forest flutes and wooden whistles, all of this mysteriously and expertly wired to an amplifier the size of a small boatbag. In front of them lay an open guitar case. Translation: Donations Welcome. It was empty.

It was hard to sort out thoughts of the distant children of Inca cloud-king warriors playing for donations from passersby in the concrete-and-steel canyons of New York. Cats played important roles in the religious lives of Latin American Indians; I had it in mind to show the Incas the snow leopard, but had no heart to add to their cultural misery.

A two-ton truck rolled slowly by. A sign on the side said, "Robots Rise." I checked the sidewalk. Nobody moved.

The waiter at the Algonquin that night explained that he was a Turk and that he had been serving tables fifteen years, all there. In five years he would qualify for a union pension and do something else. "It's hard on your legs. You have to get out. I see the whiteheads (old people)—all crazy." This applies to a lot of circumstances.

I bought some excellent flies in New York that day; the salesman congratulated me on my choices.

Upon my escape from the city I dug out my old tape of Los Indios Tabajaras and drove north, reminded that Inca cloud-kings do not stay kings forever and times change. Snow leopards end up in hotel rooms where high-priced Park Avenue hookers once plied their craft. Only tourists now visit Inca ruins.

The new flies looked wonderfully alive in the Black River, but caught no fish. If there is blame to be assigned, it is totally mine.

· 18 ·

FISHING FOR
INFORMATION

It felt like I was stalking the elusive bear again. For more than a year I had been studying Ojibwa (Chippewa) history, and had painstakingly arranged numerous meetings with various tribal officials and individuals in Michigan and Ontario, many of which never materialized. I was always there; the other party sometimes wasn't. It was similar to many of my trouting expeditions.

The no-shows simply reinforced my resolve.

One summer, after innumerable letters and phone calls, the late Arnold Sowmick, then-chairman of the Saginaw Band of Chippewas, invited me to meet him at a powwow near Mt. Pleasant. I arrived early in the morning to an awakening camp and the smell of wood smoke and coffee, the sounds of yipping dogs and happy children. Native American powwows are essentially social gatherings used concurrently to make a few bucks, politick, visit, eat, dance, put up with tourists. I had been invited, but still had to pay to get in, reminding me of my lack of standing.

The chairman was gray-haired, thin, and of medium height, with a soft voice and dark eyes. He said we could "talk" later. Then he disappeared.

As always, I had my camera along. I tried to visit with people but earned only smiles and silence.

The only person who would talk to me was a woman of thirty in a buckskin shift cut to miniskirt length. It left little to the imagination.

"You a photographer?"

"No, a writer."

"But you take pictures."

"Yes, because I have a lousy memory."

"But your pictures turn out?"

"Usually."

"You want to take some of me?" She asked this with raised eyebrows and cracked open the door of her camper.

"Natural light's better," I said.

"I'd, like, be embarrassed to be seen posing."

"You don't have to pose."

"But I wanna pose, you know?" She thumbed one of her straps. "You know, *pose?*"

She pushed the door all the way open.

"I've never done that kind of photography."

She giggled. "Hell, I've never done that kind of posing."

Before I could communicate a decision, the chairman arrived in the company of a small man with dark hair and a ruddy round face with acne scars. He was wearing a rumpled black suit.

The chairman introduced him as Mister L. I followed him to a concession stand where I bought us coffee.

"I'm Odawa," he said. "Not Ojibwa. You're writin' about Indi'n people?"

"Trying to," I answered. I laid out the plot of the novel I was writing, how an Ojibwa man had left his people, gotten a degree in dentistry and lived "white" out West, only to have his father die. When he returns to Michigan to see to his father's affairs, he has a vision and is drawn into his heritage and the tribal fishing rights dispute.

Mister L began asking me questions. Lots of them. About the details of Ojibwa history. He didn't ask anything I wasn't comfortable answering. The grilling and coffee drinking went on for nearly three hours. People watched us, but left us alone.

Finally Mister L announced, "I guess you done your homework." He was not smiling.

I thanked him.

"Only one thing more."

"What's that?"

"You'll need to go easy on the sexual stuff."

"Meaning?"

"Popular art makes us out to be wanton. I wouldn't want to read that we're wanton, you know, copulating like dogs and other animals."

I wondered if he meant frequency, selectivity, or position, but felt it the wrong time to seek clarification.

We shook hands and I watched him go to the chairman who then came directly over to me with a smile and his hand extended.

"He's a professor," the chairman said. "He says you've done your homework."

Within minutes people were approaching me with food and drink as gifts. I had been tested, passed, and accepted. At least for this one day.

Fires were lit that night. I shared beers with some drummers who had driven down from L'Anse in the U.P. Mostly we talked about high school basketball.

Then I wandered around.

"I guess the natural light's gone," a familiar voice said from behind a cigarette ember. "Wanna smoke?"

I did. It was unfiltered.

"Word is, you know about Indian people."

"Some," I said. "Learning."

"I seen you talking to L."

"He's a professor."

"He's a prude and a preacher," she said. "He lecture you about sex?"

"He said I shouldn't make Native Americans out to be wanton."

She laughed softly. "Hell, I been wantin' all day."

"That's a pun," I said.

"Yeah. You think Indians don't like sex?"

"All humans *like* sex. That's how we keep having humans."

"You've got that right. You ever think about that word you used, 'wanton'? It's like two words, want and on, which says maybe it's a woman's word. Is for me."

For reasons not clear to me I explained secondary and primary sources, and told her how I spent months reading the English translation of the *Jesuit Relations*, and the works of Parkman, Schoolcraft, Tanner, and others.

"You didn't read Indian writers?"

"Not for the period I was interested in."

She laughed. "Maybe they liked screwin' better than writin' about it?"

At that point the camper door opened behind her. A tiny voice said, "Mom, I had a bad dream."

She dropped her cigarette. "The kid's bad dream wins out. I gotta take care of the boy. Good luck with your writin'."

I slept in the car that night and fished Cedar Creek the next morning, got six small trout, and headed back to Kalamazoo, which is alleged Potawatomie for "boiling waters."

I wrote the novel and sent it to my editor at Random House, but he didn't like it. "Too much spiritual shit." He said. "It needs more sex."

So much for research and resources. Borderline insanity is good preparation for the book biz. When people ask me what the writer's life is like, I usually reply, "Which writer?"

OF YUKS AND KIDS

A t 5:45 A.M. it is so cold in Wings Stadium that someone suggests we open the doors to the outside in order to warm the concrete mausoleum. John-the-Gypsy is sharing an underground hallway with me as our players stumble by in twos and threes, dragging their equipment bags, trying to wipe sleep from their eyes. John-the-Gypsy is muttering profanely about the God-awful hours we have been forced to endure this season.

"How many practices you got today?" he asks.

"Three. And I gotta scout for move-ups, too."

Frown. The Gypsy's beady eyes lock on to me like the radar in an F-4. "Why in blazes do we do this?"

My mind gropes through the sleep mist. "Yuks . . . I guess."

"Yuks?"

"Yep, they always make me laugh."

They, of course, are the players: kids. And they are what this wacky hockey program is all about. While we adults stand in the halls grousing, the kids are in the locker rooms suiting up for practice, and there are no complaints from them. Make no mistake about it: This has been a tough year, and as long as we are forced to take the hours available (vs. those we'd like), it will continue to be like this, a tough fact for many to accept. So I look for other things to remind me that it's not so bad. We've still got a program when many cities don't. And we've got the kids and their nervous, sometimes frenzied, parents.

In almost two decades of coaching kids from the learn-to-skate through bantam levels, I had some wonderful memories, few of them relating to the outcomes of games or championships.

I am running a Mite B practice at the old Kalamazoo Ice Arena (it later morphed into a beer warehouse), trying to direct a troupe of wiggling six-year-olds in oversize skates and hand-me-down gear. "Okay, gang, raise your right hands." Frowns abound, bewilderment reigns supreme.

A brave but squeaky voice finally ventures, "Your right or ours, coach?" New approach. I remind myself that the essence of coaching is out-thinking the little buggers. I turn my back to them, raise my right hand, repeat the order to the Green Machine, and all but one player complies. All eyes turn to the individualist and the same soprano voice from earlier cracks the morning air. "Your other right, stupid!"

That one outlier is named Skipper. Before the season began, his father met with me to explain that his son had serious learning disabilities, but the family and their doctors thought socialization, discipline, and the exercise of hockey would be good for him.

We are in the locker room before a Mite A (seven- and eight-year-olds) game at that Rockne-ish moment known as "getting them ready." There has been a long, careful lecture on a portable chalkboard. The air and board are filled with Xs and Os and squiggly lines and arrows, talk about points and slots, corners, and head-manning the puck—twenty minutes of careful talk with regular pauses for questions. I talk slowly, searching eyes for comprehension or confusion. But there are no signs, no reactions other than the nervous tapping of skates on the rubber floor mats, a sort of pre-skating rapture. Eventually I say, "Okay, any questions?" Skate blades scrape, tape knobs on hockey sticks get squeezed, and finally, a brave soul ventures to speak. "Coach, I gotta question."

I smile benevolently, like Woody Hayes who knows a camera is in his snoot. "Yes, my son?"

The boy stands. "Which door do we go out when we go on the ice?" End of chalk talks in Mite A. Forever. Several players tap my leg with their sticks as they clomp by.

"Good job, coach."

We are at a preseason skating evaluation and the kids are coming on to the ice, one at a time. The six-year-olds, most of them in the no-skate category, struggle along on Jell-O ankles, wiping snow from the ice with their plummeting bodies. I watch them come through the door, deal with the sudden slipperiness of the ice and the loss of shoe support. A few aggressively bolt through the door like they've seen the pros do. Most of them inch their way out tentatively. Each of them clutches an evaluation form, which they are to hand to the coach at each evaluation station. One kid comes through the door, trips and does a belly flop, but his paper is still firmly in his oversize hockey glove. He rests there in a heap.

When a coach stops to render assistance, the kid rebukes him: "Keep your hands off me. I'm gonna do this myself," he says, maneuvering to his knees in order to stand. This, I think, is the beginning of a real hockey player—or anything else he wants to be.

Another year, another rink, another team, but again in Mite A, and we are pairing off for power skating. I am telling them the drill is not a race and each player should do it right, at his or her own pace, and not hurry. I look over and see that all but two are ready to go. I skate over.

"What's the problem here?"

"Girl," the voice in the giant black helmet says. "I gotta touch a girl, and I ain't holdin' no *girl*. You can't make me. I ain't gonna do it."

Crisis. "You want to be a hockey player?"

He nods.

"Then grab hold of this other hockey player and let's get to work." End of trauma.

At a learn-to-skate session we are working on balance. The instruction is to slide on their bellies at the sound of the whistle, then get up as quickly as they can and keep skating. All but one player hits the ice when the whistle sounds. He stands there staring at the flopping fish around him.

"What's the problem?" I ask. "Do you understand what you're supposed to do?"

"Sure," he says with a pained expression, "but I thought I came out here to learn how to stand up. I already know how to fall down!" No doubt this one will be a lawyer.

We have just finished a squirt game on the short end of a 5–3 score. Our goalie is elated and his mom and dad can't understand it; after all, he just lost!

"Boy, I was great!" he chirps jubilantly.

The parents try to hush him. "You gave up five goals," his dad hisses.

"Yeah, Dad," the kid says, "but I stopped five others, and in practice I didn't stop *any!*" You tell 'em, pal.

Another game, before the rules were changed to eliminate checking at lower levels. The stands are packed with moms and dads, brothers and sisters, grandparents, in-laws, neighbors, and they are all screaming, "Check 'em," and "Hustle!"

Two players on my bench have their heads together—in conference.

"You guys okay?" Usually they are hanging over the boards shouting at their teammates.

"Sure, Coach. We were talking about *them*." A glove is waved toward the bleachers and their rabid denizens. "They sure get excited about all this, don't they, Coach?" Right on, guys.

Another squirt game (nine- and ten-year-olds). We are in the locker room waiting for a signal that the Zamboni is done and the ice is ready for us. As a coach I am nervous, a certifiable basket case. What have I forgotten to work on? Are they ready? Behind me, players are laughing and shouting put-downs, chirping happily, and shooting tape balls off the walls and each other. Suddenly, a loud "Shusssssh!" cracks the room. My son Tim chides the others. "Keep it down, guys . . . you know how nervous he gets before games." It is abruptly silent, and gloved hands are patting me with reassurance.

My "hitter-mucker" is grinning (as he always is), and I am thinking that gunfighters were probably a lot like this kid. I explain the drill, which is meant to teach them to keep their heads up. They will race the length of the ice, each of them stickhandling a puck. Half the team will start at one end, the other half at the other end. They will need to keep their heads up or risk a collision at center ice. My mucker says in an earnest voice, "Coach, do you want us to miss them or take them out at the red line?" He is serious, not grinning, and I am hoping the powers that be protect the kids who must play against this one; the game was made for him.

I am driving home from practice. My son and a teammate are riding in back, swapping war stories and recalling the "old days" when they couldn't skate.

"My first time," the friend says, "I just walked around the edge, keeping my hand on the boards, and this coach comes over and asks me why I don't get away from the boards and I tell him, because I don't want to fall through the ice in the middle."

"Little kids sure are dumb," my son says sympathetically. They are an ancient and experienced ten. I smile and suddenly find myself wondering if I could auger a hole through the rink ice and fish there.

It's late in a squirt game and we are ahead 2–0. The third line, our weakest, is about to take the ice against our opponent's weakest unit. The five of them are clogging the open door and I ask them why they aren't on the ice yet.

"We're talking about what we're gonna do," one of the players says. "We're gonna go out there and protect our goalie's shutout."

I smile. The goalie will get a patch for a shutout. The others on the team will get nothing, but he's a teammate, and these kids are showing the beginnings of an appreciation for what teamwork and group goals are all about. I have a lump in my throat when they crunch away. The shutout stands and the lesson endures.

We've just won a difficult game, 3–2, and the teams are lined up shaking hands. I watch to see what happens when the player who had the one-on-oh breakaway meets our goalie, who stoned him. They meet, shake hands, and embrace clumsily—all smiles. "Way to stop me," says the nine-year-old, "way to stop me." Sportsmanship at its most basic.

I have a player down. I am on the ice and it doesn't seem serious, but I want a doctor to take a look. I search the stands and see one of the parents from my team. He's a doctor. I point to the injured player. He taps his chest with his thumb and mouths, "OB-Gyn." I point to another parent, also a doctor, who mouths, "Pathologist." I look up in the bleachers, ask so all can clearly hear me, "Is there a Boy Scout in the house?" I get a standing ovation.

As coaches we always set team goals, such as having every player score at least one goal and one assist during the season. Seven years later, Skipper is thirteen and still playing hockey. He has not scored a goal in his career and has seldom had even the opportunity. He can skate and has the rudiments of some of the skills, but the game is too fast, or beyond his comprehension or ability to consistently make instantaneous decisions. He can't anticipate the puck and has trouble with developing action and options. This season we taught him to go up and down the wing and how to get into position for passes and rebounds, and as the season progressed, he learned his job and the kids worked like dogs to put the puck on his stick so he could get a shot and maybe a goal. He would never score a hat trick, but one goal? Maybe, but time was running out.

It was the last game of the season in a year when we had won most of our games in the league, and all of them against other towns, and twelve of our thirteen players had scored at least one goal. With a few minutes to go in the game, our guys swooped in on the enemy net and Skipper dug frantically toward his position. We saw the puck come sliding across the ice onto his tape and with a slow-motion, single fluid motion, he buried the puck in the upper right-hand corner. There was a nanosecond pause in the arena before Skipper was overwhelmed by his teammates. Those on the ice were joined by the rest of the team spilling over the boards from the bench to pound his helmet and back with congratulations.

The coach from the other team leans around the glass as we watch the celebration. "Geez, you'd think you guys just won the Stanley Cup."

My assistant coach, a former player at the University of Minnesota (turned scientist) looks over at the other coach and said, "Nah. This is even better, eh?" Both of us had tears in our eyes as Skipper made his way to the bench and the other kids continued to pound him. The parents were in ecstasy behind us. We scored more than 150 goals that season, but I think every kid on that team remembers the one goal that did not determine the outcome of anything, other than boost the ego of a kid who did not have much going for him, but who worked like a dog to do the best he could—and on that day did what every player dreams of—putting the puck in the net and raising his hands in triumph.

PART III: ENDING THE CENTURY

We arrive at the various stages of life quite as novices.
—François de La Rochefoucauld

· 20 ·

THE REALITY
OF UNREALITY

I am at that age when the next ranks of my contemporaries are beginning to drop. The first rank went during Vietnam. Death has always been something for others, such egocentricity enabling armies to exist.

In my youth there were the usual natural deaths of aged relatives, tragic auto accidents and occasional suicides, products of unexpected genetic limits, bad luck, or behaviors that left survivors groping for explanations. Two of my friends, brothers, found their father's body hanging in the barn one morning. He left no note and no clues, and they outwardly accepted done as done and got on with living. Another man I knew used the palm of his hand to hammer a metal ballpoint refill into his temple, and when the refill bent and he was still alive, he switched hands, got a fresh refill, and finished the job on the other side, as awful an example of single-mindedness as I've come across.

There is absolutely nothing romantic about death.

Three years ago I got a 4:30 A.M. call from a friend who is as close as a brother.

His wife had shot herself. I collected another friend and we rushed two hours to the hospital through a whiteout, where we began a sixteen-hour vigil as nature took its course.

At one point my friend urged me into the room to see his wife, who had a massive bandage on her head, her face swollen beyond recognition. Some brain-stem function lingered, and now and then she shrugged a shoulder and flopped an arm. Each time this happened my friend would look at me with hope in his eyes, but I knew it was a matter of time. The bullet had blown a large hole in her skull. Normally, the swelling brain presses down on the spinal cord and cuts off blood circulation, but with the venting from the wound, the brain was swelling out the holes in her head and delaying the inevitable. A suicide is a terrible thing to witness, but the real victims are those left behind.

Having grown up in the Air Force, my brothers and I developed a certain casualness about the subject of death. The entire purpose of an armed force, regardless of its mode of transportation or operational venue, is to create deaths. Some of ours invariably die with theirs, but more of theirs is the goal. Pronouns not only encourage violence on a large scale, they enable it.

Every third or fourth house at our final base seemed to be inhabited by young interceptor pilots with young wives and children. Training accidents took a toll in preparation for the real thing. Once in a while we would come home from school to find the street jammed with cars and silent people carrying trays of food covered with aluminum foil. We had enough sensitivity to understand the signs of the extended family closing ranks. There was seldom a lot of fuss. He augured in. He bought the farm. He screwed the pooch. We kids seldom talked about this sort of thing, and our parents never did, at least with us.

Those pilots who had not augered in tended to think along the lines, "If it had been me instead of him, I would have gotten out of it."

It is a great fiction that duration of life is driven by sheer willpower.

The night my father died he suddenly sat up in the hospital bed and feebly began to try to get out of the bed. He was connected to a spaghetti of tubes, so I blocked his way.

"What do you want, Dad?"

He stared at me, unflinching. "How do you know?"

"Know what?"

He stared for what seemed like an eternity.

"You know," he said again, adding a perturbed nod.

"I don't know what you mean," I confessed.

He tsk-tsked me with paternal disgust. "The Virgin Mary and all that."

I had no idea what to say. All my life I had sought his approval. He had been my source of affirmation and reassurance, and in an instant we had unexpectedly reversed roles.

"Maybe it's like a road map," I said. "When you open a map you expect that the lines will lead you where they say they will. It comes down to faith." Great advice from an agnostic.

I watched him trying to process the metaphor. After awhile he grimaced, as if to say, "Mark that one wrong on the quiz, Bozo," and with an emphatic grunt lay back in his bed forever. When my time comes, how will I process the metaphor?

As I was writing this, my father-in-law died. He was a fine gentleman, eulogized as always having looked for fun, and having found it. One minute he was grumbling that we hadn't refilled the birdfeeder on the side lawn, and fussing around in his bed. The next minute he was openmouthed and staring at eternity. Gone.

Where? I am still searching for a metaphor to cling to.

In the past few years I have happened upon wreaths of plastic flowers on the South Branch of the Au Sable River and at the Forks of the Pere Marquette. There were no plaques or cards and no notes of explanation, and I assumed the flowers marked places where the ashes of cremated trouters had been sprinkled, earth to earth and trouter to water. I doff my hat at each finding and ask the sooty spirits to make nice trout rise to my fly. Church is where you find it.

There are days and nights on trout streams when I am convinced my sole purpose in being there is to follow the flow to its end. Life is its own meaning. All that matters is covering water as best you can, which inevitably means that we will all do it imperfectly. Birth comes with a death certificate. Only the date is missing.

21

FISH WHERE THEY ARE: STOVEPIPE BROOKIES

S outhwest Michigan is wine country, and I know a number of small streams where you can fish for browns with vineyards on the rolling hillsides around you. There are also lots of rumors down this way about local brook trout hotspots, but these places are hard to find and the fish even harder to catch unless you loose your creativity.

Mann Creek runs north into the Kalamazoo River from east of Fennville. There's a fine little Mexican restaurant in town and numerous orchards where the fall cider is sweet, plentiful, and cheap. The restaurant got its start serving migrant workers come north to pick Michigan fruit.

God and I drove up to Mann Creek on a sunny September day, and I parked on a wide gravel road. God headed downstream with his armamentarium of homemade brass spinners, and the sort of urgency that suggested the longer he took to get into the water, the fewer fish he might find. Our thinking around rivers and trout is rarely rational and I question no one, lest they question me.

Never in a hurry to jump into action on a trout stream, I leaned against my blue Bronco, had a smoke, and watched the upstream water, where salmon were rolling in about ten inches of water, scooting around like corpulent water bugs. It seemed to me that with so many big, aggressive fish in attendance, the local brookies were likely to have gone to deep cover, like a pilot downed in hostile territory.

A narrow-gauge culvert ran under the road, connecting the two segments of Mann Creek. The more I thought about it, the more I convinced myself that the brookies might have taken refuge in the culvert. Especially if the hydraulics were sending loose salmon eggs down into the tube. Cover and low-effort food: what more could a fish ask for?

After this exercise in logic and hope, I tied on a red San Juan Worm, added a split shot, stood off to one side, and drifted the fly into the tube.

I got a hit immediately and out chugged a brookie of about nine inches, fat with a pink-orange belly. I stepped into the water and released the fish, which shot frantically upstream.

Hmmm.

Later, an old man came ambling down the road. He used a cane and needed a shave. He arrived just as another brookie came out of the chute on my worm and, when released, headed upstream.

"I'll be damned," the old man said. "A brook trout out of a pipe."

I said, "Pretty lucky."

He said, "You can say that again. Word is there's no brookies left in the creek, so you probably just got yourself the last one."

I smiled and nodded.

"Even a blind pig finds an acorn once in a while," he said with a chuckle as he headed back to wherever he had come from.

He was right about there being no brookies in the stream. They were all packed in the pipe and I had caught eight of them, all eight to ten inches long, their mouths filled with salmon eggs. When G2 came back, he was grumbling. "I didn't see a single damned trout," he said disconsolately. "Just damned salmon. You do any good?"

"Eight," I said.

One of his bushy eyebrows popped up. "Where from?"

"You don't want to know," I said. Trout are where you find them.

22

THE ZEN OF TROUTING: MISTER TOM'S CABIN

I was in Japan on business and my friend and colleague Charlie Snoek arranged a weekend for us in the mountains northwest of Tokyo. Our host was the late Tom Hiyashi, then in his eighties, a retired board member of Mitsubishi Chemical, and Snooker's mentor.

Mr. Tom was a slight, short man with white hair and a wonderful smile. To virtually all things he answered, "Is that so?"

A career diplomat before his sojourn in the world of capitalism, Mr. Tom spent World War II under house arrest in Calgary, Alberta, where he was the Japanese consul. His RCMP minders escorted him on his daily walks, but after several months of wearing out longer and younger legs, the Mounties told him to just go and be back at such and such a time.

Snooker first went to Japan as a honcho in a joint venture with Mitsubishi, but very quickly found he could not get certain chemicals through Customs. In exasperation he called Mr. Tom and told him it was time to fold the joint venture.

"Is that so?" Mr. Tom said.

Snooker explained his problems.

The next day, the barriers were gone and the needed chemicals began to flow into the factory. Mr. Tom was what some in Japan call a King-Maker, one of those silent types who sits behind the curtain like the Wizard of Oz, pulling strings.

We met Hiyashi-san at his apartment in a distant suburb of Tokyo. Inside his front door was a stuffed German shepherd. He could not bear to part with his favorite pet when it passed away.

On the way to the mountains, Mr. Tom decided we should snack on some juicy Japanese pears. He stopped his car in front of a grocery store in a small town, halting it smack in the middle of the highway, got out, left his door open, and trundled into the store. Cars veered and squealed their tires going around us. I looked back at Charlie and told him no way was I playing sitting duck.

Mr. Tom's cabin was located in an artists' colony. It was secluded, overlooking a silver river at the bottom of a gorge. The house had a tower similar to those used to hang and pack parachutes, but this tower was filled with dozens of stuffed Canadian mammals and birds, gifts from the Canadian government when he was freed at the end of the war. Tom wanted a museum built when he died.

That first night we drove to an *onsen*, a mineral bath in a country inn. In Japanese public baths, as in Russia, the genders are separated.

Sort of.

First you go into a changing room, where you strip. Then you take a towel and go into another room to soap yourself and rinse. The water comes out of a low pipe in the wall. While you are soaping and rinsing before entering the bath, you are standing in full view of all bathers, all genders.

Which came as a bit of a shock when I turned around to see several female faces staring at me. They weren't giggling. Exactly.

We had the entire dining room to ourselves for dinner. We were served tiny trout, twisted brown by frying and seasoned with some sort of spice that made them sweet. I don't know how many we ate, but it was plenty. We had enough food for a large group, of which the diminutive Mr. Tom ate most.

We slept on futons on rattan floors and awoke to a cold cabin and frost on the ground. It was autumn and the valley below us was covered by a canopy of low Japanese maples turned a luxurious scarlet-orange.

The next day we went down to the river and instead of finding people fishing, we discovered dozens of men in waders with easels set up, painting away.

"No fishing here?" I asked Hiyashi-san.

"Good trout," he said, "but before you can catch a dream, you must be able to see it. To paint a fish is to see it."

Before we departed, Mr. Tom planted two trees in honor of our visit, and I wrote a poem, a Heywood Haiku, meaning clumsy. But Mr. Tom had the poem rendered into stone by a sculptor-calligrapher and placed it at the base of the trees. It is still there.

There is so much to learn in this life, and so little time to learn it. I now paint fish every chance I get. Trout, naturally.

23

TASTES LIKE CHICKEN

It used to be that if you took the hydrofoil from Hong Kong to Macao and caught the bus to the People's Republic of China (PRC) border, you would be let off near a restaurant with a white tile floor. You couldn't miss it. If you sniffed the air you'd know you had arrived.

The specialty of the house was snake, various flavors of two-steppers; venom sweetening the meat, claimed the experts. The waiters were young men, who brought sacks and wooden boxes to the table and hauled out specimens for you to choose from; hey, now *that's* a beauty.

Having made a selection, the waiter would grasp the snake behind the head and by the tail and hold it close to your face so that you could pass judgment: "Yessirree-Li, that's the one for me!" If you looked closely you would see that the waiter was holding the snake so hard that feces were squirting out. Decision confirmed, your waiter would lop off the snake's head, hold it up by the tail, run his filet knife the length of its belly (starting at the anus), strip out the guts with a sucking sound as the connecting tissues tore loose, and let the viscera fall to the white tile floor by your feet. The heads tend to tilt up toward the tabletops. Easter Island in miniature. No shoes, no service. This was a bad place to go barefoot.

You could have your snake boiled, broiled, baked, or fried, with a sauce of any hue in the rainbow, green and red being the house specialties. It was considered ill mannered to refuse such a delicacy.

While you ate, other guests were served, guts collected, and the white tile turned pink. Waiters left their flip-flop footprints. They didn't offer dessert.

White rice and green tea came with the meal. Vomiting was optional.

Jamu means "tonic" in Bahai Indonesian. You are driven through Jakarta's sprawling slums where millions live in packing crates roofed with plastic or layers of thatching of yellow and green fronds. There are no lawns to mow. Eventually the dense urban slums give way to knots of rural shacks and finally to a low-slung jungle. At the edge there is a single roadside shack with bamboo walls. Outside there is a collection of circular stairs cast in cement. The stairs are covered with green moss. You follow your host into the hut and stand in front of a stainless steel counter.

"*Jamu,*" your host says to a man on a stool behind the counter. He has a narrow black tie, shiny gray silk suit, and no shoes.

"*Jamu,*" repeats the proprietor. Conspiratorial smiles are exchanged. The proprietor opens a hinged door in the countertop. Cool: The Good Humor man used to have one of these on his rig. You are invited to peer into a metal bin filled with a slithering, writhing ball of snakes, alive and restless, startled by the intruding light, an undulating knot with multiple heads—a living Medusa. Probably they knew the score.

Your host points and looks to you for affirmation. You nod. The proprietor snares one of the snakes with a noose attached to a limber bamboo rod. The pole bends; the struggling snake is hoisted out and held up for your inspection. You think of rubber chickens at hockey games, only less lethal. Yay-up, that's a dang good reptile all right.

The snake's head is pressed firmly against the top of a V-shaped gutter of stainless steel; the gutter slants downward, call it forty degrees, expert skiers only. At the bottom of the chute there is a glass beaker. You notice that there are shelves along the back wall; the shelves are filled with more beakers, some turned mouth down, but not in any pattern you can discern. In the Air Force, when a man was lost, survivors drank a toast to him and turned his mug over. You hope that's not the custom here.

A blade flashes and the snake convulses; dark blood spills down the stainless steel channel into the glass, which begins to fill. Drained, the writhing carcass is pitched into a fiberboard barrel; the proprietor pitches without looking. Experience counts. The floor shows only faint traces of blood around the bottom of the barrel. Not his first day on the job.

The beaker is moved eight feet left to another stainless steel chute. Another door opens. This batch has stripes. Solids and stripes. Like a game of eight ball. When my dad thought somebody was mentally defective, he called them an eight ball. I'm the eight ball here. Another living knot below, another choice by nod, another catch of the day, another ritual inspection, another bleeder into the half-filled glass, another corpse consigned to the barrel with a rubbery, squishing sound.

There is little doubt where all this is headed.

Rule Two: Do not drink the blood of venomous serpents if you have sores in your mouth. The jury's still out on cavities.

The proprietor uses a delicate glass stirrer to mix the blood. The beaker is pushed over to you. All present face the cringing guest of honor.

Among international travelers this is known as "the test." It comes in many forms, but it always comes. You are in your forties now, understand the game and its only rule: to save face, you cannot refuse the offering.

You also have learned the trick. What is transmogrification if not an act of sheer faith? They want your business; they cannot afford to kill you. The red liquid in the beaker is an '87 Barolo. Look out tonsils, look out gums, stand back stomach, here she comes. "Good," you declare, wondering if you have red mustache. Wads of wrinkled, filthy rupiahs are laid out on the counter. At the exchange rate it works out to $12.50 a snake. The price does not include a towel. You use your own tissue paper, wad it up, and do not check for color.

At midnight you are still alive, a decidedly favorable observation.

Life is the accumulation of the stories we tell about ourselves, and often has nothing to do with truth in the mathematical sense.

I am troubled by a dead serpent drifting on the bottom of Campbell Creek one September—bothered that I couldn't identify it with any certainty. Twelve inches with black-and-silver-white markings, thick as my pinky, with a tail tapered to a rough awl-like point, and that menacing, trowel-shaped head. No rattles, though I am sure it should have had them.

In the snake business, and the field craft that accompanies it, it's critical to be able to quickly rule out what something ain't, meaning venomous or otherwise dangerous (anything better than lottery odds). The great constrictors of the world eat infrequently and are reputed to be harmless when sated, but how does one know, or account for interspecies gluttons and sociopaths? A plus B equals C never tells the whole story outside the lab.

A Sunday morning and I am unshaven and red-eyed, hunkered down in the aisle of my favorite bookstore, thumbing through *The Audubon Guide to North American Reptiles*, searching desperately for safe purchase in the solution of the mystery of the Campbell Creek serpent. When I turn to the vivid color plates, the photos are so lifelike that the hair stands up on my neck, and no matter how I situate my thumbs I can't seem to find a place where my fingers will be safe from a sudden strike. This effect is called the willies. Entirely irrational, I confess, but rational fears can't compete with their irrational kin. Such is the stuff of magic and state hospitals.

The Rhinecliff of my childhood was copperhead country, where grandmotherly caveats resounded: "You go out in those woods and you're gonna get bit, Mr. Smarty Pants." She was nearly right. Playing hide-and-seek during recess I nearly sat on one particularly fat and large specimen behind the schoolhouse one afternoon, inches from perdition or large-scale gluteal necrosis; such memories leave an impression.

Flying into Hell's Canyon in a Bell helicopter, the sort called a bubbletop, the Aardvark and I were flanking a heavily perspiring pilot who, by his own admission, had "not quite got the hang of hovering" in the radical thermals created by the catastrophic marriage of mountains, wind, and fire. He would do his best, he promised, to get us as close to the ground as he could, but we should be prepared to jump the final few feet. Food for thought. Meanwhile he braced the cyclical between his knees and rummaged under his seat, eventually extracting a rust-colored rubber tube for each of us, a dwarfish dildo the size and shape of a waterproof container for wooden kitchen matches.

"What's this?" I asked.

"Snakebite kit." Thumpathump, thump-thump. Was that my heart or the main rotor? The world seemed tippy. Er-ah-er, my vocabulary seemed to have plummeted into Hell's Canyon ahead of the chopper.

"Canyon's loaded with rattlers," the pilot added. "*Big* fuckers." Har-har.

Often such warnings lack substance; not this time. One of our crews killed eighteen diamondbacks with their Pulaskis along the bottom of a creek that emptied into the Snake River. It's said that this famous river was named because of its serpentine course, or perhaps for the Native American tribe that lived nearby. Not true. The name is literal—as far as it goes. Rattlesnake River would serve the interests of improved accuracy, but full disclosure would require USFS topographic maps to squeeze in the Shitload-of-Large-Aggressive-Rattlesnakes-Nobody-Tells-You-About-Until-It's-Too-Damned-Late-To-Do-Anything-About-It River. The chartmakers probably won't take this suggestion seriously.

At dawn, after an all-night fire watch, we trooped the shallow fire line that we had scraped and chopped down to mineral earth the previous afternoon. We could see where snakes had crossed, leaving distinct smudges. *Lots* of snakes.

"Good deal," one of the boys said. "They're headed away from the fire."

"So are we, asshole."

While I went through navigation training, Sandy and I had a nice apartment in Sacramento on Notre Dame Drive. The lobby had a lush atrium. My fellow classmate and friend Frank Bonham (of Auburn and Mobile, Alabama) and I were on our way to check out the fishing situation on the American River, which was a mile or two away, just past the hop fields. As I reached for the glass door, I perceived motion below, heard a dull thud, like a small ham dropped on linoleum, and instinctively jumped back and found myself face to face with a coiled, buzzing rattler.

It took an hour to convince the CHIPs to visit, two Boone and Crockett galoots with Smokey hats, .357 magnum hawglegs in holsters on their hawglegs, spit-shined boots with buckles just under the knees, well tanned in California style. They swaggered imperiously toward the glass door, come to disinfest the building of what could only be a delusional junkie or high-octane blow-head; they came, they saw, they went weak in the knees. Their tans muted.

Their exchange went something like this.

"Far out, Corporal Lance."

"Fur sure, maaan, like, it's like a damn *jungle* in there, maaaan."

It is 1968, the temperature in the mid-70s, the air as thick as 10-W-30, slow ceiling fans breaking even and not much more. We are puffing stale Rum Crooks with white plastic tips while getting our formal orientation to Southeast Asia, our lecturer a compact, rat-faced, tanned, quick-eyed NCO, the sort of feral product that crawls out of a West Virginia "holler" into the jungle and thinks, "Hey, this ain't so bad. Lousy weather, rough territory, lots of snakes—it's just like home, by God."

He says, "We got two kinds of snakes hereabouts: your two-steppers, which is to say *beaucoup* poisonous fuckers, and the other kinds'll eat you, *sirs*." He is not smiling. Welcome to Thailand; here are some generalizations you can live by. Literally. We were each given a cigarette, unfiltered.

"What's this for, Sarge?" A prize for paying attention during the orientation briefing?

"Snakebite kit, sir. Get yewerseff bit? Light that sumbitch up. Give you somepin' ta do till yew die." Har har.

We had a small wooden hut that served as our post office. My boom operator came out of the place one evening and stepped on a cobra. No harm done, but adrenaline flowed. Two Thai civilians heard the commotion and effected a rescue. One of them distracted the reptile by waving a hat in its face; the second man got behind the snake, grabbed its tail and, like an All-Star second baseman making the double-play relay to first, smacked the creature unceremoniously (albeit vigorously) against the wooded slats of the hooch wall, a clean kill.

In the aftermath, the pivotman rolled the snake around with his big toe, rubbed his belly, looked up at me, smacked his lips, and pointed down. "Good," he said, this theme previously visited: snake as gustatorial fare.

U-Tapao Air Base had been hurriedly built on a swamp along the edge of the Gulf of Siam. The rock needed to provide a platform for heavyweight aircraft came from a nearby hill; the demolition boys first blew up the top of the hill, then the Thais trucked the chunks down to the swamp where they packed it down and pounded it flat, covering the area with a several-foot-thick blanket of concrete and topped with tarmac, all of which soon cracked under the strain of too many heavyweight bombers and tankers. It was a long war.

When the spring monsoons swept in from the north, torrents of cool water ran down into the wetlands beneath the concrete shell and drove the snakes up onto the porches of our "quarters" and the raised wooden sidewalks. Russell's vipers, cobras, banded kraits, king cobras, pythons, snakes with names and snakes with no names, with more strange markings than an East Village millinery shop, all in broad daylight—countless specimens hell-bent for the high ground—a herpetologist's happy hunting ground. At night, base regs commanded, flashlights were mandatory for all personnel, to avoid the snakes. Some rules don't have to be written down or repeated.

There was a 1 A.M. curfew on base. Miss it and you were outside the fence on your own for the night. One night my copilot and I took a cab into Sattahip, the deep-water port where munitions came in for our bombers. We drank too much Singha beer and missed the curfew. Drank *way* too much, and we had to fly in the morning—*before* curfew lifted. It was drizzling the sort of steady, light rain the Vietnamese called *crachin*—rain dust. We had no choice but to crawl under the perimeter fence and swim and wade through the swamp to hard ground, trekking through snake turf to our hooch. I got the shakes in the air later that morning, not from the hangover, but from the realization of what we had done to get back in time.

Golfing on Okinawa, we had local women for caddies, mandatory for the course, an example of local pork-barrel politics, I guessed. What other reason could there be? I sliced a drive off the blue tees on number three and started down into the high grass in the rough to begin the search. One of my crewmates grabbed my arm.

"Not your job," he said.

"My ball, my problem." I have always been a strict constructionist in the laws of games and personal responsibility.

"Let the caddy do it."

"Give me one good reason."

"Habu."

"Say again?"

Local snake. Habu. Deadly. Two-stepper."

I watched the little woman in cloth boots work her way around in the rough. "What happens if she gets bit?"

Brief contemplation. "Buys the farm, I reckon." Shrug. A short life in the slow lane. Snake country breeds a certain amount of ambivalence.

We had a bamboo grove by our hooch. "Snakey," the wing veterinarian declared over beer one afternoon. The Air Force veterinarian's main job in a tropical assignment was the pursuit and destruction of salmonella, which afforded him a lot of time to drink. The Thais took a seventeen-foot, six-inch king cobra out of our bamboo grove one forenoon while we sat sunning in lawn chairs, sipping Singha, the local brew reputed to have a formaldehyde base. It took three men to carry the thing, which was thick as an NFL nose tackle's steroid-enhanced forearm. The Thais paused to show off their prize. I smacked my lips and rubbed my belly. "Good." I was learning my lines.

One morning we came upon a black-toothed Thai marine with a yellow-and-black banded krait wrapped around the top of his head like a glistening black-and-yellow turban. He did not say why. What he said was, "Day, no problem. Night, *big* problem," and spat a scarlet stream of betelnut juice for effect.

Sandy and I took our three boys to the reptile house at the Detroit zoo. Not my idea. She wasn't crazy about snakes, but she believed that if adults showed fear, it passed on to the kids, so she was always brave in the face of such things.

Some of the snakes were in glass-top drawers.

I lifted up Tim so he could see better.

His shriek immediately shattered the silence and a stampede ensued, emptying the house—with me at the front of the fleeing pack. Tim

and the rest of my family were abandoned, left behind to fend for themselves. In snake country it's tough to count past number one.

A metal pen had slipped from my pocket down the back of Tim's
shirt. His scream had emptied the place and I was in the doghouse,
which, bad as it was, wasn't as bad as being in the snakehouse. I did not
think, therefore I moved quickly and handled amends on an ad hoc
basis. A good rule to follow: Do not go in harm's way when it is avoid-
able. I no longer do reptile houses.

Away at a business meeting in the late 1970s, I called home and
learned that a legion of shotgun-toting policemen were out in force,
scouring our neighborhood for a king cobra (see how some threads never
end?), reported anonymously to have gotten loose from a secret and illegal collector. I refrained from coming home until the sweep was completed and the homeland officially declared as snake-free as the land of
my Irish ancestors. I stayed out of the basement all winter.

A neighbor kid showed up one spring day with a Massasaugas he had
found along the road north of Kalamazoo. It was coiled in a one-gallon
glass mayonnaise jar.

"Neat," he said, proud of his find and still jacked by the thrill of the
capture.

I say, "You kill it or I kill you."

It's my Irish genes no doubt. We have a few Massasaugas in Michigan, a statistically insignificant number in comparison to blackflies, mosquitoes, or vehicle–deer collisions, which is to say we can walk our
woods more or less inattentively—a bad habit if you happen to visit fishing kin in Mississippi.

There are not supposed to be any Massasaugas north of a line south
of here. Campbell Creek is well north of the line. That dead snake
preyed on my mind and drove me to the bookstore where I remembered
all this. Its identity remains at large and I haven't been back to fish
Campbell since.

In Grayling one frigid October day, Trout Bum Czar Steve Southard
told me how he used to find all sorts of Massasaugas in the marshes
around his folks' place—two hundred miles north of where the snake experts say they are.

I was in Japan, near Nikko, an establishment built among hundred-
meter high white cedars planted in rows half a millennium ago, there to

shade the shrines of shoguns, who used to head into the mountains to avoid the humidity and insects of a summer in the swamps of Edo (Tokyo).

We had reached a small mountain pass with a scenic waterfall. Ice had collected on the rocks. Near the falls there was a mom-and-pop Stop-and-Rob. Snow was in the air; nothing serious, just a few spits, winter rehearsing for the main event. We had been driving around for several hours and my legs needed stretching. The Japanese may make the best-made autos in the world, but they are also the best-made *small* autos in the world.

We walked into the shop and I cruised the narrow aisles. There was a long rack with thin packages hung on metal rods. Like crawler harnesses or jerky. There also was a mountain stream outside and this suggested unanticipated possibilities. The packages were too thin to be pickled pigs feet. Mepps spinners maybe. One could hope.

Uh, so sorry.

I reached and tensed. Under shrinkwrap I saw stiff translucent snakes, eight or nine inches long, vaguely reminiscent of sea horses. The color was what bassers would call "smoke."

"What's this?" I asked my friend and colleague, Mamoru Ohara.

"Viper," he said with a grin. "Boil it in tea. It's nutritious and healthful. Good broth, very nice."

"Flavor?"

"A little like chicken," he said with a sly grin.

· 24 ·

FISHING IN THE DARK

Standing on the banks of the Au Sable one June night, my friends God and author-guide-agent Bob Linsenman and I were standing thigh-deep in water on a sweeping outside bend. The bottom ahead of me angled sharply down. I could see nothing. A large trout splashed slapdash across the river, far beyond my reach, secure in its safety. Having fished worms and spinners with four-foot rods at night, I was totally unprepared for the sheer complexity of using a nine-foot, six-weight fly rod in absolute darkness. The ways to screw up are incalculable. You have to be sure of your footing and space for backcasts. You need to patiently await rises knowing there may be none at all, or all may be out of your reach and you can't go chasing. You need luck. You need to stick with one fly and hope you don't have to replace it in darkness. Some hope for a full moon, but personally I hope for X-ray vision, or failing that, night-vision goggles.

It struck me that being blind and night-fishing with a fly rod might be an advantage for this sort of braillish feel-your-way, stay-where-you-are angling. After all, I had bowled with Dan Dillon, a blind student at MSU, who consistently beat the hell out of me.

Two nights earlier, I stood at a bend inside a well-known riffle and watched distant fish taking emergers. I had on an *Isonychia bicolor* imitation, a White-Gloved Howdy, but got nada in takes. Later I realized they were taking Size 22–26 blue-winged olives.

There is too often an elitist image attached to fly fishing, in part because of entomological implications. It seems to me that Latinophobia keeps a lot of people away from fly rods. Some may applaud this, but I'm not one of them. You can fly-fish for all kinds of fish, including mermaids, and you don't have to be an entomologist or ichthyologist to enjoy the sport. When you're new to fly fishing, you want names you can pronounce and remember.

The problem is that bugs (like fish) don't write or read books and pretty much do what they want, which is often contrary to what the bug experts tell us.

God, Bob, and I floated the pristine Au Sable stretch from McKinley to U.S. Forest Service Bridge 4001. There are not a lot of trout in this stretch, but some of them are of gorilla proportions, and it doesn't get the beating that some of the upper stretches take. We saw a doe and fawn and watched a bald eagle soar over them as they came down to the water's edge. About 9 P.M. we pulled the boat over to the shore of a small island and took up our waiting positions. A few small fish fed. A passing canoeist said the hex (*Hexagenia limbata*) flights upstream sounded like flocks of Harley-hogs passing overhead.

"They're coming," Bob said. I sensed hope in his voice. Even with 150 days a year on the river, Bob is always optimistic.

And come they did. The air was filled with a stew of caddis, *Isonychias*, blue-winged olives, and *Hexagenia limbata*. I aimed my penlight at the water and saw that it was wing to wing with hex spinners, like a sheet of Visqueen stretched shore to shore.

Across the way under a canopy of cedars, thousands of lightning bugs mated and danced, blending into a sky filled with millions of stars.

A single fish rose near God, who patiently made more than forty blind casts before getting a strike, which amounted to one loud suck, one hard pull, followed by a muscular roll, one staccato splash, and adios. At midnight we floated on down to the takeout, our bow plowing a path through gazillions of spinners.

We were there, the bugs were there, the wind was calm, the humidity high—and no fish. This is not an unfamiliar story to fly fishers, though it is not something you hear a lot of talk about. It makes for lousy magazine articles.

"Bob, how do you explain this? All these bugs and no fish."

"Two words," Linsenman said, "Fuckin' fuckers."

Fred Lee and I were on the Muskegon River downstream from Croton Dam, our second visit in a week, both journeys aimed at intercepting a gray drake spinnerfall. Our first float found the temperature plummeting twenty degrees in thirty minutes and that was that. We counted a grand total of three drakes in the air over our riffle.

Gray drake nymphs (*Siphlonurus rapidus*) crawl to shore and emerge into trees, there to sit for twenty-four to forty-eight hours. At some point the males fly en masse out over the riffles to await the arrival of the females, who if they show, sort of buzz demolition-derby style through the male formation, inviting aerial fornication, after which the boys croak, the girls lay their eggs, and the spinners of both genders plummet to the water to be slurped with great speed. Theoretically. These are big bugs, somewhat smaller than hex flies and brown drakes but bigger than most other mayflies, and as such, their expirations mean an eager chow line. Theoretically.

When it got to be 9 P.M. we were concerned, but at 9:30 P.M., the bugs showed in force and over the next forty-five minutes literally filled the air above us. About 10 P.M. some of the girls arrived and we silently cheered as aerobatic copulation began and the whole swarm steadily descended toward the water. At 10:20 P.M. the formation was about two feet from an en masse splashdown. Ten minutes later they were gone, vanished with no evidence they had ever been there; we heard the splash of a single fish we could not see.

We shrugged and headed silently downriver. Perhaps we would find spinners over another riffle farther down river.

No such luck. At 11:30 P.M. we pulled the float boat and talked to crews of two other craft. One group had seen no drakes at all. The other had gone through the same experience that had visited us and nobody had an explanation other than the temperature drop might have caused a dearth of females, which meant less sex and fewer spinners, and most of the males had probably retreated to their trees, hoping to survive another night, but most likely croaking right there.

The central issue in hatches seems to be critical mass. On both occasions we saw cinnamon and tan caddis of various sizes, a smidge of midges, a few sulfurs and light cahills, all of which were ignored. There seems to be a requirement for the dinner table to have a certain biomass on the plate, although we saw plenty on the Au Sable and no feeding there.

At all times and under all conditions it is the fish, not the anglers, that determine acceptable critical mass, and even entomologists are frequently stumped by what the fish are not doing.

As professional guides, Fred Lee and Bob Linsenman had no real explanations for either experience, which is a quality I admire. All we could do was laugh and shake our heads. Bugs!

As it happens, Fred had had two heart attacks about the same time I was visiting Strokeville, yet there we were, him jumping out in the shallows to push the boat and at other times cussing softly and lugging the thing back up against the current so he could reset the anchor and put us where he wanted us to be. A great guide is obsessive-compulsive about positioning the boat "just so."

Guides are like airline pilots: some say little and state only the facts. Others keep up a running Aw-shucks, Chuck Yeagerish, good-ole-boy foot-by-foot travelogue.

As a career flak I admire people who make a living at the behest of the public. Guides see it all: couples en route to divorce court, brothers who carry golf-shot counters to see who catches the most fish, biz-bosses out to impress higher-ups or subordinates.

Guides come in all sizes, shapes, and personalities. Eccentrics seem to do all right in the trade, though blatant misanthropes and misogynists probably don't get much return business.

Linsenman once had a client who knew it all and missed fish all day, wouldn't listen, and blamed Bob, who finally had his fill and told the guy, "You couldn't catch AIDS in Africa."

Some guides teach; some don't. Some know all the names of the bugs; some just keep it to LBFs (Little Brown Fuckers) or BGFs (Big Green . . .). Some don't even do that. Some observe silently, while others direct casts like Forward Air Controllers giving instructions to stealth bombers: "Move it five inches upstream, seven inches left. Do a reach-pile-lift parachute-hook cast." Getting paid to guide seems pretty cool until you realize guides don't fish. Their job is to taxi anglers and act as their caddies.

Great guides share one trait: genuine excitement when a client hooks a gorilla.

Fast-forward to Linsenman standing below the boat launch showing God and me how to "pulse" and "rip the rod tip" to trigger strikes with streamers the size of horned toads.

Learning from Linsenman is like being coached by Bobby Knight or Vince Lombardi. "Rod tip, low! No, dammit, *low!* You're corkscrewing into the boat. Move the rod back! Move the tip, not the line. Shit! Set the hook, set the hook! Don't wimp out! Don't screw this up. Throw there, there, now . . . *shit!* Too late!"

"Sorry, Bob." This spoken like Droopy. *Mea maxima culpa.* We pay Linsenman and *we* apologize for our performance? Geez.

Bob and I had circled each other's orbits for nearly thirty years. Bob's sometime co-author Steve Nevala (and brother Denny) are my longtime outdoor pals and forever hockey teammates. Bob and Steve met at Oakland University. Steve became a high school English teacher. Bob went into business, made it big, did some agenting, and has led an interesting life.

"I saw you and Steve talk to a high school group years ago," Linsenman told me.

"How'd we do?"

"Pulse, pulse, keep the rod tip low!"

Linsenman's parents owned a cottage at Big Island Lake between Rose City and Mio (pronounced *My-oh* with a sort of Day-O and me-wan'-go-home Harry Belafonteish intonation). Bob grew up along the Au Sable, catching his first trout at age ten on a fly rod near Perry Creek.

"Streamer fishing is physical, demanding, all work, and not for wimps," he insists.

Ja wohl and *danke, mein* drill instructor.

After eight hours God and I had aching backs, cramped hands, stiff necks, and cravings for Jack Daniel's (lose the Coke, please).

When God and Linsenman spied a thirty-inch brown trying to avoid God's rattlesnake streamer, they shrieked in unison—like sixteen-year-old girls spotting a teen idol.

One way to escape the big doldrums and complexities is to throw streamers, which is not a leisure-time activity. The work is continuous and sweaty and a lot like flying: hours and hours of boredom interspersed with moments of excitement.

This particular day the temperature was in the mid-70s under a hot sun, followed by pounding rain, more sun, then drizzle, and sun again. And there was Linsenman, our Captain Bligh, amidships, "Rods low, boys, rod tips low, goddamn weather, we need an overcast, pulse 'em, pulse 'em, hit 'em, move it, *move it!*" Too bad Stanley Kubrick passed on. He would have loved to capture Linsenman on celluloid.

Steve Nevala says that if Linsenman likes you, he yells.

"He yells at *you?*" They are decades-old friends.

"*Especially* me."

"How do *you* react?"

"I say, yeah-yeah-yeah, and keep doing whatever the hell I want to do and remind him that he bow hunts with the finesse of Fred Flintstone."

We are moving fish, getting flashes on our offerings, and changing them every fifteen minutes or so: changing colors, changing sizes, fishing a small streamer behind a large one, constantly experimenting for the magic bullet. At one point I look at my watch and timed the casting rate: nine casts per minute. This works out to just over forty-three hundred casts over eight hours. Figure one flash per hundred casts (if it's a good day) and you quickly conclude that this is anything but efficient work. Forget ergonomics; there's no such thing as comfort in a drift boat.

"Set the hook—rip his eyes out!" Linsenman screams.

"Rip his eyes out? What happened to no kill?"

"It's a metaphor," Linsenman says.

As soon as a fish is hooked, he hovers to release the creature as if it were his own spawn. We have sometimes spent nearly thirty minutes with a fish before assuring ourselves it will be okay.

I don't rip their eyes out very well. I think about offering an explanation, but in Bob's boat, it's no kill, no booze, and no whining. Bob can whine, but his clients can't. Fair enough; he's the capitano.

Naturally, God catches fish. He always catches fish. We're covering about eight miles of big water, moving right along, fling-flunging our streamers, paying no attention to scenery or wildlife, both of us in a fishing frenzy, frothing water, focused on BIG fish—technically those over twenty inches, but knowing deep down it's the thirty-inchers we really covet.

Bob suddenly shouts, "There goes an eagle."

God never looks up. He is orgasmic with thoughts of a thirty-inch brown. All he says is, "That big bird better not be carrying a big trout."

Predictably, God takes two sixteen-inchers in the first hundred yards of the float, hardly looking at them as they are released to swim away. Later he hooks and loses a much larger fish. About 7:30 P.M. he hooks a fish with a small black Woolly Bugger. I see it flash as he fights it. Bob nudges the boat to shore, rolls overboard like frogman, and nets the fish. It is yellow-orange with huge spots and an iridescent blue spot on its gill plate. Twenty-four and a half inches. Linsenman is smiling like a proud papa.

When we resume the float, God is using a full sink line, but his casts have been jacked out to a hundred feet by pure adrenaline. He wants *more!*

God did not come willingly to fly-fishing streamers, but he has religion now because streamer fishing is as close as you can get with a fly rod to flipping spinners. Never mind that his left elbow has to be packed in ice for six months after each outing.

At the end of that day God and I repaired to the Mio Saloon, which is open until 2:30 A.M. even in no-tourist season. I tell the barkeep, "Jack Daniel's, big glasses, hold the ice and the Coke." I tell him this several times over the next few hours.

May 2001 we floated again with Bob, and God took seven browns in two days, 22–26.5 inches. That fall he took four fish in one day—20, 21, 24, and 29 inches.

Next spring or fall we'll get that thirty-incher. I'll be happy to see one.

· 25 ·

THE WOODS OF THE BLUE BRASSIERE

There is public land adjacent to my office where I try to walk every day. It's a bit less than two thousand acres, which is more than enough space to stretch heart, legs, and mind. I call the place, *Le Bois du Soutien-Gorge Bleu*, which translates from my crude French to "The Woods of the Blue Brassiere." My walking has reminded me of how little I know about what I see outdoors. As I traverse the pine duff trails I realize that I am far more knowledgeable in a kitchen where my ignorance is well established. How many of us are similarly deficient about nature?

Like a hairless bear, I amble along my daily three- or four-mile circuit, which I can finish in an hour if nothing distracts me—a rare occurrence. I walk to keep weight off and to keep my heart healthy, but more than anything else I walk to see what I can see. I walk because it pleases me.

Weight is a conundrum. I was lean for twenty-six years, obese for the next twenty-eight, and now I have shrunk again—below my high-school weight. When I left the working world I decided to conquer weight once and for all. My daughter began to call me the "family anorexic."

The formula for weight loss, like flying to the moon, is paper-simple. It's like stock trading: Buy low, sell high. Eat less, exercise more. Every day. In three years, I went from 310 to 190, where I now reside, 46 waist now a 35. I have lost a third of my former self, but I am still not svelte and never will be.

In typical fashion, I drew a chart and tracked my progress. It is attached by magnets to the refrigerator in my office.

I weigh myself every day, but record it only once a week—or so. The weigh-in entails tricks and self-deceptions. I have a medical scale of the sort you stand on in doctor's offices. Depending on where you stand you can be lighter or heavier. Foot placement on the scale is like foot placement in a heavy current on a rubble bottom—it yields different results. I weigh after bowel movements. I weigh naked, and always remove my glasses, which weigh less than a graphite one-weight.

Mind tricks aside, I remain steady and do not panic if there are fluctuations, which are inevitable in all phases of life.

The landscape I visit for my walkabouts cannot fairly be characterized as beautiful, though it is varied enough to be interesting. There is an oak and pine forest on sandy plains, several mature red pine groves, some aspen stands (which we Michiganders call popple), jungles of red willow and tag alder down along a narrow stream that contains only some soot-colored chubs. There is a lake into which the creek empties; alleged rainbow trout in the lake stem from reports of winter catches on corn and Vienna sausages that date back decades. I have recently heard of a twenty-six-inch brown taken on a leaf worm in mid-summer, but this may be a fisherman fact (one stretched to the limit of its elasticity). The small lake does contain yellow perch, bluegill, largemouth bass, pike, crappie, and perhaps trout. Its deepest hole is eighteen feet. A substantial marshland rings the lake and several low ridges follow the contours of the marsh. I'm told there are Massasaugas in the marsh.

In more than a year of rambling this turf I've seen a dozen deer (only two bucks), mallards and Canada geese (which like to nest along the creek), a pair of regal swans and their five offspring cruising the shallow coves of the lake, many gray squirrels, two foxes, one woodchuck (one of these oddly denned at the water's edge of the swamp), one rabbit, one partridge, some woodpeckers (including a pileated), doves, blue jays, and cardinals. The usual stuff. I have seen tracks of foxes, coyotes, coons, and possums. Right now, as spring comes toward us, I am accompanied each day by small coveys of juncos, whose black-and-white coloring fits the political atmosphere of a presidential election year. I've never seen a porcupine but recently read these animals copulate every day of the year, so they may be sleeping while I walk. This is not the sort of place to earn the title of gamey and attract hunters.

Despite a distinct lack of game, the ground and paths are littered with ejected shotgun shells, their colors shining in the sun like tubs of sugar sprinkles at TCBY. I have taken to sticking the empty shells on small branches of trees. I do it because it satisfies me to make something and because it may give some hunter pause and it may dawn on him to pick up his own trash and pack it out. I also make little displays where I find the shells, so in some sense, one could assume that one of my shotgun-shell trees would mark a good place for seeing game. Only there is no game to see, much less to shoot at, which doesn't seem to retard the shooters. What they are shooting at is anybody's guess. All I can say for sure is that they shoot a lot and litter a lot. The DNR has posted signs that say, NO TARGET SHOOTING. Naturally, all the signs are pocked with birdshot and buckshot holes. I also notice that as one nears a residential area, there is a NO SHOOTING: SAFETY ZONE, but as you approach a nearby apartment complex, there is no comparable safety warning posted, which leads me to wonder if local and state governments have decided that apartment dwellers have less value than people who live in houses.

In March I noticed a progression toward spring: less snow, some robins, a daffodil or two in bloom. Bumblebees skittered low over the brown fields, a few dandelions flashed yellow beside the stream. Butterflies buzzed around when the sun was out; first lavender-blue, then black, then white. Nightcrawlers appeared magically on sidewalks after soft rains.

The woods are home to bow hunters in the autumn, some of whom don't bother to follow DNR rules regarding tree blinds. In one year I have found more than two dozen blinds permanently affixed to trees (nailed and spiked in). I have also found four aluminum arrows bespeaking less than stellar marksmanship. I see ten-gauge shotgun shells in oak forests and woods. What the hell are these people shooting at?

A few hundred yards west of the lake is a pond, fed by the creek. When I found it two years ago, it was isolated and unbothered. I caught eight bass on eight consecutive casts, using a Red Humpy. Now two houses have been built on a small rise above the pond and a non-regulation soccer field has been built on its southern shore, complete with underground sprinklers, fed by a pump with a hose snaking into the pond. A dented rowboat has been installed on the bank of the pond. It won't be too long until the shrill and positive yells of soccer moms fill the air and the bass disappear.

This week in mid-March comes after a much welcomed, several-days-long spell of 70-degree weather. Last night we got a trace of snow, which was gone by mid-morning, and we all know that in southern Michigan our snow season is pretty much ended. Farther north they could still get snow into May, or later.

There are five deer carcasses in the woods this spring, the corpse of a fox, and the remains of a rabbit. It has been a light winter, not too cold, with moderate amounts of snow. The fox and deer remains are all slung back along the two-tracks, suggesting hurried discards from illegal activities, not natural winterkill.

During my wanderings I have found an azure ski hat; a purple-and-orange bicycle helmet (sans chin strap); clusters of 9 mm cartridges, a robin's egg; a blue plastic elementary school chair; five live shotgun rounds (.12 gauge, .410 and .16-gauge); a silver license plate folded like a wallet, which says CHUCK in black letters; numerous empty gas canisters for pellet guns; cherry-red firecracker packages (the blue labels say, THUNDER BOMB, Made in Kwantung, China, bespeaking the burgeoning global market); the dried-out and sun-bleached shell of an Eastern box turtle; blue jay, woodpecker, and crow feathers; a quarter; a dime; a dollar bill; a Mariah Carey disk; a NASCAR auto deodorizer; an empty Fourex condom case; a pair of pearl-colored panties; a black G-string; and a blue satin bra, size 34B (handwash only, made in Thailand, of all places—another unexpected connection to my past). The condoms and underwear suggest that more than lead projectiles get launched in The Woods of the Blue Brassiere.

I dutifully collected some of the loot and put it in plastic bags, like a crime scene technician. One day I may construct a collage.

The vast litter causes me to wonder if there is something about the woods themselves or being in them that causes some people to lose their judgment. I've always thought this when hearing the screams and clatter of canoeists, but dry-land litter seems further evidence. In Michigan we have a bottle return law that keeps the woods and roadsides fairly clear of pop and beer bottles, but we still see whiskey and wine bottles in the forest, along with candy wrappers, Skoal packages, plastic utensils (only forks and I have no idea why), cigarette packs, potato chip bags, and pint milk cartons. It is as if people suffer a continuous brain fart when they enter the forest and discard things that they would never drop even in a mall parking lot. What I see in the woods is not totally mindless. If people can get a dime at the can return, they will carry the can and toss the aluminum pull tab, for which no deposit has been left and no deposit can be redeemed, which suggests the power of money as a motivator for behaviors, good and bad. Could it be that a meager dime can alter human behavior? We must assume so.

I look forward to the day when I can walk the woods and find no litter, though I will readily confess I will also miss the garbologic loot. As a novelist I love to imagine how such things got to where I found them; but if there is nothing to find, my mind suffices to create what I need.

When people ask me why I walk so much, I tell them, fishing (or writing), which usually draws cash-register responses. I am not trying to be a smart-ass. I go into the woods to learn how to observe, and in doing so I am practicing for fishing and writing, and for life, all three of these things being inexorably linked.

I am neither Dan'l Boone nor Sherlock Holmes, but I play detective as I wander. A bird feather suggests the need to pause and look around, especially if the feather is down; flight feathers fall out from exertion or biology, but down suggests mayhem and an animal kill and usually you find the evidence not too far away. One day I followed the wispy trail of blue jay feathers from the sandy red pine flats across the stream into the swamp, where I finally found the murder/dinner scene, some two hundred yards away.

When I see something I immediately ask myself what has happened here. I smelled a fox for several days and finally followed my nose to mom and her kits. A second fox family was lodged in a den in a low berm next to the parking lot by a nearby immediate care facility.

One summer, I found four dead crows under the power line that parallels one of my walking trails. The birds were lying side by side, as if they had died simultaneously. Something struck me as odd. I was tempted to call the DNR, but never got around to it. For seven straight days I walked past the dead crows. Nothing had disturbed them. On the eighth day they were gone, and I wondered if something had finally carried them away. The next summer the news was full of reports of dead crows in more than forty Michigan counties, all of them having been infected by mosquitoes carrying West Nile Virus. I had found my crows nearly a year before the first detection of the virus in a bird in the state. Could it be I saw some of the first? It's not a comforting thought.

There are, to be certain, no true wilderness areas remaining in Michigan. There are some places in the U.P. that seem like wilderness, but they aren't. Most of our game and fishes are here artificially and managed like hothouse potted plants—to be marketed for consumer consumption. Fish and game laws of our DNR have done wonders to create the illusion of wild places. My game area is such a place and I am thankful for it.

I could walk anywhere, but prefer The Woods of the Blue Brassiere.

· 26 ·

TURNING THE CORNER: SOME PRACTICAL THOUGHTS ABOUT FISHING DOWNSTREAM OF A STROKE

Slowly and inexorably, aging erodes not only the capability of our bodies, but our confidence in them. Over time we begin to entertain doubts about things we had previously taken for granted.

Disease and ill health accelerate the ebb in confidence and accentuate our sense of mortality. Having had a number of brushes with death during my life, I had never given it much thought except to acknowledge that sooner or later we all have to take the inevitable dirt nap. In the Air Force we stupidly believed that only the unlucky bought the farm first and early. I had spent nearly fifty-six years doing and living, not wanting to accede to caution, seldom contemplating danger or death, and when I did pause to think about what I was about to do, I made the skimpiest of ballpark assessments and got on with getting on. Giving in to fear can paralyze anyone. Courage is not the absence of fear. It's doing what you need to do despite it. I learned that in the Air Force, too.

Two days ago I was on my way to the mall to meet God and his fiancée (The Lovely Laurie) for prenuptial shopping. The wedding was coming and I was to be best man. A coyote ambled hurriedly across the boulevard not two blocks from my house, and I took it as a propitious omen. God and I were slated to go up to the Au Sable for the hex hatch and we had always heard coyotes yapping when we camped at Canoe Harbor on the South Branch. I imagined the coyote was passing the word from his kind for us to head north. Two weeks before this, Fred Lee and I had been headed for the Muskegon River when we saw another one. Clearly, a good trend was in the making.

The day after shopping was Father's Day, and my daughter gave me a black T-shirt proclaiming in white letters: MIND CONFUSED, TENDS TO WANDER. At least it didn't say Stroke Boy, her latest name for me.

The morning after Father's Day I headed north. It was nearing summer solstice, seven months and two days post-stroke. This would be the first time I would fish alone. God was supposed to be with me, but got held up until the next day, so I drove alone the two hundred miles to Mio.

If I had given in to fear and been totally attentive to my condition and more considerate of the feelings of Sandy and the kids, I might not have ventured out to fish alone. Or I might have notified the Oscoda County Sheriff's Department, DNR, or USFS of my intended whereabouts. I might even have stuck a CB in my vest because my Nextel cell phone doesn't work six miles east of Grayling. But I did none of these things. Instead, I dutifully packed aspirin, Life Savers, and nitroglycerin tabs in my fishing vest and drove to Kellogg's Bridge on the North Branch of the Au Sable.

I craved solace and selfishly wanted to fish the way I had for a long time; alone, enjoying the time to observe and think and daydream, paying minimal heed to time or risk.

The fishing was almost secondary. I had known for a long time that I was not a fisherman who writes, but a writer who fishes. Catching trout is neither instinctive nor easy for me. It is the mystery and puzzles that compel me. And the environs.

I had done what my doctors wanted and what I could. I stopped smoking; I walked an average of one hour a day, seven days a week; I kept to my diet, counted carbohydrates, and had kept my blood sugar in normal range for six months—without an oral agent. So far, so good. Despite all this, I remained keenly aware that if my body decided to crap out, then it would happen and I would have done all I could. This reality exists for all of us. It is called fate.

Someone once said we are only free when we have nothing to lose. I disagree. Real freedom is when we have everything to lose and still find the courage to act.

I was antsy as I sat beside the bridge tying on a brown drake emerger and watching gray clouds sweep overhead. This was not just another fishing trip, but *the* trip, out alone, separated from all support systems. I looked upon the outing as a test, self-imposed.

I caught a nine-inch brookie on my first cast and kept him too long in the net as I ogled the creature's beauty. The nearby whump of outgoing artillery at one of Camp Grayling's ranges shattered my reverie. I moved upstream in relative contentment until two bozos crashed into the river directly in front of me and began whipping casts over the hole I had been moving to. I kept my mouth shut and waded back downstream, allowing the current to gently nudge me along.

That night the sky cleared as I headed east of Mio and hiked into the Eagle, a stretch of fishy water well known to river guides. I sat on the bank while fish fed in a frenzy and the sun sank. I saw no floating bugs and not many flies in the air. There were the ubiquitous caddis, but below Mio there is so much food the trout there ignore caddis. Probably too much work for too small a yield. Naturally, I tried to solve the puzzle, but I never did. I didn't catch a fish and let the darkness begin to settle. Night sometimes reveals life we cannot see in the light, life we can only sense and sometimes brush up against. It is as if night is a separate and parallel dimension. Romantic thoughts aside, there are practical lessons in the darkness too. No matter how long I fish with a fly rod at night, I never feel more than the slightest remove from stupidom.

Shards of lavender twilight lingered in the treetops until nearly 11 P.M. when I began to stumble up the loose-cobble shallows, climbed the bank under leaning cedars, and set out through the woods. There were fresh ferns up to my waist and I was engulfed by the fragrances of wintergreen, pines, and Russian olives. Fireflies hung above me and the air was filled with fluttering, pale orange moths whose wings caught the remains of the failing sun and glittered like gently falling flakes of gold.

Having chosen to bushwhack rather than take a trail, I got a bit disoriented during the hike and it occurred to me that if I succumbed here, it might be awhile before my remains would be discovered, and there was an even-money chance that coyotes and other of nature's vacuum cleaners would turn me into organic fertilizer.

I decided this wouldn't be a bad way to check out.

None of us know our future. We never have. Life is risky and something eventually cuts down all of us. I accept this. Meanwhile, I have a brain, a heart, plenty of juice, an abundance of curiosity, a love of the perfume of pines, a weakness for forget-me-nots and the music of rivers, and a passion for chasing trout and writing.

After the stroke I had a lot of motivations to get better and troutchasing was an important one. That night I think I turned a corner, and my mind shifted from the past and covered waters to life yet to be lived and waters yet to be waded in.

Bottom line: I was lucky.

It could have been much worse and left me with no choices.

There is a move afoot in the medical community to call strokes "brain attacks," which is thought to be a more descriptive term.

Not all brain attacks are the same, and both the immediate short-term and long-term consequences depend on several factors: how much and how long the brain is denied blood; what part of the brain takes the hit; and, what treatment you get and when, meaning as quickly as possible. Genetics also plays a role, yet undetermined. All such events tend to be individualized, but there are some common downstream events and phenomena, that all stroke victims share to some extent.

Doctors and hospitals have a lot of pamphlets about brain attacks, but few deal with the question most victims want the answer to: How normal will I be? My first concern, human relations aside, was the effect on my ability to think, create, and write. Then my mind turned to trout.

My strokes were in the right brain, which caused temporary paralysis to the left side of my body. The paralysis passed quickly, but my left hand lost dexterity. My balance wasn't what it once was. The not-so-steep stairs suddenly looked like K-2. Some menial tasks became difficult, like alphabetizing, filing, or arranging chapter numbers. I still have trouble opening envelopes.

Fear of more to come, another shoe to drop, is also a normal feeling after an attack. What if it happened while I was driving or fishing?

The worst effect of all was the erosion of physical confidence. I didn't really need a cane, but I used one for a few weeks like a security blanket. When I got better and tried to skate, I felt minor vertigo and lasted only thirty minutes. Worse, the blades of my hockey skates no longer were connected to my brain and no longer operated on automatic. I had to think about every step.

I literally developed cold feet, which caused a minor debate between my family physician and the neurologist. One said the circulation problem was a stroke deficit, while the other one held out for diabetic neuropathy. The jury remains out on this issue, which for the doctors is academic. My concern was practical. Would cold feet make wet wading in a cold trout stream untenable? I felt pretty certain my wet-wading days were over, which I would miss, but wading was the point, not how I might be dressed when I was doing it.

Fortunately, my legs were in pretty good shape. Even so, a bit of unsteadiness in the bell tower makes loose cobble more than a distant irritation.

Luckily, I never lost consciousness or the ability to hear or speak or comprehend, but sometimes I would start to do something and forget what it was. We have all done this, but now it seemed different. I had always been blessed with an ability to do multiple tasks simultaneously. Now I found I was forcing myself to do things sequentially, finishing one thing before moving on to the next.

I was more easily frustrated and my temper more easily ignited. It still is at times, but not as frequently. My daughter, Tara, told people I had developed Tourette's Syndrome.

I relate all this not for sympathy but because I know other trouters have or might have similar experiences, and I want to share my observations and suggestions to help them get back into the water and the flow of life.

So let's talk about the pragmatic side of fishing after a stroke.

Top of the list is to do what the doctors say to reduce the risk of a recurrence, understanding that even if you do everything by the numbers, there is no guarantee. For me that meant no smokes and keeping my blood sugar under control, both of which increase the risk of further strokes and death. If you are overweight, over fifty, and have diabetes in your family, get your blood glucose checked regularly. So much for proselytizing. Fifty-fifty hindsight is as flawless as it is obnoxious.

With luck and some work and determination, you will be able to wade and fish again. You might not be able to do it like you want to or used to, but you will be able to return to something you love. Trouting is about solving puzzles. Recovery from a brain attack is just one more puzzle to assemble into the picture you want.

This said, recovery from brain attack is seldom quick or dramatic. It is more a matter of slow improvement over time.

Once you start fishing again, there are some things to consider.

At the beginning, take a friend to help, then *let* him or her. Remember, macho and moron both start with "M" and have five letters.

Move deliberately. Easy does it. You used to wade eight hours nonstop in a river with Class V rapids. So what? You're in the water again. Think about it. This is what counts, right?

In your early trips after a brain attack, lower your expectations.

If you get in the water and feel dizzy, get out and talk to your doctor. Over time things will get better, but don't try to force it. Remember, baby steps beat no steps.

Do as many preparations as you can before you get to the river. Experience teaches us to walk to the water's edge and observe goings-on before we select a fly. Early after a stroke, forget that. Pick a fly, either for a predicted hatch or for searching and tie it on at the car. Help yourself by avoiding 6X–8X tippets for a while. Practicing knots at home will pay dividends later. If you have used nail knots to tie leaders to your fly line, think about converting to loops to simplify the process.

Keep everything as simple as possible at the start.

Don't expect to constantly change flies. Pick a couple and stick with them.

S-L-O-W down. Be deliberate in all things.

One time out, concentrate on dry flies. Next time let it be nymphs or streamers. Don't bother with droppers. Keep it simple. Like a rehabbing athlete, you have to relearn and modify a number of skills you may have taken for granted.

Safety is critical. Avoid tough, high rivers with hat-floating holes. Wear your PFD, a wading belt that fits properly, and use a wading staff. Fish close to your companion. You don't need to be far apart. Besides, your companion will be focused on you, not his or her fishing, and before you take umbrage, remember that you'd do the same for him or her. Give into it and accept help and concern. Carry a cell phone, CB, or other kind of radio if you are fishing a bit apart. Always tell somebody where you are going. Think about where the nearest hospitals and medical care are located.

Even with all this, shit will still happen: wind knots will be hopeless tangles, trees will gobble backcasts, gear will be dropped and lost. All of this has happened before, but there is a tendency during recovery to blame it on the stroke. Don't. How you respond to events may affect your health; it will affect your peace of mind, so roll with the imagined punches. I have lost sunglasses, car keys, retractors, clippers, nets, shirts, wading belts, boxes of flies, reels, batteries, lights. I have always lost this stuff and I still do. And at least once a year I leave my rod on the car top and drive away. Blame it on Murphy.

Depending on the extent of your deficits and how hard you work at recovering, there may be some things you can no longer do physically. If coordination is a problem, try to compensate by becoming a more competent on-stream observer and use what you see and learn to work the water safely and more intelligently.

There is no magic in this advice, but these things have helped me. I hope that if you experience a brain attack, in the aftermath this counsel will help you get your feet wet again.

27

WENDING THE WINDING ROAD TO FISH CAMP

T he rules for the annual trek to fishing camp on the Pere Marquette require that we drive on as much dirt as possible and that the drive take absolutely as long as passengers' glutes can tolerate. Our record is in excess of eleven hours for a drive on macadam that can be made comfortably and legally in two hours flat.

If one's meanderings harvest some looks at deer, fox, coyotes, wild turkeys, blue herons, geese, ducks, owls, hawks, turkey buzzards, and so forth, so much the better.

A satisfactory journey should begin well before noon, include a stop at the meat market for fresh steaks, a modicum of political discussion, and as many outrageous tales and outright lies as can be recalled or fabricated on any topic other than work.

Road beers are verboten nowadays, but they weren't always.

Regular stops to mosey through country stores or gas stations that sell tackle on the side (the older the establishment, the better) are encouraged. Conversations with local indigenous persons (LIPs), however, must be limited to what's being caught and on what. Or snowmobiling. What's everybody riding up this way these days?

Homegrown fresh corn, tomatoes, zukes, and cukes may be purchased from roadside stands. The salt and pepper shakers are in the glove box. From last year. Try the corn called peaches and cream; excellent raw.

See an interesting glade off to the left? Let's stop and stretch our legs. Delete expeditious from your vocabulary. Expeditions with this group are never expeditious.

When night comes, stop and ooh-ah the stars. Make sure you turn off the motor. The stars shine brighter in silence. Polaris is between the Big Dipper and the Chair of Cassiopeia, the tilting W.

How many elk nowadays in the pens at Sippy Flats?

Is the venison jerky at MarV's Shell as good this year as last? How're the moist muffies?

Let's swing over to the upper reaches of the White River and see how the brookie water fared over winter.

Look for the redhead in the white string bikini on the houseboat on the Muskegon. She likes to sun herself here in June.

Counting roadkill is all right, but once you're off the hardtop there's not much to count. Federal standards require that major highways be engineered to handle traffic at 85 mph; a good road to fish camp should leave some doubt that it can handle any vehicle at any speed.

To take eight or nine hours to drive what can be driven in two is to allow for decompression to the slower pace that woods and trout water deserve.

Honk the horn as you approach camp. The early birds will come out to meet you with a cold beer.

After we get our gear stowed, we will ceremoniously slice my daughter Tara's rum cake and take it with some pepperoni slices or a hot prosciutto cured in a cool ethnic Italian cellar in the Soo. Eat with your fingers. This saves dishwashing.

The cabin is old, nearly a century, its chinking yellow and cracked. Sit on the screened porch and stare out at the moon, sipping *pertsovka*. Did the loons come back this year?

Old man what's-his-face's grandson at the end of the lake is adding a porch. Why the hell did he go and ruin the old place?

On a clear night the lake is glass and this is not Earth and we have two moons, both full and white. The bass politely refrain from jumping until we've had our fill of the view.

No need to say anything, now or for the next week. This is how it is when you want to do it right.

We call it fish camp.

The summer of 2002 marked the twenty-fifth year that I have gone to fishing camp with the same five men. A lot of marriages don't last as long.

It doesn't matter how we met; there is that old saw about there being only six degrees of separation between all passengers on the Spaceship

Earth and we have all seen ample evidence of this in our lives to at least suspend disbelief.

One snowless December I drove up to Lake Perrault south of Houghton. The DNR plants sterile male brookies there to grow them into trophies. I've never fished the lake but often stop just to look. I have never seen a fish feeding on the surface, though once I saw a dozen drunks feeding on the shoreline.

A pickup truck arrived moments after me. A man was driving; a boy in a Cub Scout shirt and jeans accompanied him. They were delivering popcorn from the annual fund-raiser. Delivering and looking around, a grand sport in the Yoop.

"Seen the moose?" The pickuppie asked.

"Nope."

"Been around a coupla weeks, eh?"

"Bull or cow?"

"Oh, she'd be a bull, eh?"

Icebreakers complete, we moved to the customary and compulsory exchange of bona fides in order to determine how far this conversation could proceed. In the Yoop you are most likely still the new person in town at the twenty-year mark. I told him how I'd gone to Rudyard High School [WELCOME TO BULLDOG COUNTRY!], which was about three hundred miles east of where we stood, but still in the Upper Peninsula.

"No kidding, eh? You know Rosie Lingren?"

In fact, I *did* know her. "She was my girlfriend in high school."

"Yah? No shit! Her husband Kenny is my cousin. Rosie's a great gal, eh?"

In my fifteenth year I had ridden my bike east from home nearly every day to fish for trout in the Little Munoscong. In my sixteenth year, I rode my bike west about every other day to see Rose. It was a seven-mile haul, one way. We dated for nearly three years and as her cousin-in-law said, she was indeed a great gal. Our paths had split thirty-seven years before and here, staring at a lake, I had run smack into my past.

It often happens this way.

"She and Kenny live out to Misery Bay," my informant announced.

I knew there were good steelhead runs out that way, and some sneaky little trout streams, and I liked knowing that Rose and her husband had settled into such a grand place.

The point is that when you allow your nomadic impulses to have free rein, you open the door for connections, old and new.

We call our fishing camp the Little L Lake Baldwin Bullshido Club because all six of us like to argue about anything and everything; arguing, I believe, is a verbal form of the Japanese warrior Code of Bushido. We use crude and blunt wit instead of sharp steel.

One of our members caught his first trout at camp, not on the Little South Branch of the Pere Marquette, but at a pay-and-catch commercial pond where we paid so much per inch in order to give him the experience. He is now one of the most accomplished fly fishermen I have ever waded with. Small beginnings can grow into substance.

Over more than two decades, camp has evolved through various stages. The constants have been good company and exquisite food. Some years we imbibed a lot more than we fished. But we always managed to play nickel-dime poker into the wee hours and over twenty-four camps the margin between big winner and big loser is about twenty bucks. Neither Monte Carlo nor Reno, most nights we play every hand, wormy cards or not.

Our cook is Robochef Bob Peterson, who rides a two-wheel Beamer, skis, kayaks, canoes, and has enough energy for several people. At last year's camp we had the usual fine menu. Tuesday night we began with a gorgonzola pine-nut salad with balsamic vinegar dressing. This was followed by shrimp-and-scallop Creole, washed down with a couple of bottles of 1994 Remelluri.

The next night it was Greek salad followed by pork tenderloin rolled in fresh rosemary and served with baguettes on a bed of risotto. The wine was Cinsaut.

Thursday is traditional steak night, and this time we started with a Chinese noodle napa cabbage salad, and then came the filets. We had 'shrooms and onions glazed in marsala wine, steamed fresh green beans and baby carrots, baked potatoes, and an apple pie I had gotten from a delectable source. The vins du jour were a 1995 St. Emillion and 1988 Château Musar.

This is how we eat at *every* camp, which may explain why everybody keeps returning.

One of the tricks to a successful camp is to divide the scut-work duties. Peterson cooks. Reg and Lars wash dishes. Al makes fires and does all grilling. Dickie Bird is the vacuum-cleaner specialist. I am camp cartoonist. (Stop grinning: It's tough duty!) Over twenty-four years I have filled two books and started a third of cartoons retelling the events and adventures of each year's camp. Some day we will have six copies printed and pass them on to our families. Or the Museum of Odd Americans.

Important glue for a camp is memories.

On the other hand, camp isn't about anything except hanging out and spending time with friends.

The thing about these special men is that they are always there for each other, even though most of us live far apart.

Reg got married in 1999 and Al VanDenBerg flew up from South Carolina and Bob and I drove down to Fort Wayne from Kalamazoo. Lars Hjalmquist had a flight reserved from Florida but developed an inner ear infection and got grounded by his sawbones. Dick Chamberlin's wife was ill, which kept him home, where he belonged.

At the rehearsal dinner, wedding, and reception, we had a fine time mixing with family and friends of the hitching couple. People kept asking if we had really fished together for more than twenty years.

I was proud to say that we had and I know we are all better for it.

When you're young, there is a tendency to think of a friend as virtually anyone you know, but as you grow older and perhaps a tad wiser, you discover that a real friend is a rare commodity, one of life's true gifts.

Our camp has bass-filled Little L Lake out the front door and the Little South Branch of the Pere Marquette a short walk out of the other end of the cabin. No motors are allowed on the lake, not even silent electronic trolling rigs.

There is a quiet that engulfs the little cabin, which was built early in the century. At one time the log cabins on the lake hosted Georgie Jessel, Sophie Tucker, and George Burns and Gracie Allen for a summer as they practiced new vaudeville routines for the coming winter.

For several years our next-door neighbor was a retired Marine brigadier general, a mustang who rose through the ranks and spent most of his time in World War II fighting alongside Chiang Kai-shek. The general and a three-legged beagle named Butch visited one afternoon and stayed late into the night helping us consume margaritas. We were spellbound as the general recounted his adventures and struck by his integrity and common sense. We carried the general home and the next morning the general's wife, a watercolorist, dropped by to tell us he had enjoyed himself thoroughly and that for him, it had been like being with his boys again. He was hungover the rest of the week. Maybe longer.

The general died a few years later. We still drink a toast to him on steak dinner night, but margos, as of this writing, are no longer allowed in camp.

In twenty-four years, we have killed precisely two trout, a fourteen- or fifteen-inch brown, and a seventeen-incher. Our campmate Lars, who celebrated his birthday in camp one summer, said one morning that he had not tasted fresh trout since he had been a kid growing up in Iron-wood in the western Yoop; so when Reg hooked a nice brown, he looked over at me and we both nodded, and he took the fish to the shore and cleaned it. Friends take care of each other. Reg took the larger fish home to his new bride, Christine, probably to prove to her that we can actually catch the damn things and not just consume alcoholic beverages. We've seen sicknesses and medical problems, one divorce, two marriages, lost two spouses, had three retirements, and too many job and career changes to count.

The day will come when each of us reaches our biological end, but there will always be memories, and I hope that whoever gets to where we are going first finds us a fine camp for eternity.

It's difficult, I think, to spend much time in natural settings and not conclude that the intricacy and subtlety of our planet suggests a creative force. God is known by different names to different people, but I am certain that if there is a Heaven, there will be trout and loved ones and friends, and that's enough for me.

28

HUNTING HUNTERS
IN THE U.P.

It is the afternoon before the 2001 firearms deer season is to begin and we are bumping along a Class VI road (a road in name only) near Hemlock Rapids on the Paint River in Michigan's very rugged and hilly western Yoop. Michigan's wolf guru, Jim Hammill, has gotten a radio call from one of his pilots reporting a mortality signal from a radio-collared wolf. A mortality signal sounds if a wolf is still for four hours. We are asked to help locate the animal. I'm along because I am doing research for a novel.

"Wolves," DNR Sergeant Mike Webster says with a grimace. With deer season in their faces, conservation officers have their minds set on deer hunters and their likely antics. Tracking a wolf can take a lot of time and remove officers from preparations for the two-week dance that is about to begin. Time is a major issue for officers and each of them tries to use their time judiciously, but reality often intervenes to change their plans.

Just yesterday CO Steve Burton and I went to find a man who had brought a bobcat into the District 3 Office in Crystal Falls to be sealed as an animal taken under a fur-harvesting license (meaning it was trapped). An hour later the biologist mentioned to someone in Law Enforcement that the animal had a large hole in its side and maybe everything wasn't copasetic.

We found two old men at a small frame house in the old mining town of Gaastra. One of the men was using a cane to pull the truck door closed behind him. Steve asked about the bobcat, which belongs to the brother of one of the men.

"Already gone taxidermist," he said in Yooperese.

Steve pressed him gently. "You're *sure?*"

"Well, we look da garage, eh?" the old fellow said, leading the way back to the garage and opening the door.

There lay the cat with the gaping hole in its side. Steve said, "That looks like a gunshot wound."

"Nah," the man said. "She was a bow, eh?"

The man's brother had shot the bobcat while bow-hunting for deer, then went to get a post facto fur harvester's license, hoping to pass it off. This almost worked. Steve confiscated the carcass and told the man there was a problem with the tagging, and for his brother to call him. Instead, the brother called CO Dave Painter last night and confessed to him. Dave passed word to Steve and told him the hunter is worried about not being able to keep the bobcat. It will take three days before the spooked cat-killer will come in to face Steve. The poacher won't get the animal back. You don't get to keep a stolen car either.

After the bobcat deal, Steve and I went to court in Iron Mountain where he testified at a hearing to condemn a weapon. He had found a loaded and cocked .45-caliber in a glove compartment last summer. The judge required him to testify with the deputy prosecutor. The condemnation was uncontested and it seemed to me this could have been handled without a court proceeding, but it is instructive to watch and to listen to Steve and the prosecutor prepare for the brief hearing. This was supposed to be Steve's day off. So much for that notion. We were two days from deer season and all officers were already mentally into the tasks and challenges looming ahead.

So our sergeant isn't happy to be chasing a wolf today because it takes away from preparations for deer season. There is also another factor. When cattle or sheep get killed, or hunting dogs get chomped by wolves, it's often the officers who get the complaints and bear the brunt of criticism. Having spent three decades in corporate PR, I know what it's like to serve in an organization's fecal shield.

But we have a job to do and head out. The road is bad and there has been a lot of recent logging in the area, which has left it crisscrossed with a varicosity of trails that lead nowhere. We have a section number for a location, which we have marked in a section map book; we have to stop, get out, and check little orange tags on trees to determine where we are. My old Air Force navigation skills are not a detriment to the effort.

Linda, the area forester, and Monica, Jim Hammill's wolf technician, are thirty minutes behind us in another vehicle. They have a GPS and a portable antenna. Eventually we all rendezvous. Monica turns on the antenna, which is shaped like an H and makes clicking sounds. She holds it over her head and swivels herself in a three-sixty.

"Down there," she says, pointing.

"Cedar swamp," Mike mutters. "Let's hope we don't go swimming." He strips off his gray uniform blouse and Kevlar vest and heads into the swamp in his T-shirt.

Monica walks with the antenna over her head and we all stop periodically to listen, to help pinpoint where the sound is strongest. The river is about a half-mile away and we know that the pilot got the signal somewhere in this section, so the search could be long or short, but we get lucky and find the animal within two hundred yards of where we are parked. Mike is the one to find the animal, a classically colored gray wolf lying on its right side with a red plastic tag in its left ear: Wolf No. 159. It looks like it stretched out to take a nap. The ground is covered with lush green moss. I begin taking photographs. It is a male, maybe seventy pounds, and looks healthy. No sign of mange, a common problem. Mike and Linda drag the animal out to the trucks. The stench when they lift it tells us it has been dead for a while, maybe from the day before. Anything that dies in this weather will rot and stink fast. Hunters will need to get their deer to processors, or risk the meat spoiling.

The dead wolf goes with Monica and Linda back to the District Office in Crystal Falls, where it will be x-rayed before it is sent to the Rose Lake Lab near Lansing for a full necropsy. The X ray can show any traces of metal from a bullet or arrow.

This appears to be a natural death, but within three days hunters will shoot three more wolves. This happens every deer season and nobody takes responsibility. In all of this fall's shootings, the hunters turn themselves in.

Not all the shooters get away with it. Detective Steve Johnson of the Wildlife Resources Protection Unit tracked a wolf-killer for a year, and finally nailed him—in Wisconsin. COs in different states often help each other with investigations, and if some yahoo from Michigan pulls a bonehead deal in Colorado, chances are that Michigan COs will help their Colorado brethren to bring the offender to justice. I think most outdoors people don't really understand the level of cooperation among COs, or their dedication to protecting fish and game.

* * * * *

I am standing in the bed of a DNR patrol truck. It is the night before the firearms deer season, and we have backed the truck up a two-track into a copse of popples. From our position we can see vehicles approaching on the hardtop a half-mile away. I am with Sergeant Mike Webster and Officer Dave Painter. Mike lives in Crystal Falls and supervises COs in Iron, Dickinson, and Gogebic Counties. Mike grew up BTB (below the bridge). Dave is originally from Clinton County (also BTB) and now lives in Crystal Falls and handles Iron County. For two hours this afternoon the two officers had a running discussion about finding an appropriate field to "sit on" tonight in anticipation of jack-lighters. COs are highly motivated and because there are so few of them with so much territory to cover, they find themselves torn between where they are and where they might be. I am often similarly conflicted when I am trout fishing.

The night air is cool, but this is November and the air should be frigid. Instead, it is almost soft, like a spring night, a harbinger of the unseasonably warm deer season to follow.

We sit in total silence for three hours but see little and hear no wayward shots. A couple of vehicles look like the drivers might be thinking about headlighting, but no spotlights come on and they pass by us into darkness. We know there are deer in the potato fields in front of us because we counted thirty or so with a quick glance as Dave backed the truck into position.

The western U.P. is on central time—an hour behind the rest of the state—and we have darkness by 4:30. We figure that our chances of picking off shiners might be better after the bars close, but we also have to think about getting sleep before tomorrow morning, when BOB, the Blaze Orange Brigade, will be afield in force. In Michigan this season about 750,000 hunters will be toting their shotguns and rifles around the woods. Usually there are more than one million hunters out during gun season, but last winter was a tough one up north, and the deer herd estimates are down for the Yoop. Add to this the weather not being conducive to hunting this year, and the combination of these two factors may contribute to fewer hunters being out and about.

We are tucked into a two-track with barren potato fields on either side of us and another one across the narrow ribbon of blacktop. In the swamp beyond the field across the road we hear a truck motor grinding and roaring. It sounds like it is trying to get down a muddy road and not doing well, and this prompts some second-guessing about our positioning. The sounds go on for almost an hour.

"Maybe we should be down on the other side of that field," Dave says as the unseen vehicle continues to whine and sputter and struggle.

Mike shrugs and says, "It really sucks to be that guy." We are on surveillance for poachers and can't leave our post to help.

* * * * *

Opening morning we are on foot, humping up a ridge to some illegal blinds that an area forester alerted Dave to. The foresters are responsible for surveying huge tracts of land and often see things that they pass on to the law enforcement personnel.

Mike and Dave fly up the steep grade like gazelles and I lag behind. At one point Mike looks back and says, "We're not going to have a heart attack, are we?"

I'm too winded to even make a wisecrack. I shake my head and keep climbing and puffing.

We find a twenty-something man from Wisconsin sitting in an illegal blind. He has been placed there by his grandfather and is under the impression he is on private land, when it is actually public. He also has shot a five-point buck, which Mike goes down to check.

Mike will retire this coming spring with twenty-five years of service, and he has the scars of a quarter-century, including a bad back from several vehicle accidents and mishaps. You'd never know it to watch him move, but he constantly berates the younger officers for their driving. One afternoon with Steve Burton, Mike jokingly shouted for him to stop and back up. Steve asked why.

"Because you missed a rock back there and since you've hit all the rest of them, I didn't want you to miss that one, Officer!"

The deer is properly tagged, but Dave tickets the young man for the illegal blind and tells him that if his grandfather is a stand-up guy, he ought to pay the ticket for him because he put him in the position and ought to know the law. Dave reminds him he will also have to remove the blind, even though it belongs to his grandfather. "The law says the user is responsible," Dave informs him. The cheesehead shrugs.

* * * * *

We are on the road and about to pass a vehicle rolling slowly toward us. Dave says excitedly to Mike, "Stop!" Dave immediately bails out, cuts behind our truck and across the front of the other vehicle. Mike gets out more deliberately. A slovenly man and a passenger get out of the other truck. The driver grins insipidly at Mike.

"You guys have any luck this morning?" Mike asks.

"Nah, too hot."

Mike checks their cased rifles. They are unloaded.

Dave comes around the back of the truck and the driver gets a goofy look and says sarcastically, "If it ain't Deputy Doolittle."

Dave maintains his cool, but it is clear there is some history at work here.

Back in the truck he's agitated and tells Mike he's busted the guy several times before, that he's up from Chicago and his camp is a mess. Dave says, "Bums."

"Do you need a hug, Officer Painter?" Mike asks with a laugh.

"The guy's a jerk," Dave says disgustedly.

* * * * *

Two hours later we are cruising a narrow gravel road when a pickup comes skidding around a curve too fast and Mike is forced to put our right side almost into the ditch. The driver may be intoxicated.

"Get 'im!" Dave yelps. We make a tight one-eighty and Mike pursues. We make the stop, parking our vehicle at an angle across the left front fender of the truck. Two guys get out. They are also from Chicago and the driver denies he was going too fast. They insist they aren't hunting. Mike and Dave check their licenses and cased rifles. The driver pulls out a wad of money as thick as the slide on a shotgun. Mike calls the Law Enforcement Information Network (LEIN) on the radio to check outstanding warrants. Nothing. The two men tell Dave where they are staying and that they were out gambling last night and are headed back to the casino again tonight. They say it's too hot to hunt. Mike lets the driver off with a warning.

"Did you see that wad of dough?" I ask Dave, who laughs.

"He pulled out *another* roll while you guys were on the radio!"

* * * * *

We find a camp along a nearby road. There is an uncased rifle across the seat of a four-wheeler.

"Uh-oh," Mike says. "What we have here is a gonna-happen moment."

We drive down the road and wait. Eventually a four-wheeler comes down the road, but cuts to our left before it gets to where we are waiting.

Mike quickly follows the tracks on the hard dirt and we eventually find an elderly woman wearing orange and red, sitting on a log five yards off the tote road.

"Did you come in on the four-wheeler?" Dave calls over to her.

"Yah, with my husband."

We drive farther on and find the four-wheeler. The driver is frail and elderly. He is taking his loaded Model 90 Winchester off the handlebars. No helmets in sight.

Mike talks to him. He hunted this area with his brother fifty years ago and wanted to come back and see it again.

Dave checks his license and sees that his age is late eighty-something. He asks the man what he ascribes his long life to.

"Good whiskey and a hot woman," the old guy says, grinning.

Mike lets him off with a gentle warning. "We can't bust an old geezer," he says when we are back in the truck. Mike lets over-seventies from his church hunt his property in Crystal Falls. The sergeant sometimes comes across as gruff, but he has a soft spot for people, and deep empathy. In fact, empathy seems to be a trait all officers share. In a job that requires them to make judgments continuously, they are notably nonjudgmental. I also see no evidence of professional paranoia. They accept the world as it is and do their jobs the best they can. This is fascinating insight.

"Slow day," Dave says. "With this warm weather hunters are staying put in their blinds. When the weather's cold they're usually road-hunting by 10 A.M."

Later that day Mike will tell someone that we are experiencing a "widespread outbreak of legality."

It's in the low sixties and it is November 15.

"Good whiskey and a hot woman?" Mike says.

All three of us laugh.

* * * * *

On another road we find a young man hoofing down the shoulder with his rifle slung. We stop and chat. He's a Marine, home on leave, hunting with his father.

We find the father farther on. He is sitting in a lawn chair by the bed of his truck, his arm hooked to a portable dialysis unit. He says he's seen no deer, "but it's nice to be out."

Dave and Mike move his chair back so he's not in danger of being hit by passing vehicles and wish him good luck.

"That was something," Dave says, his voice starting to crack. "Hooked up to that thing and still hunting." Dave has young sons and is teaching them to hunt and fish. I think he has projected himself into the future.

* * * * *

Late that afternoon we are far away in another part of the county, checking camps. Mike and Dave know a camp where there is sign of a lot of recent four-wheeler activity and damage.

Mike says, "Find four-wheelers, find trouble." Many COs end up loathing four-wheelers, jet-skis, snowmobiles, and dirt bikes.

The first camp we look at has six relatively new pickup trucks, two expensive RVs, and two large trailers for four-wheelers. There is also a smaller and older camper-trailer. A few beer cans are on the ground, but the camp is clean by most hunting camp standards. There are two bucks hung on the camp pole, a nine-point and a spikehorn. Nobody home. Mike and Dave decide they like the look of the camp. We withdraw with a plan of coming back at dark to intercept hunters returning from the field.

"This will be a good one," Mike says. His statement is prophetic.

Meanwhile, we motor to another camp we saw earlier in the day. It is a new camp and Dave is curious. Hunting groups in the western U.P. tend to camp on the same spots on public land year in and year out, some groups for decades in the same place. COs get to know the camps and their inhabitants. This is a new one. There are several vehicles and two new large wall tents from Cabela's. The tents are the color of eggshells.

We coast the truck into camp and quietly get out, not latching our doors. Dave circles the camp in the woods looking for gut piles. Mike and I walk through the camp, looking in vehicle windows. By one of the tents, Mike waves a hand to get my attention. The end flaps have been folded up and the end of the tent is wide open. Two people are asleep on cots inside. We continue the walk-around. Dave finds some blue jay and grouse feathers in the woods, but nothing else. The sleepers never wake up, never even know we are there.

"I'll come back later," Dave says.

As we drive back to the first camp Mike is on the radio. Margie, the District 3 dispatcher, has called to ask if we have had contact today with Steve Burton, who is on patrol somewhere in Dickinson County.

"Not since early this morning," Mike reports.

"The computer shows his truck hasn't moved all day," Margie says. All DNR vehicles are equipped with the Automatic Vehicle Locator—or AVL—which is tied into the Global Positioning System and enables an officer's truck to be located at all times. We can look at the rolling map in our vehicle's laptop computer and see each other, and so can the district offices and Lansing—which COs call Station 20. Margie has asked Officer Dan Helms to do a drive-by. Danny and Steve share Dickinson County and often work together.

I tell Mike that Steve told me two days ago that he intended to patrol by four-wheeler on opening day.

By dark we are back in the first camp. Around 4:15 P.M. we hear a single shot.

Mike gets another radio call from Margie. Danny Helms has found Steve's truck but there is no sign of Steve. Mike asks Margie to ask Danny to remain in the area and for her to alert Tom Courchaine, the district's lieutenant who is working with officers in Delta County today.

"Problem?" I ask.

"Burton's aggressive," Mike says. "He won't back down from anybody." His tone is something between admiration and concern. Because COs spend most of their time alone, it's dangerous work. With the lieutenant in a distant county, Mike is the ranking officer in the district. He tells Margie to give him a bump on the radio as soon as she hears anything more.

Dave asks, "You want to move over to Dickinson County?" That's where Steve's truck is.

"Not yet," Mike says, silently weighing factors. We have a terse discussion about what it would take to mount a night search, how we would go about it, who we would need, and how to contact them. Then we turn our attention back to the business at hand.

Twenty minutes after the solo gunshot we see the lights of a four-wheeler jiggling and bouncing toward camp. We shine our Maglites to stop them.

There is a heavyset, middle-aged man driving and a boy of twelve on the back. No helmets, riding double, both of them with loaded rifles.

Safety first. The guns get unloaded.

Dave asks about the two deer on the buck pole. Who do they belong to?

"The nine-point belongs to the guy in the camper," the man says. "The spikehorn is my dad's."

"Where's your dad, still out hunting?" Dave asks.

"No, he went back to Detroit."

Dave arches an eyebrow in my direction. "Your dad drove ten hours to Iron County, shot a buck, and drove all the way back to Detroit this morning?"

"Yeah, he had things to do."

"Grandpa had to leave," the boy says, chiming in.

Dave asks for the grandfather's phone number.

When he starts to walk back to our truck, the man calls out, "Wait, wait, that's my number. I always get them confused."

Dave gets a second number, which he calls in to Station 20 and asks them to call and ask if the man has been hunting in the U.P. today, and if so, where, and if so, did he have any luck, and if so, what?

Meanwhile, Dave checks licenses and talks to the man and his son. No helmets, riding double, loaded guns on a vehicle, and loaded guns after dark. They already have four strikes against them. While Dave talks to the pair, Mike is on the radio again with Margie, checking on Steve Burton. He asks her to hang in the office until we know what's going on with Steve.

Lansing calls back to report that the father in Detroit says he's never hunted and that his son asked him to buy a license so he could use it.

Dave confronts the man, who tries to stare at his feet over a beer belly and begins to hem and haw. He tells Dave his father has Alzheimer's, and had asked him to get a deer for him.

Dave ignores the obvious lie. "Who shot the spike?" he asks firmly.

"I did," the man says, and then he begins to apologize.

Dave tells him an illegal deer here is $1,500, but he is not going to zap him with that. Instead, he walks the man over to the buck, has him remove the illegal tag and replace it with his own.

"You're done hunting," Dave tells him. With the son out of earshot, Dave pointedly tells the man he's disgusted that he has a twelve-year-old lying for him. The man stares at his boots. Dave also writes a no-helmet ticket.

"How many other four-wheelers?" Mike asks.

"Four," the man says.

"Five more," the boy says, correcting his father.

"Which is it, four or five?" Mike asks.

"Six counting us," the man says.

I say, "I heard a shot."

The man quickly says, "That was me. I took a neck shot and missed a doe." I don't ask if he has a doe permit. I have no official capacity and am strictly riding along as an observer, but I let Dave and Mike know what I've heard.

Over the course of my patrols I serve as a quasi-Voluntary Conservation Officer or VCO. VCOs are trained, and many have related jobs either in the DNR or other law enforcement or government agencies. Before taking off, I ask each officer what they want me to do, and they tell me how to play each situation and I follow orders. I am here to help and gather information, not to hinder. An officer's most important tool is his brain, but two people are more of a deterrent to escalating trouble than one. Especially after dark.

When the other five vehicles return, the first four have two hunters on each machine, no helmets, and all of them with loaded weapons. The last vehicle has a lone rider with a helmet, but his rifle is loaded. We take the firearms and Dave unloads them while I hold the light so he can see. Then he collects the cartridges and clips and writes tickets using the truck seat as a desk.

Meanwhile, Mike is on the radio again, checking on Steve Burton's status.

The first man is telling other young hunters coming in that he screwed up and that they have to follow the rules, but I hear the first man's son tell the other boys in hushed tones that he took the shot at a doe at dark and missed. His old man lied about this, too. Probably trying to protect the son, but from what isn't clear to me.

One camp, a myriad of infractions, and nine tickets. There could have been more written.

A little after 5 P.M. we hear Steve Burton check in on the radio. Mike is visibly relieved. This is to be Mike's final deer season in uniform; these are "his boys," and he doesn't want to lose anyone. His pride in his officers and the job are palpable. He strikes me as the prototypical warrior leader, not an administrator.

Back on the main road it is pitch black, and a four-wheeler comes hurtling down the shoulder toward us. Mike turns around and we catch up. The driver is a fifteen-year-old boy and he's wearing his helmet, but he also has a loaded rifle in a case across the handlebars of the vehicle. He says he's headed for his parents' camp. We unload the rifle and follow him. The father comes out on the deck of the new cedar log cabin; Dave explains the situation, and gives the father a ticket for not supervising, explaining four-wheeler and hunting rules. The boy was driving down a federal highway closed to snowmobiles and four-wheelers. The boy swears he wasn't hunting. He just drove to a friend's camp to see a buck that was shot there. He says he didn't know the rifle was loaded. Dave writes the appropriate citation for the father, who makes no comment and shows no emotion.

It was too hot for the deer to be moving today, but we bipeds covered more than two hundred miles and walked another two or three during our twelve-hour patrol.

On the way back to Crystal Falls, Mike calls home and learns that J. D., his father-in-law, shot a three-point this morning from the blind Mike built for him on the side of Mt. Webster. Mike shakes his head. Before meeting Dave and me early this morning, Mike fetched J. D.'s lunch up to the cliff-side blind because his father-in-law had forgotten it. His last words of the morning had been, "No spikes or forks, right, J. D.?" and his father-in-law had said, "Right."

Mike's wife, Sue, is a Michigan State Police sergeant in Wakefield, and she has already taken a four-wheeler out and fetched her dad's deer back to their house. She will retire next year too.

"Three-point," Mike says, shaking his head. Ironically, Mike is fairly new to hunting and is ambivalent about getting a deer. By contrast, Dave and Steve are lifelong hunters and outdoorsmen. Later in the season, Mike will hunt from his father-in-law's blind and spend two days reading a novel.

"Did you see any deer?" I asked him a couple of weeks later.

"Nope. I was reading."

"You'd better be nice to your father-in-law," Dave tells Mike, tongue-in-cheek.

"I know the drill," Mike says, grinning.

Dave also calls home to check on his wife who has gotten a buck two consecutive years, but she has seen only does today. "Too warm," she says. "The deer weren't moving."

*****

On the second day I meet Steve Burton at a gas station-convenience store in Sagola at 4:30 A.M., and away we go with coffee and donuts. I tell him everybody was worried about him yesterday. He nods and that's the last we speak of it. Within thirty minutes we are checking five four-wheeler drivers who are just getting ready to head out before dawn. When Steve asks about helmets, they hunt frantically around in their pickups to find them.

Steve is a genuine Yooper from Ishpeming, a former state trooper, and now an officer in the Army National Guard. He's also currently working on his master's degree in public administration at Northern Michigan University. He grew up hunting deer at the family camp on the Peshekee River, near the McCormick Wilderness Area.

When vehicles we've already checked pass by us in a small convoy, the drivers all have on their helmets and are riding single. They each wave. "Law-abiding citizens all," Steve says. "Yesterday morning there must have been twenty of them," he adds. "Word must be out that we're here."

After daylight we check a camp where there is a nice eight-point hanging. Only one man is in camp and he acts hinky in our presence. His campmates are in the woods.

"Something's not right back there," Steve says afterward. He'll revisit the camp later. I'm tempted to write off his feelings, but I know that good cops develop instincts about situations and master the art of situational awareness. Something has triggered Steve's concern, even if he can't verbalize it and I can't sense it.

Early in the afternoon we are at another location where there was an illegal camp with litter all around, including spent condom packs.

"I think I know who these guys are. Couple of yahoos from town. They're gonna clean up this mess," Steve said with steely resolve, and in fact, they will do so.

Farther up the road we find a tent with four bucks hanging from a nearby tree. One of the animals is half-skinned, but all of them are tagged legally. There is no sign of the hunters. It looks like they split in the middle of the skinning job. The meat will spoil in this heat.

A small pickup with a man and a woman pass us, moving slowly. Slow-moving vehicles during the last two weeks of November strongly suggest road-hunting.

When we catch up to them later, they are backed into an open spot near some trees.

"How's the hunting?" Steve asks. He always approaches the driver. I always approach the passenger side.

"Not hunting," the pudgy driver says.

No guns, no licenses needed, so we move on.

"They're not deer hunters," I tell my partner for the day. "The woman was scrambling to pull up her jeans. They were down to her knees."

Steve grins. "Oh."

At dark we sit on a camp to intercept hunters coming back in. Both Dave and Steve make a point not to go traipsing into the woods during the first or final thirty minutes of shooting time. The last thing they want to do is disturb peoples' hunting experience. So we wait. Late this afternoon we found a fourteen-year-old boy hunting alone with a shotgun in an illegal blind his dad took him to. We wait for dad to get back, and of course, he is last to arrive. Steve takes the man aside, explains about the blind and that he has to hunt with his son. The man was hunting miles away from the boy. By law he needs to be directly supervising his son. There are so many rules I can't keep them straight. When somebody asks me a question, I refer them to the officer.

Pulling out of the camp we get a call from Dickinson County. Can we handle a bear–truck accident? The animal is causing a traffic hazard and the Troop and county units are on other calls.

"Okay, but we're thirty miles away," Steve tells the dispatcher, and away we go, humming along at high speed with our blue lights flashing. It is a surreal ride and a lot of cars ignore our lights and don't pull aside as state law requires. Our siren whirps us through towns and villages. We both try to keep an eye out for deer. I can't help myself. I feel the exhilaration of a six-year-old riding in a fire truck. My unabashed glee embarrasses me. The COs are professionals. I am a professional. I am not allowed juvenile feelings like this. But they are there and I have to laugh. Doofus, I chide myself.

At the accident scene the bear is in a twisted sprawl on the side of the right lane. A truck is pulled over farther on. We park behind the truck. An elderly man is driving with a son who looks like Fatty Arbuckle.

Steve gets out the needed forms and starts taking information. As a former U.P. Troop, he has a lot of experience with accidents and reports. I ask the driver if he's looked at the animal.

"Nope; since we hit it, I been sittin' here tryin' not to shit my pants," he says. "The bloody thing come outta nowheres."

"Bears," Steve grumbles as he writes.

After the truck hit the bear, two more vehicles struck it, dragging it down the highway. An oncoming eighteen-wheeler was being tailgated by a woman, who picked that moment to pass, pulled out, saw the bear, and swerved back behind the truck too sharply, sending her spinning down onto the grassy shoulder, stopping within feet of a drop-off—a near disaster—but she and the eighteen-wheeler are gone by the time we arrive.

I walk back to the point of impact and pace it off. There is a huge splash of blood and about thirty yards of intestine chunks down the right lane, just inside the center line. It is 211 yards to where the bear lies. It's a jet-black female yearling, maybe 175–200 pounds. Most female black bears are in hibernation by October 15, regardless of the weather. Too bad this girl was still out and about. The injuries are what a pathologist would call massive trauma, and I can't help thinking what damage a truck would do to a human being as I drag the bloody animal down into the ditch to prevent accidents from gawkers.

It's raining when Steve drops me at my truck in Sagola so I can head for Crystal Falls, twelve miles to the west. Tom and Sherie Courchaine were expecting me for dinner at six, and I am late. Tom is District 3's senior officer. We met when he was in a similar position at District 12 in Plainwell, near my home. He served as a CO and sergeant before his latest promotion. He is a veteran of the Native American fishing-treaty rights battles of the Garden Peninsula in the seventies that nearly led to bloodshed. Sherie is a former diabetes educator. They met and married when Tom was a CO assigned to Escanaba. Sherie's dad, Jack, joins us for dinner. He is over from his place in Newberry in the eastern Yoop to hunt the back of Tom and Sherie's place.

I knock on the door and Sherie immediately sees the blood on my hands and arms and laughs pleasantly. "Spent the day as a working warden, eh?" She points me to the bathroom to wash up. After a wonderful dinner and sharing a couple of bottles of a French Bordeaux, I can hardly stay awake and head for Iron River. It is drizzling and there are deer to dodge all the way. My fifty-eight-year-old ass is dragging and it is only day three of my eight days of patrol.

*****

I am no longer sure of the day. I have not heard news or read a paper, and know nothing about what's going on in the world except the work we are doing.

It is night again and Dave Painter and I have driven down a two-track to a camp. We park and get out. Three hunters have just returned to their tent and are in the process of getting a fire going. Dave is chatting with them when another vehicle comes along the road headed past the camp into the woods. Dave walks over and flags down the driver, who turns out to be a retired police officer from Detroit. He says he's staying in a cabin just over the border in Wisconsin, and he's going down the road to look for a hatchet he left back in the woods. He also says he was expecting a pal to meet him, but he probably stayed in the cabin instead of hunting. Just then two more vehicles come down the road heading back to where this guy also was headed. Dave talks to them briefly and they head on. The two men in the second truck are sullen and do not want to talk. Their answers are monosyllabic, issued through scowls.

Dave says to me, "They're all together." Obviously his instincts are aroused. Meanwhile, the first three hunters get in their truck and disappear. When the other two vehicles return after ten minutes, Dave intercepts them again. Dave goes back to the second truck to look at it.

As I start to follow him, the former non-talkers in the first truck roll down their window and suddenly become effusive and want to play "Twenty Questions." They ask me if there's a DNR in every state, and I say yes, but the function has different names in different states. They start to ask me questions about the U.S. Fish & Wildlife Service, and if there are enough conservation officers, yada-yada, and I tell them to direct their questions to their state representative or the governor, and go to join Dave. The guys in the first truck were trying to divert me. I've dealt with enough reporters and other folks to recognize the tactic. Besides, to them I am just another CO of some unknown flavor. I am big with a short green parka, a big black flashlight, and a hunter's orange cap, dressed much like Dave. In the dark we probably look the same.

Dave has found two doe heads in the second truck—and the missing hatchet. One of the deer is not tagged. He quickly learns that it belongs to the retired police officer, who doesn't have a doe tag. Dave writes a ticket and keeps the head for evidence. All of this takes place at night over about thirty minutes, and it is so dark that I literally can't see my hand when I hold it up. After we get an address for the cabin where they are staying, and the hunters have departed, we drive back to where they were and look around. Dave suspects there is another deer back here and that our sudden appearance has caused them to abandon it. We spend thirty minutes bumping around in the fields, using spotlights mounted on the sides of the truck to read tracks in the grass to see where they have been. We find a place where a vehicle was stuck and some branches cut to help get them out of the mud. Dave decides to come back at first light tomorrow to look around and see what he can find. He's sure there is something more.

I have dinner at 9:30 P.M. It consists of a donut from a gas station in Crystal Falls and a decaf coffee with amaretto creamer. I don't remember having lunch. In fact, I can't remember any lunches during the week except for my supply of energy bars and a day-old pasty that Steve Burton and I shared during one of our patrols. My breakfasts have been donuts and orange juice from the same gas station.

Each morning I plop a paper bag by the cash register and the sleepy female asks in Yooperese, "Fresh bakery?"

I nod. "With holes." Donuts with holes are cheaper than those without holes. I never bother to find out why.

Riding back-wrenching roads all day and trying to concentrate on seeing everything we can see is leaving me bushed every night. This is definitely a job for younger people.

* * * * *

Day eight and Dave Painter and I are patrolling somewhere between Iron River and Crystal Falls. It's a quiet day. Many hunters have broken camp and headed home. The day before yesterday we crossed a flimsy beaver dam and hoofed into blinds in northern Iron County and had a spell in the morning checking guys carrying handguns. Later, we cruised a road past a cabin Dave had been called out to around Halloween.

Earlier this fall, the resident had beaten another man with a baseball bat in Crystal Falls. The Iron County deputies had gone out to his house to find him, and discovered a blood splash and deer hair. Dave got the call at 2 A.M., and found an illegal deer when he got there. He didn't get home until 4:30 that morning. He explains that the assailant works on a pipeline out of state. Dave has been cruising by the house since then in case the man comes back. There is a warrant for his arrest for both the assault and the illegal deer.

Dave also tells me about another incident where an ex-con violated a restraining order by entering his ex-wife's house and beating her. Then he took her gun and shot a deer. Dave got called out in the middle of the night for that one, too.

"There's a larger fine for killing the deer than for beating his ex," Dave says, shaking his head.

About an hour ago we were driving along when a woman suddenly popped up on the road, dragging a deer. We stopped. She had shot the six-point, gutted it, and dragged it up a steep hill to the road in about twenty minutes. We threw the deer in the back of the truck and drove her to her house, a third of a mile away. She was going to drag it and didn't want to bother us, but we take her anyway. Dave tells me she's a Native American and he has busted her father for illegally taking a bear. She is built like a linebacker, with a rosy complexion. Dave congratulates her on her success and earns a big smile.

Last night Steve Burton and I crept up on a hunter with an illegal bait pile. Steve led the way. It was approaching dark and Steve didn't want to disturb anyone, but he recognized a vehicle as one belonging to a young man he had ticketed in the same place last season for the same violation. The twenty-something guy says he doesn't remember Steve or the incident.

Later, we found a truck parked along a remote tote road well after dark and stopped. After awhile we heard voices in the thick woods and got glimpses of flashlights. Maybe they were dragging a deer out. We quickly determined they were lost in the dense underbrush. The weather was finally getting cold and we slapped our hands against our sides to keep warm while we waited. Three men emerged on the road without a deer. One man was packing a loaded 44. magnum hogleg, which we didn't see right away because it was under his coat. When Steve saw it, he asked the man to make it visible. The man was unhappy about this, but Steve patiently explained the concealed weapons law, and reminded the man he could confiscate the weapon and ask for the court to condemn it. This calmed the man down. Steve took the pistol and unloaded it. The man didn't have a concealed weapons permit. Absent such a permit, you have to keep a pistol visible and in plain sight. He didn't.

One of the hunters told us he shot at a deer, but couldn't find blood. He fetched his pals and they went with him to look for a trail. The law allows for finding and dispatching a wounded deer after shooting hours, which end thirty minutes after sundown, but the guy had a loaded pistol and they had three lights. It would be okay to take a weapon, but it would make sense to carry the ammo and load up only when the weapon was needed. Steve senses this story isn't what it ought to be and issues a citation. The pistol-packer says he's not going to carry the damn thing anymore.

But that was last night, and today has been pretty quiet. The sun is out, the air cooling down, and we are passing a pasture when I spy an animal in the field.

"Is that a deer?" I ask.

"Hand me the glasses," Dave says, stopping the truck.

He looks, hands them back to me. "Wolf."

I take them and look. Sure enough. I grab my camera with the 300-mm lens and get out. This wolf is about a hundred yards away, light-colored and massive. It stares at me while I snap photos, praying the animal doesn't spook and bolt, but it stands there, majestically alternating looks at us and the other end of the field, which we can't see. I kick myself for not having the 1,000-mm.

A red pickup truck pulls over to the shoulder just past me and the driver jumps out.

"What is it?" he asks excitedly.

"Wolf," Dave says.

I keep snapping away.

Suddenly I see a rifle rising in my peripheral vision and instinctively I reach over and push the barrel down toward the ground. "You can't shoot a wolf!" I whine.

The man says, "I know, I just want to look through the scope, eh!"

Dave says, "There's a second wolf along the hedgerow, guys."

I get a glimpse, but no photo. It is black, smaller.

Two wolves at one time.

Back in the truck, I tell Dave I'm sorry I grabbed the guy's rifle.

He says, "I almost did the same thing when he pulled it out of the case from the back of his truck, but I saw him make sure the chamber was clear and I knew it wasn't loaded." He is amused, either at my naïveté, my reaction, or both.

Several hundred yards down the road we see cattle herded against a fence in the same field the wolves were in.

"Better tell Jim Hammill about this," I say. "They may have been stalking the cattle."

Dave nods.

Three weeks later at the post-season deer feed at retired Officer Mike Holmes's camp near Iron Mountain, I learned that the man with the scoped rifle was one of Steve Burton's National Guard sergeants. He told Steve about the wolves and how Dave Painter was with "some old guy with a camera."

It's good to make an impression, I guess.

I am back at the American Inn in Iron River by nine and fast asleep within thirty minutes. Tomorrow I will make the drive home to Portage. It will take about twelve hours and it is supposed to snow along the way.

* * * * *

We have about 240 people in the Law Enforcement Division of the Michigan Department of Natural Resources, and about 160 of them are in the field doing the actual enforcing. That's 160 people for one of the biggest states in the country. Michigan's Upper Peninsula alone is the size of New Hampshire and Vermont combined. Marquette County is the biggest county east of the Mississippi, and is larger than Rhode Island.

In my travels I have met a CO who shot a felon in a shootout in which he and his partner came to the aid of Michigan State Police officers. And I met a retired officer who saw his partner run down and killed at night during a stakeout of bear poachers. Others were involved in near-lethal outcomes in the wars over Native American fishing rights during the seventies and eighties in the Garden Peninsula, and another stopped a man from shooting his partner and him during a night stop. It turned out that the would-be shooter had said publicly he would shoot the next cop he encountered. The State Police had issued a warning, and the COs had not yet gotten it. Only their own competence kept that incident from leading to a lethal outcome.

A national study has shown that conservation officers are eight times more likely to be injured in the line of duty than any other police officer. In some ways this is intuitive: COs work among citizens who are recreating and armed, and the bad guys often work at night when the COs are too often alone.

Most people don't realize that conservation officers in Michigan enforce all the laws that other police officers enforce—*plus* fish and game laws.

State economies ebb and flow in cycles, but our land is finite. What we have is all we are going to have, and unless we take care of it, it will erode and be gone.

Michigan hired the nation's first uniformed and salaried game warden in 1887, and our COs have served with honor and distinction ever since, but we need more COs in Michigan.

29

CAMP FISHHEAD: EYE-EEE!

It is an autumn road trip. Robochef and I are wedged into the Green-streamer I, a Suburban packed to the gunwales with gear we might only possibly and theoretically need, and enough streamers to cro-chet a blanket for a mastodon. Our first night out we wandered the trails of Starved Rock State Park on the Illinois River, about ten miles west of Ottawa, discovering there a magnificent old log lodge on a par with Old Faithful Inn, but somewhat easier on the gas budget. It had been built by the Civilian Conservation Corps (CCC) in the way-back-when and still stands as evidence of some of the wonderful things that program pro-vided our country. Why the CCC has never been repeated is a question national policy planners ought to ponder.

After walking some of the park trails, we dined with Jameson and Caroline Campaigne in Ottawa. Jameson (Rush) is publisher of Jame-son Books, and served up a thick and tasty duck gumbo washed down with a couple of bottles of '95 Amarone. Caroline went off to tennis, leav-ing the boys to talk trout-chasing, books, and politics as we dined under the pining eyes of two dogs and two cats, one of which bit and clawed me to blood.

We were rolling the next morning by 5 A.M., and in St. Louis at Hargrove's Fly Shop in Brentwood by 9 A.M., there to rendezvous with the advance team that would sortie south to Camp Fishhead (CFH) on the North Fork of the White River in the Devil's Backbone Wilderness. Jeff Bryan (Hoosier) and Colorado ski/fly-fishing guide Steve Wiggins (Wigs) led the way, and provided a continuous and seldom stellar travel-ogue ("That would be a rock. That would be a tree. . . .") via handheld Motorolas while attorney John Hinde (Leroy DeVine, from Le Roi du Vin) rode trail, making sure we "Yankee boys" didn't stray off into serious squeal-like-a-pig territory.

According to Jeff Bryan, "The St. Louis Fishheads date back to the 1970s when radical fringe elements of the Ozark Fly Fishers sort of 'found' each other, this the result of a gravitational pull from common beliefs in serious, hard-core traditional fly-fishing values, and cocktails." Jeff insists the Fishheads were Trout Bums before the term was coined.

The original Fishheads would gather for lunch on Fridays at Culpepper's in SinLooey. Lunches often lasted the remainder of the day, with Fishheads rushing to their homes for dinner. Palaver tended toward fly fishing, with lubrication by beverage spawning far-ranging discussions of other subjects. Over time the Fishheads invited others to join (after vetting to eliminate A-holes). Eventually the older members faded away. Jeff concludes his history lecture with the point that while the people may change, some worthy philosophies live on. The actual number of Fishheads is unclear. Eye-eeeee!

In the Ozarks, every church and storefront along the way had patriotic slogans on their marquees. Flags fluttered from buildings, poles, trucks, cars, SUVs, and bicycles. It was only two weeks after September 11, and Middle America was in high patriotic dudgeon.

Pressing south, the roads grew narrower and the terrain hillier until we pulled down a pitted gravel road into Sunrise Ranch, where the Fishhead gang had been gathering for many years. The Fishheads were allotted one end of the camp and other campers were warned to ignore any sounds coming from our end.

Steve (Old Scrot) and Cel Southard of Grayling were already in camp, having been fishing in Arkansas for most of the week. The Southards run The Fly Factory in Grayling and Steve is the soul guide of the Trout Bums that congregate there. Steve and Cel introduced me to the Fishheads at the previous July's Trout Bum Bar-B-Que.

Cel immediately told me about crawling out of her tent one morning at a previous camp and nearly stepping on a copperhead. Hoosier grinned. "We played with that boy some, then let him loose up on the hill." I made a point of finding out which hill and carefully avoided it the rest of the week.

Meanwhile, Robochef pulled me aside. "Jesus, this is like being asked to go play a round of casual golf and finding out you have to play with Tiger Woods, Jack Nicklaus, and Arnie."

I just grinned.

The first night we plied the waters of the North Branch of the White River in Missouri, wading the cobble below Patrick Bridge. The water was cool, but low, and small chubs were active but not a lot of trout. I caught one dink brown. Most fish taken were in the deeper riffles.

The next day we were in canoes on the Eleven Point River in the Irish Wilderness Area, a paddling between towering cave-pocked ridges and hills of sandstone and limestone. The water in some of the glides and flat-water runs was deep, and every rock far beneath us clearly visible. We stopped at riffles to look for wild rainbows and Bob hooked and lost a nice fish in his first ten minutes. I hit and lost two others.

The riffles were sparkling with high-noon sunlight and white-silver flashes of nymphing trout, but nothing we passed in front of their noses seemed to interest them. Correction: nothing Robochef and I used interested them. Wigs seemed to be catching them just fine and was bounding down the riffles like our old pal God.

Fishing remained slow for the two neo-Ozarkians until Hargrove and Jim Heese (Bobber Boy) lugged their canoe up on the gravel and decided it was time to get serious and try what Hargrove announced with great moment as, "the science experiment."

Tommy Hargrove is known in the group as the Drunk Monkey, a moniker stemming from a time when he attended a Federation of Fly Fishers (FFF) conclave in Mountain Home, Arkansas. The shindig was held at a hotel with rooms overlooking an indoor swimming pool. Hargrove had opened the window of his ground-floor room into the patio and started tying flies and jawing amiably with passersby. When the night's fund-raiser auction started, Hargrove sat in his window with his bidding paddle. At some fated moment the auctioneer looked back at the bearded face and balding pate, struck his gavel with a resounding whack, and announced to the assemblage, "*Sold* to the drunk monkey in the window in back!" How the name migrated back to SinLooey is not written in Fishhead annals, only that it did.

So now the Drunk Monkey wanted us to try a "science experiment" and we agreed. We tied yarn eggs below nymphs, started high-sticking like boys trying to lift pies off grandma's windowsill, and began regularly hitting fish, twelve- to fifteen-inchers, all of them good scrappers. In fact, the fishing got so good that we were ninety minutes late to the rendezvous with our car shuttle man, who talked about September 11 and how he wasn't much worried about terrorists invading the Ozarks because "We're too far inside to get to."

Robochef was not a month back from the Boundary Waters with wife, Julie, and daughter Laura, and more than a tad nervous about having my inattentive hulk perched up front of the canoe. I had been cited as the primary cause of the disaster in every canoe I was ever in, and late that day his fears proved well founded. We had just shoved off from shore, when the ass-end of our craft hung on a rock. Robo, *mein Kanoekapitan*, said *nein. Nyet—nada—zilch.* I leaned forward and low, not moving, scarcely breathing. When the canoe began to seriously pitch to my right I instinctively leaned left. (Note: Instincts in a canoe are rarely the correct ones.) We heeled left, teetered momentarily, and flipped over. Wigs shot photos the whole time, offering to keep them off the Internet—for a price. Robo and I came up sputtering. He blamed me; I blamed him. Eye-eeeee! The others brayed like Missouri mules on Ozarkian LSD. Robo got the worst of it and finished the float trip in his bathing suit. We gathered float bags and sundry flotsam and jetsam, brushed off *mein Kanoekapitan*'s ego, regained our equilibrium, and headed downstream.

Attorney John Walker is the Fishhead Prez. He is alleged to be a bit physically unstable wading rivers, but has allegedly caught trout from sundry unusual attitudes. Because of his accomplishments, Fishheads now reverently refer to any unusually hooked fish (e.g., falling down, over the shoulder, dragging a fly while wading upstream, etc.) as "Walkering" a trout. By midafternoon we had rolled our canoe and Robo had Walkered a rainbow, an auspicious beginning to our first Ozark interlude.

Having loaded our gear and strapped the canoes to the roofs, we repaired to West Plains in search of camp pumpkins to carve, a CFH tradition. This stop made us very late to camp that night, but Bobber, the Fishhead Fire Marshal, quickly cranked up a blazing, crackling conflagration of six-foot-long white oak logs. Fire-watchers and heat-seekers backed their chairs up to ten feet and as the night went on, the flames rose higher, and the chairline continued to retreat. It had been down to 34 degrees our first morning, and remained in the mid-40s the rest of the week, but Bobber's fires threw off enough heat to warm the twenty-plus tents through most of the nights. At various interludes firebugs brought forth bundles of hand-cut Ozark cane, which they pitched on the fire, causing them to explode with new energy, roaring and hissing and spitting sparks in a homegrown fireworks display.

There aren't a lot of rules at CFH, but one is that the first person up stokes last night's fire's remains and starts the coffee. Usually it was Cel and me who were the early risers in the heavy morning dews. That first morning I noticed a rubber chicken hung in a noose over the cooking area, but I kept this observation to myself and sought no clarification.

Every morning we all sat around the rekindled fire, drinking coffee or tea and watching as Tommy Thompson (Pubes) of North Carolina emerged like some sort of giant nymph. He had somehow forgotten his tent poles and had resigned himself to sleeping on the ground in the open under the stars, with a bright blue tarp over his electric blue mummy bag. The morning emergence was fascinating and became a camp spectacle. First, the blue lump would begin to tremble and undulate; then, it would fold up as if hinged and suddenly a face would pop into view, the head wrapped in a towel that looked like an Afghan turban. Tommy didn't talk much when he first awoke, but when he did, the talk turned quickly to fishing, which was pretty much the standard conversational fare of camp. These were serious trout-chasers.

Camp had one anxious moment. Hank Reifess (Frank) and Steve Adams (Vice President of Stupidity and Evil) had driven down the day before us to chase smallies. As they got ready to launch their canoe, Hank had bad feelings (we don't say pain) in his chest, so they backtracked to St. Louis where Hank was admitted to the hospital. This naturally garnered great concern among the Fishheads, but Adams reported in his gravelly voice, "He ain't dead and he ain't dying. How's the fishing?" Priorities are priorities. Adams was a nuclear submariner in another life, and had not had a haircut or beard trim in more than thirty years. I had met him in July at the Trout Bum Bar-B-Que when his head and facial hairs were shaved by auction and raised something like six grand for Au Sable River projects.

Hargrove's fly shop in Brentwood is a quasi-meeting place for the Fishheads. The idea of auctioning Adam's hair had been hatched there during Friday night Vespers (we don't say Happy Hour hooch sessions).

At Vespers there is a whole set of fine-based infractions, such as using excessive Latin bug names: $10; or being unusually influenced by, and submissive to, the spouse: $10—unless he/she is hot or a new spouse, in which case the fine is usually reduced or waived. Accumulated fines are periodically recycled into bottles of single malt scotches and placed in the liquor-larder in the Drunk Monkey's back room (we don't say clubhouse).

Our second day on the Eleven Point was less productive than the upper reaches of the previous day, but the scenery was no less spectacular. Robochef ordered me not to paddle on day two, but there was a lot of flat water and eventually the stubborn Swede relented.

Arriving at the launch point, Hoosier's van got a flat front right tire, which Robochef changed, while Hoosier and Bobber drove up the mountain to try to find a place where a cell phone worked so we could get the tire repaired while we fished. As we unloaded and began to stack gear along a rock wall, something inside me whispered, "snakes." We set our rods and bags by the wall and seconds later a small copperhead darted along the base of the rocks and shot into a crevice to hide. I moved my gear down to the water's edge. One look at the terrain shouted copperhead, but it also looked like rattlesnake country. The Fishheads weren't so sure about this, but our car shuttle man told us he runs over dozens of them every summer. When my little voice speaks about snakes, I listen. Eye-eeee!

Late that afternoon we reached the takeout early, and found a gathering in the making. An older gent wandered over to talk to us and said it was a bachelor party with fifty or so celebrants expected to roll in. By the sounds we could hear the likkering-up phase in fine process. He said later they would take their jet boats out on the river and spear some suckers.

"You gonna have women and strippers?" Hoosier asked.

The man gave him a squinty look and said, "Ain't goan be no wimmen."

We then contented ourselves with playing with Wigs's two-weight and catching one-inch chubs until our shuttle man showed.

That night in camp we had a band, and Hank Reifess had checked himself out of the hospital and showed up to be part of the festivities. The band had two guitars and a young girl singing. The stage was the back of an ORV trailer and the singer, a lithe, sixteen-year-old blonde named Kristin, sang songs from the thirties and forties. When Walker asked her to sing "Mood Indigo," she looked him in the eye and said, "Ah don't think ah know it, hon." The next night she knew it well enough to bring the camp to a full stop as she crooned, and lyrics wafted over tents and uplifted faces like magic spells.

On day four, a dozen of us drove down to Rim Shoals on the White River in Arkansas and spent the afternoon catching rainbows in two-foot-deep riffles.

Our last night in camp, Detroiter Jeff McGowan (Pie Boy) used five Dutch ovens to bake fresh apple pies in the fire, and served the confections with ice cream and cheese.

Eye-eee!

30

A MODEST PROPOSAL

I t's one thing to rail at the DNR for not taking care of our fish, and yet another to have a stretch of river and know that if the fish are to survive, it's my problem too.

Parties of anglers in the nineteenth century took hundreds of grayling from northern Michigan waters—sometimes in one day of fishing. There are ample photographic records in fading sepia. Elk, moose, wolves, pigeons—the same thing—all shot out or trapped out or driven out. Only hominids are truly wanton. Absent rules we might very well be living in barren geography. Take Detroit. Please.

Yet the mistakes of yesteryear can be corrected as a buffer against future problems. I wrote earlier of the return of turkeys. We also have an estimated two thousand elk in the state now, a thousand moose in the Yoop, and almost three hundred gray wolves: Game and fish management works. But even with grounding in rules and laws, the sheer force of population continues to pressure habitat, and everything wild that we treasure is at risk and will continue to be so. I read recently that 97 percent of the state's population lives in southern Michigan, where only 2 percent of the land is publicly owned. My three favorite birding spots now sprout houses; the pheasants, quail, pat, deer, and migratory ducks that were there have permanently migrated.

The English rules, and they are peculiarly English (the Welsh, Scots, and Irish fish more the way we do), seem to me to be like those arbitrary cultural practices that have international businessmen still wearing ties and most of us eating dessert last when there is no good moral or scientific biochemical or nutritional rationale for either practice.

Some action is necessary.

Thus, I propose that every American who cares to be a trouter be allotted five hundred trout to be caught (defined as brought to net or hand) during his or her lifetime. Caught but not killed. A kill would cost you ten. If each of us had to spread five hundred trout over our lives, we would have to savor each one, and our approach to the fish might be quite different. Remember that young man and his baby girl at the culvert on Campbell Creek. "Used to catch our limit here every Sunday morning."

When trouters reached the five-hundredth fish, TU or FFF could present them with a medal on a gaudy ribbon in the pattern of an Adams (Michigan's most famous fly). Local colleges could record their reminiscences on tape so that those to follow would benefit, not so much from the technical aspects as from the context of the insight gained, how each fish is precious and how not a single one can be taken for granted when a lifetime equals a mere five hundred.

Dinks, smolts, and hawgs would count equally.

God naturally scoffs at the idea. "Unenforceable," he says.

Perhaps. But what I'm proposing hearkens to earlier times and centers more on a personal code of honor, the willful adherence to limits. It seems to me that creel limits are already more a matter of honor than legal enforcement; I've run into the odd CO in my hunting days, and only once while fishing, which as a practical exercise already makes adherence to creel limits and legal methods a matter of personal responsibility.

In this light the move to a five-hundred-fish-per-lifetime limit does not seem such a far reach.

The most important thing would be to inculcate the new values in our children. What they grow up with they embrace, and if you doubt this, try tossing something out the car window when there's a kid eight or older riding shotgun, or try to pitch a glass bottle into the trash instead of the recycling bin. Values gotten early tend to stick.

31

RETIRING TO LIFE

I was certain I wanted to retire during a sojourn in France when I learned that corporate offices were moving to New Jersey, but my epiphany came during a video conference as our new marketing guru in New Jersey never looked up from the document I had sent her a week before (at her insistence), and which obviously she had never bothered to look at until the cameras began to roll. When the meeting ended I walked directly from the videoconferencing room to my boss's office and told him to color me *finito*. He stared at me in disbelief.

The next day the word was out and colleagues began to drop by my office.

One of them asked, "What will you do?"

"Fish," I said.

"You mean like a vacation?"

"Yeah, forever."

I left on May Day, liking the revolutionary connotation. That was more than four years ago and since then, I've fished all over my beloved Michigan.

The first thing I did was put exercise back into my life. I ice-skated every morning (except fishing days) with Bob Lemieux and God (whom at sixty three Bob taught to ice-skate). I shucked about seventy pounds in that first year and began to have pecs again. Sort of. Some aspects of aging can't be entirely undone.

Bob and I met when he was coaching the Kalamazoo Wings in the International Hockey league and have been friends ever since. He was not a fly fisher when we met, and of course, I wanted to introduce him to the sport. It is a bit twisted that the most inept of fly fishers would be proselytizing, but you don't need to be an expert to be a zealot. I wanted all my friends to share what I loved so much.

As longtime friends, Bob and I shared some common fishing experiences. One Easter years before, we had taken his son Danny and my son Tim to the Outer Banks to chase blues migrating to Long Island

and points north. The boys were in their early teens and more insatiable for food than fishing. But we all fished hard and because I had no real oceanic experience, I had no expectations. I had seen photographs of blues, but that was the extent of it. We fished with disgusting live bait called bloodworms and every tug on the line brought forth a surprise.

One night on Hatteras Point, where the Atlantic's two great currents smack into each other, the boys threatened to go on strike unless they got food. Bob drove them back to the village to feed them, while I remained behind to watch rods stuck in sand spikes. I had a heavy Hudson's Bay blanket wrapped around my shoulders to protect against the wind, cold ocean spray, and peppering sand. We were ostensibly fishing for black drum that night and simply put out our baits and let them sit on the bottom. During the day we saw anglers using balloons to haul their baits hundreds of yards offshore.

While Bob and the boys filled their maws I spent my time trying to avoid being debrided by blowing sand and now and then checking the lines with my flashlight. I had never caught a black drum, but I knew what they looked like and that they could be big, and I assumed sluggish.

Eventually, I spied a line inching its way out.

I got to my feet, picked up the rod, and reefed it to set the hook.

It was like jerking a cement sarcophagus.

After an hour of crank-and-yank and intermittent cursing, a huge fish slithered onto the sand from the surf. Not a black drum, but a shark, between five and six feet long, its tail sweeping around in obvious displeasure.

I stepped back to think.

During previous days we had watched fishermen gut sharks and throw them back into the ocean. Or gut them and leave them to die and rot on the beach. I couldn't do either. I used my pliers to snip the wire leader, got the beast by the tail, and hauled it back into two feet of water, where it wiggled off into the black.

Bob came back after midnight. I related the events and he smiled. "Good decision."

Our paths went separate ways after that, him into professional sports management, and me doing my corporate America.

When I retired, we hooked up and I suggested he try fly fishing, and off we went to the Pere Marquette River, where in the first hour he caught two thirteen-inch browns on dry flies, with no hatch in progress.

I then crossed the river and climbed up the bank to show him where to cast. On his second try with an oak hopper he shacked the cast, hitting the V of a sweeper and log parallel to the bank.

I told him never to look away from his fly. Warned him repeatedly. But he did.

Like we've all done.

He looked away just as the biggest brown I'd ever seen in the Pere Marquette rose from the depths like a Polaris missile egressing a submarine to slash lustily at the bug, which a startled Bob jerked out of its wide-open white mouth, a trout in the twenty-five to thirty-inch range, a hog, a gorilla—you choose the word, it was a breath-taker.

His first time out.

Later that summer he caught an eighteen-inch brookie on the South Branch of the Au Sable just as a bald eagle soared over him, covering him and his fish in its shadow.

Turns out, he's one of the 5-percenters.

Early that September we camped at Canoe Harbor and drove over to Mio to catch the ephoron hatch. This was one time I knew I could see the bugs and know for sure what they were. Find them we did. We caught and caught and released and released until well after dark, as rafts and beer-propelled paddlers of all descriptions floated by us. The last group consisted of a huge raft with five people, towing a smaller raft with a man and woman in it. One of the women in the tow-craft was shrill and shaking her fist at the couple behind them as they passed by me. "If you two hadn't stopped to fuck for an hour, we'd be off the damn river and dry and warm by now!"

The offending couple remained silent. Moot point, I thought.

Bob said from somewhere in the dark, "This fly fishing is *so cool.*"

Three months later Bob and I took a week's trip to the U.P. About four miles above Seney, on the Fox River Road, a gray wolf (not to be confused with a gray Wulff) crossed the road in front of the Green-streamer. It was a large, powerful animal that leaped the eighteen-foot road and berm and headed for cover, pausing once to look back at us. I got one photograph and followed on foot trying to intercept it, but never saw it again. Still, I have one nice shot of a lobo looking back at us.

That time on the Pere Marquette with Bob it was evening, and I was fishing a long, fast riffle with some depth, using a Montana lightning bug, a glittering gewgaw of a nymph I had ordered from tier Bob Brent in Helena, Montana. I lost a big fish by my leg after it tugged me downriver toward a twenty-something man who was watching the contest with great interest.

"My God," he squawked. "That fish was huge! What did it hit?"

I clipped off the nymph and handed it to him. He looked at me like I had just given him a Ferrari.

It was then that I noticed a young woman sitting on a boulder on the bank. I asked the young man if she was with him.

He nodded. "We're engaged."

I said, "Promise me something?"

"Sure."

"Does she fish?"

He looked perplexed. "Not that I know of."

"You ever ask her?"

"Not in so many words."

"How about asking her now? If she wants to, let her use the lightning bug."

He waded over to the woman.

I couldn't hear what was said, but she got up smiling, threw her arms around him, and waded out, rod in hand.

I put six more lightning bugs on a rock along the bank, got the young man's attention to show him where they were, waved, and went to find Bob.

Back in camp we mixed Jack Daniel's with Diet Pepsi and goosed our fire to life.

I stared up at the canopy of stars, many of which had helped me navigate all around the world, and thought they were still offering me direction. Coyotes began to bark.

Bob and I were silent, clicked our cups together, and drank to the day.

Life is sweet and retirement even sweeter, but life along a singing river is sweetest of all.

I have covered a lot of water and with luck, I may cover a lot more. Hell, in time, I may even start catching trout. And if not, so what? For me, every day is Saturday.

GETTING OUT OF
THE BOAT

Capricious life continues its snicker-snack ways. I had ended the book with feel-good prattling about every day being a Saturday, but life has its own schedule, and death is an unscheduled flight. On June 18, 2002, I was at my office preparing to leave the next morning for a week of hex fishing around Grayling. My daughter, Tara, called, her voice hard and shrill. "Mom's passed out and she's not breathing. You have to come *now!*"

I was behind the wheel and charging before it dawned on me to ask Tara if she had called 911. In a blink I decided she had, because she is her mother's daughter and her mother never panics in the face of trauma.

I arrived at the house to find neighbors gathered, a police car, an EMS truck, and my daughter and her friend Emily Castillo, sobbing. She and Emily have been pals since kindergarten and Emily was with Tara when they found Sandy.

The girls had planned to watch a TV program with Sandy. She and Tara had been to the market that afternoon and stocked up on fresh fruit. I saw them briefly at John Rollins bookstore where I was picking up my son Trev for a quick dinner. Sandy was in a happy mood. When they got home, Tara took a nap on the couch in the family room. Emily waltzed in and woke her up so they could go get an ice cream before the show. As they started to leave, Tara called out to her mother, who did not answer. That's when they found her on the floor beside the dining room table. Emily started CPR and Tara called a 911 operator, who instructed her to get help. Our neighbor Michelle Placke came over and relieved Emily just as EMS arrived.

I found six paramedics crowded into the dining room, trying to clear an air passage for Sandy, who was on her back. Her blue-gray color and the faces of the rescuers told me it was too late. After awhile the doctor on the other end of the telephone told the EMS people to stop resuscitation efforts, and the official pronouncement of death was made. We would learn from the autopsy that the cause of death was catastrophic aortic dissection with cardiac tamponade, brought on by atherosclerosis. Her death had been about as close to instantaneous as can be. There had been some signs, as there always are, but Sandy did not want to be "bothered" by doctors, and she was not a woman you could force to do something she didn't want to do.

My immediate concern was for Tara and Emily. Their experience was ripe for classic post-traumatic stress.

I called my eldest son in New York City. Tim was, as Sandy's mother said, Sandy's "first-born and first love." I called my mom and my brothers, and Sandy's mom and sister and brother. My other sons began to arrive, as did friends and neighbors. In our community Sandy had touched a lot of lives and hearts, and people rallied as they always do when death visits.

As Sandy wanted, we kept things simple: cremation, family-only at graveside, a memorial service celebrating her life, and a wake. She was interred in the cemetery in the middle of town, as close to the library as we could get her. The memorial was held at the Celery Flats Hayloft Amphitheater, which was in the midst of a Shakespeare festival. We made no effort to clear away stage props. Sandy loved the theater from behind the scenes, and it was fitting that she be remembered under such conditions. At the end of the memorial we announced to our friends that Tim and Ms. Leann Reinecke of Muskegon were engaged. Sandy was anticipating this, but died before they could make it official. The kids and I felt it important to mark a new beginning as Sandy's life ended.

Sandy and I had been married for almost thirty seven years. I had been convinced she would outlive me by decades.

I never expected the label widower, but there it is. Dad cannot replace mom, but he can be dad. At night I sat on the back deck watching Shanny, our Newfoundland-Lab puppy, charging after fireflies, while a pair of cardinals sang to each other. Life brings burdens all humans must bear. Not every day can be Saturday, but we can treat every day as sweet in its own right.

Weeks afterward I made the trek north to Bullshido camp near Baldwin, our twenty-fifth gathering; and though I felt no desire for rivers or trout, I went knowing that time heals, and that wading into the Pere Marquette and renewing friendships of decades would serve as a sort of church for me.

In July after camp I floated the upper Manistee river, from Cameron Bridge down to Long's. The water was 61 degrees, the air 85, the sun white-hot in a bluebird sky, and there was no reason to think the fishing would amount to much, but we had fish on dry flies all day and into the night, and out of nowhere, a hex spinner fall after dark. For bugs and humans and fish, life remains a mystery, and we are—all creatures—driven by forces science only scratches at understanding.

I am reminded of a scene from *Apocalypse Now*, where sailors in a patrol boat encountered a tiger, and one sailor took up the mantra, "Don't get off the boat. Never get off the boat." The tiger, of course, is a metaphor for the unknown. But remaining on the boat cannot spare us from experiences that frighten and humble us.

Life is a voyage into the unknown, and getting off the boat is what we humans were born to do. I plan to keep covering waters as well as I can, for as long as I can.